THE
YELLOW JOSS

and other Tales

ION IDRIESS

INTRODUCED BY TONY GREY

ET T IMPRINT
Exile Bay

This 12th edition published by ETT Imprint, Exile Bay in 2024.

First published in Australia in 1934 by Angus & Robertson
as *The Yellow Joss and other Stories*.
Reprinted 1934, 1936, 1939, 1940, 1941, 1944, 1948, 1951.
First electronic edition by ETT Imprint in 2020.
First published by ETT Imprint in 2020. New edition 2020.
Published as an Imprint Classic in 2024.

ETT Imprint
PO Box R1906
Royal Exchange NSW 1225
Australia

ISBN   978-1-923024-66-3   (pbk)
ISBN   978-0-6487390-3-6   (ebk)

Cover: Pearl sorting on Thursday Island, 1920s, photograph by Frank Hurley.

Designed by Tom Thompson.

INTRODUCTION

In *The Yellow Joss*, Ion Idriess OBE plunges us into a world fascinatingly close to our own in many respects, but one that has profoundly altered since 1934 when this collection of colourful and well-structured stories was first published. The contrast is engrossing, particularly since the characters, with their emotions of love, of hate, of pride, of fear, of greed and the rest, let loose in these gripping tales, are as relevant today as then. The expectation that this feature, so entertainingly crafted in the yarns, would stir a contemporary interest has led to the publication of this edition.

With authenticity that sometimes surprises the reader, Idriess introduces us to Aboriginals from Northern Australia, Papuan head-hunters, and Islanders around the Great Barrier Reef, all still in the colonial phase of European contact. Chinese gold diggers appear too, well before the rise of China. Idriess knew these individuals; he met them, lived with them, before the contemporary world had a chance to make so much difference. The first peoples in the stories are in their tribal state, infused with age-old traditions and behavioral norms, proud but fearful of the white colonialists. It wasn't so long ago – barely three generations. That closeness in time can be said to offer a benefit to the reader; to some extent it helps us understand better their descendants who are alive today and within our society's reach.

Idriess, who was born in Sydney and became one of Australia's most productive and influential authors (writing more than fifty books) was a knock about bloke, wide-ranging in his jobs, all at the practical level, and never staying in one place for long. A denizen of the Great Depression when opportunity had to be searched for and grabbed before it dissolved, his life journey took him to tin mining in Cairns and Cooktown, harvesting sandalwood in Cape York, pearl diving in the Torres Strait Islands and gold digging in Papua New Guinea.

For a while he lived with an Aboriginal clan in the York Peninsula, where he paid keen attention to its customs, attitudes and lifestyle. At times he displays a sympathetic understanding of Aboriginal closeness to the spirit of Nature and country – unusual for a white man then. The broken English spoken by Aboriginal characters is difficult to understand in detail but the reader can get the general drift; and it does add authenticity.

A word should be said about the old fashioned epithets the author applies to his non-white characters. While they imply a lack of respect we do not tolerate today, they were in common use at the time and demonstrate a historically accurate attitude. In the era of these stories the superiority of the white man, the colonizer, over people of colour was perceived as part of an immutable natural order. Of course attitudes have since evolved to a more refined and inclusive state, but merit exists in seeing how natural such racial biases seemed to be at a time not far removed from our own, particularly when encased in writing as fluent and evocative as Idriess'.

It should be pointed out that in some cases his white characters actually demonstrate a certain admiration for qualities they observe in the "natives" and that moderates somewhat the pervading convention of comfortable superiority, softening it. That tendency extends to the " Yellow race" where he speaks kindly of a Japanese diver entangled with him in the branches of a sea tree at the end of their lifelines. Ironically when he wrote this, tensions were rising in the Pacific, which led to the attack on Pearl Harbour less than a decade later.

While the short story has been around for centuries, it took until the second half of the 19th century for it to hit its stride, aided in no small measure by Edgar Allan Poe's imaginative writing. That the genre is literature is well accepted. Certainly Idriess' effort here demands that accolade. Perhaps Poe influenced him; for instance, in *The Death Stone*, and *The Bones of Leon Chang* where "dead folk walk by night" the spooky atmosphere builds into a mood as macabre and foreboding as in *The Fall of the House of Usher*. For a long time, which extended into the 1930's and beyond, dark matters of the spirit were in vogue; séances and clairvoyants created other-worldly domains that many people weren't sure did not exist.

Although these short stories are individually crafted, with each forming a cohesive plot studded by conflict, contrast and suspense, somehow, together they seem to form an identifiable whole, akin to a full-length novel. While the plots may be different, the characters keep reappearing, be they Aboriginal, Papuan, Torres Strait Islanders, Chinese artisanal gold miners, or white daredevils. They have a commonality of adventurism, courage, thirst for risk and reward and a sense of the supernatural, which informs their view on life and death. And always at their back the unfeeling hand of fate steers them to their prearranged destination.

Throughout the plots, Nature, which is constantly described and in moving detail, acts like a spiritual force, dispensing benefit and harm. And the Stoic attitude in regulating human behavior, prominent in

Western civilization until recently, is present everywhere – in the first peoples, in Chinese prospectors, as well as white characters. Long Toby, a white man in The Sandalwood Getters, is described in stoical terms – "His quiet face told of the bush philosopher, of a nature that took things as they came."

The lure of wealth, to be extracted from land or sea, from near surface gold occurrences, from deep-water pearls, compels the characters to disdain the constraints of safety and willingly risk incurring the wrath of the spirits. In each story, Idriess builds the effects of these typically masculine instincts into pacey climaxes that create high-level suspense. It's easy for the reader to accept the fateful compulsion of the protagonists because the local colour and the *dramatis personae* emerge from the author's intimate, first hand knowledge. The descriptions of the danger, particularly the hazards of diving in clumsy suits and helmets with the lifeline easily snagged by outliers of coral deep below or snapping when the diver falls into a hole, come from the time he hobnobbed with pearl divers of the tropical seas and actually dived himself. Every story proceeds in anticipation of something inevitable happening, but when the ending comes, it's as startling as a cattle whip cracked from behind. Each one has its own intrigue, its own characters, its own tensions and its own identity, all linked together by a master story teller who is sharing with the reader his lifetime of personal experience and keen observation of human nature. All in all, this book contains a chain of most enjoyable reads.

Tony Grey

Chinese workers punting bananas at Innisfail, 1885.

AUTHOR'S NOTE

THE stories in this volume record happenings or incidents in men's lives which interested me during years of wandering among the bushmen and natives of Cape York Peninsula; the pearlers, trochus and *bêche-de-mer* getters of the Coral Sea; the native islanders of Torres Strait; the "beachcombers" of the Great Barrier Reef; and along the eastern coast and in the Arafura Sea towards the west.

With two exceptions, all are transcripts of fact or are largely based on fact, unusual though an occasional one may seem. In such stories as "The City of Silence" and "The Squatting Devil of Samarai" I have taken the personal stories of old French Louis, the diver, and others, as trustworthy.

In several personal stories I am called "Jack." I never used my baptismal name, Ion, in the North or elsewhere.

I hope Colonel Woodman, Bert Vidgen of Thursday Island, Bert Jardine of Somerset, and others, will not mind their names being mentioned. My old mate Dick Welch, I know, will not; neither will "Scandalous" Graham. "Scandalous" may swear a lot and say harsh things about me, then quietly show the book in almost every shearing-shed in New South Wales and Queensland. That is, if he's "out of trouble."

I never realized how out of the ordinary these occasional picturesque incidents were until I came recently to live in the cities.

Some of these stories have been printed before. For courtesy in granting permission to reproduce them I thank the editors of the *Bulletin; Daily Mail,* Brisbane; *Sunday Sun,* Sydney; and *Burns Philp Queensland Monthly.*

For the photographs in this book my thanks are due to Alan Queale and William Shephard of Queensland, Colin Simpson of *Sun* Newspapers Ltd., Sydney, McIntosh Murray of Darnley Island, and H.L.A. Frankford of Sydney.

ION IDRIESS

CONTENTS

The Yellow Joss   8
The Sniper   16
The Cockatoo   22
The King's Colour   33
The Piebald's Bell   40
The Miracle   47
The Squatting Devil Of Samarai   53
The Death Stone   59
A Smile From Neptune   63
The Cruise Of The Greyhound   69
The Booya   77
The Bones Of Leon Chang   85
The Call Of The Pack   91
A Fisher Of Maubiag   94
The City Of Silence   99
The Sandalwood Getters   105
The Yellow Lily   114
The Pearls Of Gungadool   120
"And God Gave Man Dominion"   128
The Castaway   133
The Endless Mystery   138
The Vanishing Dream   145
The White Witch   152
Golden Hair   162
Account Rendered   168
The Bridge   176
The Rivals And A Devil-Fish   182
The Woes Of "Scandalous" Graham   187

THE YELLOW JOSS

IT was in the middle of a prospecting trip several years ago that my mate and I rode on the abandoned Chinese camp. We stared at those huts, even then overgrown with jungle. Such an obviously foreign camp had no right to be on Australian soil. In that isolated place it could mean only one thing; so we unpacked the horses and camped, and next day tried dish prospects up along the worked-out creek. We proved that creek to have once been surprisingly rich with gold, and felt very bitter because, but for the yellow trespassers, we would have found that wealth ourselves. A hefty buck of the Starcke River tribe told me those few parts of the story which I was unable to piece together. Here is the story; but beforehand know that about eighty miles north of Cooktown the Starcke River tumbles noisily from its craggy birthplace down to the sea. Much gold has been won along its short length by white men, but it is now abandoned and has gone back almost to the loneliness of the days when Captain Cook beached the *Endeavour* in Cooktown's bay. Its head creeks gurgle down from precipitous ranges that are clothed in entangling scrub, while many of its rock-walled gorges and gloomy ravines even yet have echoed to no human tread save the pad of the hunting aborigines.

A thousand feet up among the rocks in the main river gorge, and forty feet above a rushing creek that disgorges into the headwaters of the river, there was three years ago a little camp of Chinese gold-diggers. The camp site is well hidden deep down between rocky spurs and huge mountain bluffs, screened by the dark green of tropical scrub on one side and thick forest timber on the other. A luxuriant growth of man-high blady grass, choking the very tree-butts, was screening everything. On the site five cosy camps clustered together. Four of them were oblong, cleverly built of supple sapling framework; thatched entirely over with blady grass, nigger fashion; and having one manhole for ingress and egress, The other was square, a little larger than the rest. All were barely five feet high.

Thirteen men worked the camp. In the larger hut slept the serang and the cook, with the Joss. Between their mountain camp and the coast (as the crow flies a short twenty miles) are a series of small hills all forest clad. The party had been quietly landed from a *bêche-de-mer* lugger financed by a group of Thursday Island Chinese merchants. Their object was to seek for gold on the practically uninhabited Cape York Peninsula coast. Six months' supply of stores the party had carried in their baskets, jogging over the bush foot-hills and then struggling doggedly on up the jagged mountain gorge. At six-month intervals the lugger crept to anchor at an agreed on point on the lonely coast, landing fresh supplies. At such times the serang handed over to the representative of the merchant syndicate its share of the gold won. Then silently the string of Chinamen, with their enormously heavy loads, disappeared again into the great bush. They should not have been there. The law allows no Asiatic to mine. But the Chinaman smiles – "Eye no see-ee, heart no grieve-ee."

The chance of detection was very slight. Only two white men lived anywhere near: down near the mouth of the river a cattleman isolated in his bush home and interested in cattle alone; and an old, old fossicker in a weird camp among the foot-hills. The only dread of the Chinese was the wandering prospector, that nomad who may appear with the unexpectedness of a cloud in the most unlikely places. As for the blacks, they were given opium charcoal, which made them the serang's helpless slaves. The nearest town was little Cooktown, eighty miles south over the ranges. None but a decent bushman could follow that seldom trodden track that like a goat-pad crosses the mountains.

The first thing the yellow men did on picking their camp (even before seeking gold) was to make a Joss; for no Chinese undertaking can be successful without its Joss. And these men, far from their own kin, were trespassers deep within a strange and inhospitable land. They needed help indeed from the gods of luck. So with much thought and care and many mutterings they constructed a squat image of red clay. It was hideous; but Chang Ho, the serang, fashioned its face tenderly so that it seemed to smile – such a smile as a father might wear while quietly watching the tribulations of his children. That smile of rare sympathy promised good fortune for the yellow men.

The night that saw it completed, they sat there, Joss in state in the centre of the larger hut, and solemnly burned sandalwood sticks before him, their waxen faces looking strained and reverent as the closed-in place filled with a rich, heavy incense. Then Chang Ho knelt down and, with a whispered prayer that came from the heart, pressed heavily into the idol's forehead a pellet of dull yellow gold. That gold had come from the Chinese diggers' paradise, the Palmer River. This pellet was the eye of the Joss, and the symbol of what he must find for them.

Happy, happy thought of Chang Ho! The thirteen Chinese bowed low in the incense-filled hut with a happy song in their hearts that the omen was good.

It was Chang Ho who with trembling hands washed the first prospect in the new creek next morning. He stared with his slant eyes widening as the gravel swirled in the bottom of the dish, then with an exultant cry held up for all to see a little nugget of gold! The size of a pea, it flashed in the sunlight the rich yellow flash of the Starcke gold. Instantly thirteen pairs of Chinese eyes glittered at this miraculous realization of wonderful dreams. Feverish excitement held them clustered around Chang Ho and the little yellow pea. A wild gabble of shrill Chinese sounded among the quiet Australian trees.

Soon this madness would give place to systematic, intense toil; but first the thirteen, headed by the serang, marched one behind the other to the big hut. With shaking limbs they crawled inside to bow before the Joss; and there, with outspread finger-tips and foreheads they touched the earthern floor. This object of their reverence promised to be a most beneficent Joss. They kissed his clay belly in turn. With whispered beseechings Yuan Cheng, the cook, bathed the idol's face with his tears as he breathed to it of a flower-girl on the far off Yangtze Kiang, and the grandee's robe for himself. Chang Ho, with adoration shining from his strong flat face, offered his whispered promise of the ten best years of his manhood and strength if the Joss would but make the gold payable throughout the length of the creek. Then he firmly inserted that bright piece of gold into the clay forehead below the duller yellow of the Palmer metal. A gift to the Joss; forerunner of rich gifts to come! The Chinese bent very low. Yet again had Chang Ho shown grace to a good joss and propitiated him to win favour for all.

With the tireless energy of their kind the Chinese worked the creek. Out in the icy cold water while it was yet too dark for the awakening of the birds, one gang would cut away the bushes, then pick out and heave aside the larger stones. The gang following would throw out the smaller stones; while the third gang would sluice the creek gravel into the water race, where the yellow metal was concentrated. They toiled, with only one pause for a quick meal, right throughout the day; systematically, methodically, so that the work advanced with the precision of a machine. When the evening grew too dark for them to see the job, they had accomplished each day an amount of work that would have staggered a similar number of white men. The cook toiled with the others, grudging the time needed to prepare their meals.

Each night, after the hungry evening meal, the party would light the floating shark-oil lamp in the serang's hut, burn new, sweet sandalwood sticks before their Joss, and pay him homage. First Chang Ho, the serang, the expression of the Sphinx on his big flat face, would with scrupulous fairness divide the day's clean-up of gold. First, the portion which went to the Chinese merchants who had equipped the expedition; then his own portion; then the twelve other portions. Each portion exact to the weight of a breath on the delicate Chinese scales before the fixed, unwavering eyes of every man present.

Then, in the deep silence of the hut, Chang Ho would take the largest piece from the merchants' portion and embed it in the clay of the Joss. From his own portion likewise he would take the largest piece, and with muttered prayer press it into the Joss with his strong, squat thumb. And each other man of the twelve would do the same from his own portion. Then all would retire quickly for the few remaining hours of night to gather strength from sleep to gain yet more gold from the white man's land on the morrow.

The creek proved very rich, the gold held out strongly, in size mostly from a quarter to half weight pieces-like golden peas and beans. At the end of three months all knew that, if the Joss held true, each one of them at the end of two years, provided the dreaded white men did not find them, would go home to China to live a grandee for the remainder of his life.

Too short were the long, long days of toil. Too long were the short night hours when they must sleep. Then to Chang Ho came another happy thought. By day he took the Joss and sat him on a boulder that overlooked the creek. Every man by the upraising of an eye could see him smiling down upon him, glittering with his fast-growing coat of bright Starcke gold. And they would bend their backs still more till wonder was that human frames could stand it. The listless blacks sitting in the long grass of the creek-bank, with bloodshot eyes and drug hungry, would dumbly wonder at these yellow men, who were madder in their thirst for the useless yellow stone than even the mad white men.

The Joss now was an ugly-shaped thing of flashing beauty in the sunlight. The clay was almost hidden by the devotees' gifts. Chang Ho still strove to keep the warm smile on the face, but the constant insertion of gold pellets had turned the mouth corners down until it leered on the sweltering workers with a cynical grin.

And a change came over the camp. No longer did they retire straightway at night; instead, the gambling cards and the dice came out in the serang's hut immediately the Joss had been propitiated. The concentrated strength of the working day gave place at night to the intense brainthrill of the gambler, they then forgot their Joss to worship individual greed. They crouched low in the smoking hut and gazed at the rolling dice as they stole the precious little yellow heaps from some men and stacked them on the fast growing heaps before others. Just the click of the dice, a sharp drawn breath and lingering sigh, the slithering as a clammy hand reached out to draw its golden gains across the table. Often now the newborn sun would beat warm on the serang's hut and find them still at play – tragic play. The work too was different. There was no diminution of toil, but as they swung their heavy picks the hearts of eight men had ceased to sing. Months of toil, with their resultant heaps of yellow gold, had gone to others. Little devils dwelt within them. And still each night they played away what they had sweated for by day, in a frantic attempt to regain what was lost. And the ever-yellowing Joss leered over all.

When they met the lugger at the end of the first six months two of the thirteen went on board. They could live in China as grandees now. They would not take the chance of the dice any longer; nor the chance of the unstable gold "cutting out" nor the chance of some wandering white men discovering their creek. The remainder went loping back up the big mountain retreat carrying their heavy loads of food-stuffs and their heavier hearts. So another six months crept by. Days of panting toil; nights of feverish gamble. And the grin of the Joss grew distorted like the hearts of the yellow demons working and playing beneath its sneering stare.

Again two men left on the lugger that sailed for Thursday Island, there to ship for Lotus Land. This trip the lugger brought new men to replace those who had left, for the distant merchant-syndicate wanted the work carried on while the luck held good.

Feng Shu, crouching broken and motionless in the serang's hut, could swear that the Joss laughed at him, laughed, this grinning thing that his own hands had helped to fashion! As though all the demons of the nethermost hell were not already clawing at his heart! For the first time a feeling of animosity stole over Feng Shu against this Wonderful Joss. He glared back, a surge of hatred slowly gathering within him, and the yellow thing gave him stare for stare, deliberately. It seemed to possess life itself, this thing of gold. Gold! Feng Shu caught his breath guiltily, stealthily glancing round the smoke-filled hut.

But his companions were crouched around the playing mat, tensely gazing on the rolling dice. Feng Shu slowly turned his bloodshot eyes to the Joss. It blinked back knowingly, tauntingly.

A dawn came when the serang opened his heavy eyes and looked wearily to the Joss. Gone! It was gone! The Wonderful Joss was gone!

Chang Ho sprang from his bunk with a yell that brought the fear of death to every man in camp. They rushed from their bunks to find the serang mad. The Wonderful Joss was gone!

The serang ran for the creek. No, the Joss was not on the boulder where he sat by day. After one hopeless stare the serang jumped into the creek and feverishly dug a prospect where work had been left off the night before. He found not a colour of gold in the dish! He tried another prospect, and another. The gold was finished. It had "cut out!"

With tragedy in his eyes the serang gazed up at the Chinamen watching, breathless, on the bank. He stood thus holding the empty dish in his hand, empty as all men knew now the creek to be. It was "worked out." It was then that Yuan Cheng, the cook, discovered that Feng Shu was missing. And his washing-dish was missing too! With a cry like animals about to stampede they rushed to his hut. He was gone!

A black man standing by pointed to hurried tracks leading away from the camp towards the coast side. Then the serang spoke. But it was not his voice. It was the growl of a snarling animal with the blood-lust clutching its throat.

"The Wonderful Joss has made the gold cut out because Feng Shu has stolen him. We must catch Feng Shu with the Wonderful Joss and bring him back!"

They started off immediately, just as they were; and the whole tribe of aborigines, eager at the promised reward of an enormous quantity of opium charcoal, ran along the plain tracks of the doomed man like children at play.

Feng Shu had done remarkably well, all things considered, during the night. He had found the sea. He was a stranger in a strange land, with far worse things than death at his heels. He did not know where he was when the welcome daylight broke, but had a hazy notion that there was a white man's city called Cooktown down the coast. He knew a Chinatown was there, and felt he would be safe if once he could mix with countrymen of his, because he had gold – much gold. And gold is every man's friend. He glared cunningly at the heavy, glittering Joss in his arms.

He was not afraid now in this brave, warm sunlight.

They would never catch him, he had too much start; besides, they did not know what direction he had taken. All he had to do was to follow the seashore until he came to Cooktown.

Feng Shu had not the slightest idea of distances in this great white man's land, of the vast spaces without habitation. He didn't dream that, behind him, even the piccaninnies of the Starcke tribe were laughing at the plain tale his tracks told. He knew nothing of the sinuosities of the coastline, its maze of mangrove swamps, its tidal rivers to cross, with their deep holes, their crocodiles and sharks. More fatal than all, Feng Shu knew nothing of a thing called "bushmanship." If he had understood the meaning of that word not all the demons from behind the veil of death could have forced him to steal the Joss.

Soon the nice walking on the firm white sand led him in among trees, low trees, countless trees, trees seemingly thick as the sands upon the shore itself. But now there was no sand, and no shore. He was walking through mud, and could only glimpse the sea in random patches, through the thickly foliaged trees.

Presently the trees grew many roots that bunched out strangely from high above their butts. These trees grew so thickly together that their gnarled, tangled roots interlaced, strangely reminiscent of the demon trees that artists picture as growing in the land of the devils. Soon he was walking on the tree-roots. Often they snapped under his weight with a sharp, pistol-like report and he went down through the roots into the mud, jerking his head around in startled fear. (That sticky mud smelt like a charnel-house.) Then he must pull himself up and climb over the roots again, hugging the Wonderful Joss that was now growing heavier.

Feng Shu became very tired. Hungry, too. He longed to see the sky. Anxiously he peered around through the twisted branches for sight of the sea, but only heard a dreamy murmur. He rested, and ate the small supply of food he had brought with him. But there was no water to quench his thirst; the only water was salt. Dimly he began to realize that matters were not going well.

Starting off again, an hour's hard work over the roots made him dreadfully tired. He turned, and walked over the roots towards the sound of the sea. Surely there must be sand to walk upon out there.

There was, but it was many feet under water. A little wave splashed in among the tree-trunks and came gurgling to his knees. With a sudden fear Feng Shu remembered the tide! He turned abruptly, crashed through the tree-roots and felt mud clasping at his knees. Thick, oily, blue-black mud that swelled slowly up his limbs as it clung with a dreadful, sucking caress.

It was a pale-faced Chinaman who struggled desperately back through the mangroves. How heavy the Joss was! He stared down at it, thinking rapidly. Of course, it was heavy with clay! And he carried his washing-dish with him! All he had to do was to break up the Joss, wash the clay out in his dish and throw the dish away. He would thus be rid of the weight of the dish and the clay and have the gold only!

As Feng Shu crushed the head of the Joss he shuddered. Somehow his spine turned icy so that his trembling hands could hardly wash out the derisive grin from between the clay and the gold.

And at that work they caught him, the bright red clay streaming into the sea water, the dish weighed down into the muddy sand with glittering yellow gold. Crouched there, with the dish in his hands, Feng Shu never moved – just stared drawn-eyed at the triumphant black men shouting to the labouring Chinese to hurry up.

It was the serang's tragic cry that drew their attention to the clay that was once the Joss, now but a fast-receding stain on the rippling water. The Wonderful Joss was gone!

They took Feng Shu all the way back to the mountain camp. They put him to death by the Thousand Cuts. But Yuan Cheng, the cook, who was operator and only an amateur, could administer no more than three hundred.

But the gold came not back to the creek.

Chinese gold-miner, Queensland 1860 , by Richard Daintree.

THE SNIPER

CURIOUS how at times, when a man is steadily working, some quite random thought will carry his mind in a flash back years ago.

So it was with me this morning. I was back in the galloping squadrons as we swung under cover behind some low hilly rises during the Gaza-Beersheba stunt. Our squadron hastily dismounted at the extreme end of one of these. A man immediately collapsed with a bullet through a lung. There was a rush to pull the panting horses as close under the sheltering rise as possible, for the dread thought "sniper" flashed through every mind. The enemy were lining the low hills in front of us, but our man had been shot from out on the right flank.

"Crack! Thud!" A horse crashed on its belly as a high velocity bullet whistled into its flank. "Crack! Thud!" A good-looking chestnut reared surprisingly in the air, pawed frantically in an attempt to regain its balance, then crashed backward to earth, the soft brown eyes growing pitifully big as it struggled gamely to rise.

The trooper-owner stared down at it, intense feeling spreading over his hard, drawn face. A mate rushed out from cover and jerked the man's arm; even as he did so a vicious, crackling whistle had come and gone. The emu feathers on the trooper's hat fell to his shoulder, sheared clean off to the hat-rim.

The anxious squadron crouched close against the rise, each man with his precious horse pulled well in. The sniper evidently could see partly around the extreme corner of the rise, judging by the angle from which the man and the two horses had been shot.

Nothing got more quickly on the nerves of the troops than a sniper. Under several conditions, a thousand men within the range of one solitary sniper could not hit back. Each man simply had to crouch low wherever he was, while the hidden menace systematically picked his targets one by one. That sort of thing on the nerves is ghastly; compared with it, shell-fire is merely in the day's routine.

We felt it intensely that morning. Our brigade was in reserve; at any moment we might be called upon to join in a galloping charge. On the other hand we might have to remain totally inactive for long hours, perhaps all day, with, as far as our squadron was concerned, that searching sniper shooting at our extreme right flank.

Very gingerly I looked from the side of the rise through a pair of splendid field-glasses, "souvenired" from an Austrian officer of artillery.

I had the reputation of being a sniper myself. Now, every man knows that when he has built a reputation, or has had a reputation thrust upon him, something forces him to try to live up to it, no matter what his heart may be whispering. So I nonchalantly examined the field of barley on our right flank, whence, apparently, the shots had come. But, inside, I *knew*.

It was a beautiful, sun-kissed field. Emerald-green.

The crop just about a foot high, and as level as a billiard table. High in the clear air above the centre of the little field a brown lark trilled as only larks can. But of life in the field there was not a sign. I knew there would not be. Over every yard, then every foot of its greenness, I searchingly played those high-powered glasses. No slightest depression in the ground, no almost invisible green mound anywhere where green mound ought not to be; absolutely nothing whatever behind, or in, or between which a man could hide. But I well knew that a trained man can lie perfectly still facing you not a hundred yards away on hard, brown earth without even a grass-blade on it, and you can stare at the muzzle of his rifle for ten minutes without seeing him. At Enoggera in peaceful Australia we had been taught this, months before the Landing. And now, somewhere within that field of barley a highly-trained sniper lay easily concealed.

Between us and the edge of the field, just at the foot of the gentle slope which ran down from our sheltering rise, and only a hundred yards away, was a narrow waddy; or gully as we would call it in our own good language. Throwing off haversack and water-bottle, I suddenly jumped from behind the rise and tore down the slope in a crouching run, jerking from left to right, not for three seconds keeping to one straight line. The crackling hisses as the sniper tried to get me by rapid fire were reminiscent of the breath of white-hot iron.

I landed sprawling in the sheltering waddy-bottom, and gasped in long, thankful breaths. The first point in the game was won, anyway. I filled my pipe, lit it, and commenced slowly walking up the waddy. The banks were about eight feet high, and I blew the smoke upward so that its dying spirals just cleared the bank and drifted into the air above. When the bank became high I pocketed the pipe, and doubled quickly back to where I had first sprawled into the waddy.

Pulling barley from the edge of the bank was the next thing; then arranging the foot-long stalks in a row around the hat-band, and carefully spreading barley in flat sheaves over my back under and over the bandolier and bayonet-belt. Each stalk had to be done so very carefully, for if a barley-stalk drooped where every stalk should be standing– Then came the stealthy climb up the waddy-bank and into the barley-field. Inch by inch. First the length of the rifle (how heavy the familiar weapon quickly became!) poked gently on ahead, full-length of the arms, through the barley-stalks; then rested gently on the earth, palms of the hands cupped protectingly around the firing mechanism. Then careful craning forward of the head, chin pressed to the ground; then dragging of the entire taut body along by leverage of the elbows. Just one foot advance for each complete drag, just one inch at a time; chin, chest, belly, and toes pressed tight against the earth, while the heart thumped.

A man's mind could *feel* when a single barley-stalk, among those through which he crawled, quivered the slightest bit more than it should. Then one long, waiting breath, and, very slowly, on again.

But what a strain on the ears! For it was the ears more than the eyes which might win the next point in this game. Somewhere in that field lay the waiting sniper. Where, I knew not. He would not move. But his eyes would be seeing, his ears would be hearing. And he would shoot.

My mates back on the rise would go through all the old tricks to attract his fire and attention: a gently-moving hat held just above the sky-line with a stick; a rifle poked above a sand-mound with a hat slanting on the butt. If this had no effect, a man would dash from cover, then back again, lively – anything so that I might locate the sniper by the crack of his rifle.

So on I crawled, if possible slower and more cautious than before. The farther in the barley I was when his rifle cracked the better chance of locating him correctly.

He wouldn't move. From his position, the movement of his eyes alone would naturally show him all up the gentle slope of the rise and around the corner where the squadron was crouching.

If he raised his head the least bit too high above the barley to look for me he would fall to my rifle, just as I would fall to his should I raise *my* head.

He would simply wait, every instinct, every nerve, every sense tuned to the uttermost with the thrill of longing to put a bullet through my brain. How I understood the feelings of the hidden man, because they were my very own! But his rifle did not crack; he was too cunning a bird to fall to the tricks of my mates. He was waiting for me.

High in the cloudless sky the lark still carolled. From away on the right came a spasmodic crackling, drowned by the fierce, concentrated roar as a brigade burst into sudden rifle-fire. Machine-guns butted in with a harsh, metallic chattering. A battery of eighteen-pounders, then two more batteries roared in with a thundering crescendo.

"The En Zeds are into it again," the mind subconsciously whispered.

High in the air came the drone of planes. "Our planes are going to lay some eggs!" the mind announced. Then came splitting crashes up in the sky. "Turkish anti-aircraft!" whispered the busy brain. But I saw none of these things, and heard them only as in some other, far-away world. The whole battle today, the battle forever for me or for him, lay waiting in this peaceful barley-field. Though one nation rose and one fell by this evening, it would matter not at all to him or to me.

Without lifting chin from the ground, my eyes would naturally rise slightly to the sky on each pause for breath. Each time they would alight on the carolling lark, as it hovered so wonderfully balanced in the air, only to rise almost out of sight in an apparent attempt to sing its way to heaven, to reappear with miraculous rapidity, and hover, shrilly singing – and it seemed as I wormed farther and farther into the field to hover constantly over one particular spot!

I watched the lark for what seemed a long time; then a breathless realization gripped the mind and tingled through the body until it tautened at the roots of the scalp. I felt my mouth open a little and eyes suddenly widen as I pressed back the rifle safety-catch and gripped hard the splendid weapon. Then twisting very s lightly to the left, so as to be in line with the hovering lark, I crawled off again. No mother ever nursed her first-born more gently than I nursed my way through those tender barley-stalks that were so easily bruised and swayed.

Sound! What a medley of sound there was! Each stalk harboured life that constantly hummed or hissed or chirped. And things to see! There were countless live things in that barley, some of them swarming over the stalks, things so minute that I never dreamt anything but a microscope could have seen them. And as for the stalks themselves-each had taken on an individual shape; some were tall, some short; some were bent, some straight. Wonderful, too, how far a still man, chin pressed to the ground, could see through that dim, green maze of stalks. Some had wee tufts of grass growing around their butts, and an odd wild flower or two. One scarlet poppy pushed up its crimson cup for sunlight and life. And over all was the song of the lark.

I raised straining eyes, while taking long, steady breaths of the warm earth. How very earthy it smelt! In the air the lark was hovering now, not so very high. At any other time a man could hardly have distinguished that little brown head pointing towards me, now held a little sideways, peering straight down. I wormed a little farther on. Slow, tense minutes passed in withdrawing the field-glasses and carefully raising them just above the ground.

How the barley-stalks leapt into prominence! How much farther a man could see! The distance a few yards ahead had before merged into vague greenness; now, far beyond that, one could make out spaces between the barley-stalks, and the minute sand pellets around the earthworms' holes looked like brown clods.

Then something moved. It was only the turn of his cheekbone, but it allowed me to focus right into the eyes of my man. Blazing black eyes that had gazed into the haze of the desert seeking the silhouette of the camel caravans many and many a time. Only partly could I see the big brown nose, hawk-shaped, for two twisted barleystalks camouflaged his black *burnous*. The perfectly shaped, tiny black dot of his rifle-muzzle I could see, and below the telescopic sight the bony brown finger-knuckles that gripped around the weapon. A Bedouin, with the eyes of a hawk! How my heart thumped!

As carefully as myself he brought something towards his face. Tilting forward the barley-covered hat, I lay for long minutes, eyelids pressed to the rough earth.

"Field-glasses. Best German make for sure," flashed the racing brain as I lay there motionless – and waited.

At last I raised the head; then slowly, breathlessly, brought the glasses up again. His eyes now were continually roving in a motionless face, from left to right, from right to left. And I could almost *hear* him listening!

Very patiently, between all the many barley-stalks I concentrated on those two stalks which still crossed his nose. With craning neck I aligned them perfectly, then put the field-glasses gently down while never for the faintest breath of time letting my eyes miss his eyes.

Then the calculation on which one life would depend.

Dearly I would have loved to level the rifle foresight fair between those two black eyes-the desire grew almost overwhelming. But many barley-stalks besides the two crossed ones were in the way. Such a tiny thing might deflect a bullet – and a man would be allowed only one shot.

I could see the butt of the two stalks as they crossed down his nose in a straight line past the centre of his chin where the black beard hid them.

"Aim right at the butt of the stalks, exactly where the beard covers them. The bullet then should strike that little hollow below the throat at the base of the neck between the two bones, and go right down through his body. He should never move after that I"

Then the indrawing of a deep breath, the raising of the rifle, the easing of the racing nerves as the familiar weapon settled its iron-shod butt reassuringly into the hollow of the shoulder, the absolute steadiness as the trigger-finger took the "first pull" and the foresight lowered on the barley-stalk down past the eyes, past the mouth, slowly past the chin, until, engaging in the rear sight, stopped dead where the beard hid the butt of the barleystalk.

"I shall cut the stalk dead in two," whispered the mind in that last fraction of a second of complete steadiness.

"Crack

I bounded out of the barley and was on the spot even as he rolled over. He was dying. His flashing black eyes fastened on mine in a gaze of instant realization and deathless hate. He attempted to raise his arm, the sinews tautened in the thick brown wrist as he tried vainly to clench his fist. I knew he was beseeching all the curses of the Prophet upon this Christian dog who had taken his life. But as his wordless lips bared back in the last of the choking gasps I only thought:

"I wish I had your splendid teeth, Blackbeard. They are no use to you now!" Looking down at him, like a great fallen hawk in the crushed barley, I felt no remorse; only hot pride that in fair warfare I had taken the life of a strong man – hot pride that this man, older and stronger physically than I, this man reared from babyhood to regard warfare as the life of a man and splendid sport, this desert irregular knowing every inch of the country, had fallen to a stranger from a peaceful land who knew only three years of war!

Quickly I looked him over for the inevitable souvenirs.

Strung on a camel sinew around his neck were thirty eight identification disks, mostly those of British troops, but with a sprinkling of Australian and one Maoriland badge. A Mohammedan goes to Paradise if he can kill a Christian. So this good religionist had thirty-eight keys to the pearly gates. There was a special silver medal also, and a parchment deed of recognition from the Sultan.

Presently I turned and examined the barley-roots closely. But it was not until a couple of fellows from the squadron came running over that we found what we sought. Within a foot of the Bedouin's body, cunningly interwoven between four stalks of barley, was a little nest, and in it one solitary fledgeling, its eyes still shut, but hungry mouth wide open. Such an insignificant thing to cause the death of a man!

THE COCKATOO

JOHN MARKHAM lit an after-breakfast pipe while gazing through the open doorway at the brown water-ways surrounding wooded islands that cluster at the mouth of the Fly. A mighty river, rising far back in the mysterious heart of grim New Guinea. Its forty-mile-wide estuary is a vista of brown waters where the sea breaks sullenly on treacherous sand-banks. Within the mighty mouth of the Auwo Oroma itself, the banks are invisible; and many are the islands, all flat, luxuriant with coconut palm, and overtopped by the thorny sago palm whose pithy heart is one of the staffs of life for mankind.

Thousands of savage men, brown and black, live on the mothering river; thousands more, elusive and shadowy people, live in the great swamp villages farther inland. The gardens of some down-river villages show a mastery of agriculture that would lead the traveller to think these people were far advanced in culture. Maybe, judged by savage standards; but the heads of white, brown, black, and yellow men, have bleached within those great *Dtirimu* houses.

This day, smoke was drifting lazily from big Asasai village, from Warubi, from Gamobobo and Wabiri and other human hives all around the thirty-mile strip of heavily foliaged mud that is Kiwai Island. From big Wabudu and Purutu islands, from Aibinio and Gebaro and lesser isles the early morning smoke was rising too.

Markham's isle was within distant hail of Mibu Island, enticing now with the sun streaming on its avenues of palm-tops. Markham gazed with the light almost of love in his steady grey eyes. This was his home, he had carved it out himself, won it from this sinister land against the forces of nature and of man.

"Call up the boys, Cocky!" he ordered.

Straightway the plantation rang to piercing screeches accompanied by a voice that rasped through the palms to screech away over the waters.

"Line up, line up you swabs! Quick feller boy line up! My heaven! Come along! You lazy dingbats. Line up! Line up! Line up!"

Markham smilingly strolled out on to the veranda.

"Give it to 'em, Cocky," he encouraged. "Liven the beggars up!"

The cockatoo obliged with a crescendo of screechings as he shuffled backwards and forwards along the veranda rail, mimicking all the fury of a navvy foreman, screeching "Ramu," "Suvani," "Bali," "Dogoro," "Sasa," until from the distant village came laughing voices and shortly afterwards a troop of "boys" came winding through the *sacsac* (sago-palm) swamp to emerge at the plantation palms fronting the house veranda.

Markham in his loneliness had put his soul into the training of his friend the cockatoo.

Mostly Kiwaians and Moattans, the plantation labourers were hefty fellows, as black as the ace of spades, muscular brutes in their short lava-lavas; their keen, Semitic faces strong looking and reliant. They grinned up good-humouredly at the cocky "boss" abusing them over the veranda rail. The bungalow was built high up on piles, a precaution against the lake-like floods of the Fly.

Dragging his long chain, the cockatoo waddled backwards and forwards along the veranda railing, his head cocked belligerently, glaring down at the chattering boys. The poor bird possessed only one eye, but that saw all things.

Markham quietly gave his orders to the head boy, ordering so many boys to the drying sheds, so many to bag copra, so many to husk nuts, so many for field work.

The labourers trooped away followed by a screeching string of commands. "You husk him plenty feller nuts Goboro, you lazy dugong! Husk him big feller quick feller nut! You dry 'em plenty feller copra! Plenty feller bag 'im copra longa Taubada good feller master! You lazy mud turtle, Samsu! Oh this cursed chain!"

Markham laughed as the energetic bird threatened the boys, in hilarious frenzy tugging and screeching at the limit of its chain. This daily pantomime amused both Markham and his labour crew. He had a warm spot in his heart for the bird. He reached out a caressing hand under which it nestled its head, closed its one eye and clucked contentedly.

Cocky was a pathetic travesty of a sulphur-crested cockatoo. It sported no crest; its bald pate was seared with scars; and it was featherless, except for a lonely specimen that stuck out stiffly from its tail. The naked flesh of the tail gripped around this feather in bulging scars rather awful to contemplate. The blue-grey of its shrivelled body was pockmarked with scars; all that was left of one eye was a scarred socket; one wing drooped helplessly – it had been cruelly broken years ago.

"Poor old Cocky!" sympathized Markham. "Had a rough time in your day, eh!" The bird shut its bright eye and croaked softly. "You're a great old character, Cocky; you deserve lots of sympathy, but I can't scratch you all day long. Now I must go and write some letters before Cap'n Dick comes."

Instantly the bird screeched: "Cap'n Dick's a gentleman!"

"I didn't say he wasn't," laughed Markham, "though he and his crew have taught you some very ungentlemanly language. Now watch out for your friend, Cocky, while I write those letters."

He walked inside, the cockatoo hobbling after until brought up short.

"This cursed chain!" it declared decisively.

Markham, sitting at his table, spoke across the veranda.

"Now, Cocky, you know as well as I do that I daren't let you off the chain lest the natives steal you. While you are on the chain you are Taubada's property. Now go and watch out for Cap'n Dick."

He bent to his writing while the cockatoo grumbled its way across the veranda and climbed back on the rail.

The morning wore softly away. Into the cool, thatched bungalow floated the greeting call of natives as a canoe lazed by from the great Abaura fishing-grounds, the soft echo of flails as women beat sago in a distant *sac-sac* swamp. The scratch of Markham's pen was interrupted by the ear-splitting screech of the cockatoo.

"John Cowling! John Cowling! Joh-n Cow-ling-ing!"

"Damn you, Cocky, shut up!" expostulated Markham as he threw down the pen and strode out on the veranda. "What's your game? I didn't tell you to call up Cowling!"

The bird's bright eye gazed invitingly up, its old bald pate reached towards Markham's hand. He chuckled and obliged.

"I might have known that was what you wanted, you scamp. But I'll put you out on the back veranda if you raise any more false alarms!"

Distantly across the water a figure appeared on the veranda of John Cowling's house on Mibu. The cocky raised its head and screeched vociferously:

"John Cowling of Maubiag! Who found the copper ingots?"

The distant figure waved a white cloth. Markham replied in kind. The figure walked along the veranda back into the house.

"There now, see what you've done," scolded Markham.

"Mrs Cowling was very likely making cakes for John's dinner. Don't you dare call Cowling unless I tell you."

He struck a match to light his pipe and was pained at the instinctive flinch of the bird. "Silly old goat," he admonished. "You know very well I won't hurt you!" He stroked the scarred old head before returning to his writing.

The morning wore on to the scratching of the pen, with an occasional scolding outburst from the cockatoo as natives strolled past to the village. They answered his eerily human greetings with laughing words of cheer or abuse just as his remarks invited. Presently he called loudly but in a mimicking, crooning tease: "La-la's-got-a-ba-by! La-la's-got-a-ba-by!"

Markham smiled. He knew well what that cunning bird wanted. He put down his pipe. From the room, he could see out on to the veranda without being seen.

The cocky climbed down from the rail on to the veranda floor and poked out his pathetically comical head between the palm-wood lathes, crooning: "La-la's-got-a-ba-by."

A shy little native girl with the brown skin of one of the up-river tribes, her head shaved to a tuft of reed-plaited hair, stole noiselessly to the veranda, a tiny brown babe in her arms. The girl-mother's face was all smiles, her big eyes bright. "La-la's-got-a-ba-by," softly crooned the cockatoo in nodding accent to the words.

The little mother stood on tiptoes and held up her pride. She could just reach the veranda rail. "La-la's-got-a-ba-by," crooned the bird.

The little mother reached up and scratched the scarred old crown. Markham chuckled quietly. When he thought the cocky had imposed on the mother-instinct long enough, he recommenced writing. But the scratch of the pen was audible. Like a startled rabbit, the girl vanished. The cockatoo clucked angrily and burst out:

"This cursed chain! To hell with it!" and dragged the thing noisily the width of the veranda.

Later, there came an unusual, an oppressive, silence.

Markham glanced instinctively towards the veranda and his fine face clouded, for the cockatoo was all hunched up, a shrunken ball of crippled ugliness. Its head drooped sideways, its good eye distorted by an expression of waiting terror. It screeched piercingly:

"Livamada! Livamada! Livamada!"

Markham frowned. He put down the pen and watched as the shivering bird dragged itself towards his room. With its head nodding upon the veranda lathes it wheezed groaningly.

"My God! This cursed chain! This cursed chain!" Under a papaw-tree fronting the veranda appeared Livamada the sorcerer, friend of snakes. His malign influence swayed the entire estuary of the Fly. Naked and bald of head as the cockatoo, he was deceptively old, for the wrinkles emphasizing his repulsive face were really the imprints of wickedness. His one eye gleamed with a cold, fish-like stare. Red saliva of betel-nut dribbled from his moveless lips as he glared towards the cockatoo.

The bird kept rocking its head from side to side, voicing a wheezy moan, its beak tapping the floor. It was fighting hopelessly to stare around while mumbling "Livamada! Livamada! This cursed chain! This cursed chain!"

Markham pushed aside his papers and strode out on to the veranda. He detested the sorcerer because he came almost daily to torture the bird with his presence. Otherwise, Livamada had done him no harm. But he could – and serious harm, for he was one of the Sumai people; a nasty crowd, famous for their casting of spells. Relying, now, only on the fear of their black magic, these arrogant savages have even measured their spears against the bullets of a white magistrate.

The two men stood frowning, Livamada at the bird, Markham at Livamada. Markham could do nothing, for Livamada had done nothing. And Markham dared not offend him without just cause. The sorcerer's influence could breed devilry among the one hundred plantation boys if he so wished. When the native walked away, Markham picked up the nerveless bird: "He can't hurt you Cocky, old man," he soothed. "Why don't you stand up to him as you do to the others?"

But the bird was uncannily like a human from whom the spirit has been tortured. "This cursed chain!" it sobbed.

"Poor old goat!" comforted Markham. "You are Taubada's bird when on the chain; you belong to the world without it. There now, he's gone! He won't torment you again today. Sit up there on the rail and watch for Cap'n Dick."

With an interrupted mind, Markham returned to his correspondence. The only worry in his life at present was this man who would torment a bird-without saying a word or doing a thing. It was absurdly real. Every native throughout the estuary knew that Livamada, through his power over a bird, was making the Taubada "all same mad!" And yet Taubada dare not say a word – it would be so childish!

Markham frowned thoughtfully. The native is dangerous when he can covertly sneer at the white master.

"Cap'n Dick!" screeched the cockatoo. Markham dropped the pen and sprang to the veranda, his face wreathed in smiles. Very lonely men can smile that way.

"Cap'n Dick! Cap'n Dick! Yo-ho-ho an' a cask O' rum! My God here comes Cap'n Dick. Cap'n Dick! Cap'n Dick!"

Markham smiled at the sail of the *Aramia* just rounding Kiwai Island, hurried by the wind and the tide. "That's right Cocky old man, let him hear we know he's coming!"

The cockatoo, uncontrollably excited, hobbled the veranda rail, trying desperately not to overbalance, while flapping its uninjured wing. Its ear-splitting screech rang far over the water, "Cap'n Dick! Cap'n Dick! Cap'n Dick! Take the wind Cap'n Dick take the wind! Bully boy Cap'n Dick. Yo ho!"

A monkey-like figure shinned up the *Aramia's* masthead and waved. Markham waved his white cloth; on distant Mibu, John Cowling and his wife waved from the veranda. The villages awakened; crowds strolled to the water's edge. Conch-shells blared from island to island, rivalled harshly by blasts from the mainland. Canoes shot out from Kiwai, from island after island. The calls of natives echoed across the water-ways, and were returned by their kinsmen manning the *Aramia.*

The cockatoo fell over the railing from excitement. At his maddening screeches as he dangled in mid-air Markham laughed as he hauled back on the rail the flabbergasted bird that never ceased its screeching. "Cap'n Dick! Cap'n Dick! Cap'n Dick! My God Cap'n Dick! Swing her head up th' channel, Cap'n Dick! Poke her nose in th' sun, Cap'n Dick! Bully boy lad bully boy!"

As the *Aramia* came gliding up the channel, the cockatoo gave his berthing orders. "Shove it inter her Cap'n Dick! Down jib! Down mains'! Let her go, you b--ds! Let her go! Down fores'l! What ho! Hear them rattlin' halliards! Grease them blocks! Over with the mud hook me hearties! Over ya go! Make all fast forrard!"

As the anchor chain shrieked out to the boys' sing-song chorus, the bird screeched: "That cursed chain! It'll hold her! That cursed chain!"

Captain Dick Reynolds jumped ashore and gripped hands with Markham, but his first laughing words were:

"How's Cocky?"

"He speaks for himself," smiled Markham as he grabbed his mail-bag; "he thinks you are the most wonderful thing afloat. You've taught him all the English language and some other as well. There he goes again!"

"Cap'n Dick! Cap'n Dick! How's the girls in Sydnee town? Have a spot Cap'n Dick. Have a spot."

"We'll accept his advice," smiled Markham as they strolled up the path.

"Right!" agreed Reynolds. "Then you can open your mail and see what sort of a tale she tells this time, while I teach Cocky something new. He'll choke himself if he's not careful."

"My heaven!" declared the bird from the extreme end of its chain, "you're a hell of a time coming Cap'n Dick."

"Liar!" answered Reynolds definitely. "We put up a record trip."

"Liar be damned!" screeched the delighted bird.

"You're a hell of a boy Cap'n Dick – a hell of a boy!"

That evening, the men smoked on the veranda while Reynolds scratched the old bird's head.

"Do you know, Dick," said Markham with an almost boyish smile, "if my luck only holds for just two years more, I'll be in easy street. I've got two hundred acres planted now, ten thousand trees, most of them bearing, which means half a ton of copra per acre per year. With copra even as low as £12 per ton, that means £1200 a year."

"Good luck to you!" answered Reynolds cordially. "A man who carves out a home in this nigger-ridden hole deserves all the luck he gets. You're set as regards the labour question too. They like you. But always keep a weather eye on that black dog Livamada. What the hell's wrong with Cocky? Still scared of the name even! I thought people say birds haven't got memories!"

"He's had good cause to remember," replied Markham soberly. "And that black swine still comes and torments him by simply mesmerizing from a distance."

"Poor old Cocky," comforted Reynolds to the trembling bird. "I think of him every time I see the featherless wretches captive in the villages. The bucks just pull out a feather or two for any impromptu dance; there's always some flash buck wants an extra feather in his head-dress. But few are as unlucky as old Cocky here. Each time one of his feathers was pulled out, that black dog would hold a red-hot fire-stick to the spot so that the feather would not grow again. Some kink in his torturing mind made him leave this one big feather in the tail. He'd squat and watch the bird for hours, and when it was mesmerized so dumb that it couldn't give him any more sport, he'd pad over on his big feet, catch hold of the feather, pull it slowly about half-way out, then push it hard back, and hold a fire-stick to the tail around the roots to make the flesh grip tight again. That was the cause of its growing to such a prodigious size. And the bigger and firmer it grew the more painful each time the devil pulled it, I suppose."

"I thought the poor old bird was going to peg out one night after your last visit," said Markham. "Hammond spent a night here on patrol. Sitting as you are, scratching Cocky and yarning, he blew the ash off his cigarette and the bird collapsed."

"Oh, that's how Livamada – blast my tongue! Never mind, Cocky, old boy, I'm spoiling your evening's fun altogether! That's how the black swine fixed the poor bird's eye. Lala told me. He had mesmerized the bird, and was heating a cane in a slow fire. Now and again he'd withdraw the stick, examine the glowing end, peer across at Cocky, twist the stick and poke it back in the fire. Finally he took it out and sneaked across to the paralysed bird, just looked at it and said: 'Why should a bird have two eyes while I have only one!' He blew the stick into a glow and held it to Cocky's eye."

"They are fiendishly cruel," said Markham after a while, "but luckily not always with the purposely vindictive cruelty of the sorcerers. I don't think his thumbnail marks on the bird's wing will ever close together."

"No hope," said Reynolds. "He used to hold the wing strained with the thumbs pressed into it while the bird kept up that low gurgling moan waiting for him to break the wing as he had broken the other. Watch that black devil always, Mark; he plays the waiting game. He has sworn to rid the Fly of white men in such a way that no tribesman will taste the government jail. He must keep his boast for prestige sake. He burnt me out of my nice little plantation on the Oreomo – I wish I could prove it!"

"Everything is quiet here," said Markham uneasily. "All the tribes are contented."

"Yes – and watching. Four white men amongst thousands, and the other two of you located miles up the Fly. Well, offer me another spot, old man, before I go to bunk. By the way, I'm making a quick return trip, recruiting for the Thursday Island pearling-fleets. But don't breathe a word or that black dog will get busy and put the boys up to refusing to sign on."

The following days were a delight to the cockatoo.

From the veranda rail he supervised the loading of the *Aramia*, hastening the boys with a stream of commands, encouragement, and vituperation, answered in kind by the husky natives as they slung aboard the copra bags. But his greatest joy was in a few hours private conversation with the Cap'n.

The morning that the *Aramia* sailed saw the bird in great form, hobbling along the railing to the rattling of his chain. "Up jib!" he screeched to the song of the labouring crew. "Haul you beauts, haul! Give it 'em, Cap'n!" he screeched in excited echo to Reynolds's sharp commands. "Man the windlass! Up anchor! Wind, you beauts, wind! Up fores'l! Haul-haul-haul! Swing her head round, Cap'n. Swing her round! My God! This cursed chain! Up mains'l! Haul, you beauts, haul! Good-bye, Cap'n Dick. Good-bye. Come agen, Cap'n Dick. Come agen!"

Markham smiled by the excited bird as the *Aramia* faded away across the estuary.

One night a fortnight later, Markham went contentedly to bed. Hours later he awoke to a curdling screech:

"Livamada! Livamada! Livamada!"

Markham snatched his automatic and jumped out on to the veranda. The night was dark and still, the cockatoo, its beak tapping dazedly on the floor, was moaning: "This cursed chain! This cursed chain!"

Markham picked the bird up. "What's the matter? You old fool! You scared the life *out* of me. There's no one here!"

"Livamada!" hissed the bird throatily.

"Rats! Oh, I'm not going to leave you. Come with me then and we'll search the house."

He undid the chain and exclaimed as the terrified bird clenched its claws in his shoulder. Carefully he searched the house, then peered below among the dark piles beneath.

"I'm as much a fool as you are, Cocky," he assured the bird as he climbed back into bed. "He would have vanished immediately you called out had he been there at all. You can sleep here to-night but raise no more false alarms, you scraggy old fat-head."

But the bird was tongue-tied for once. It clung to the bed-rail in abject fear. Next day, while Markham was away down at the copra shed supervising drying operations, a sudden awful screech rang out from the house. He ran out of the shed and away through the palms to see a little brown figure flying up the house steps. When almost breathlessly he got there, Lala was kneeling on the veranda, the prostrate bird in her hands, her tears bathing its panting breast. The pained eye of the bird gazed up at Markham. Its last big tail-feather had been torn out by the roots.

Markham went about his work next day with a very uneasy mind. He knew that this pulling of a feather from a bird meant an attempt at the demoralization of a white man. The native mind works often in devious ways. The cockatoo no longer cheered the day with its noisy prattle. A very sick bird, it clung to Markham's shoulder wherever he went. He realized that both plantation and village people were covertly watching him; that particulars of his every movement were discussed on the surrounding islands, even on the mainland, at night.

But none were hostile; his own boys did their work well. He had no cause to complain of anyone. He felt he was duelling against an invisible menace.

Following nights of almost sleepless watching he fell into a trance-like slumber from which he gradually became aware of the faintest rubbing; through ages of time it seemed, there came something most urgently rubbing his ear; subconsciously he raised his hand and it rested reassuringly on the cockatoo's body. Fighting to retain sleep, his consciousness gradually awakened to that ceaseless agitated whispering: "Livamada! Livamada! Livamada! My God, Taubada! Livamada!"

Markham's hand pressed the crouching bird on his pillow, its beak to his ear. It "froze," gasping. Without moving, he forced his consciousness to full awakening. The room was inky dark, with not even a rustle from the palm-leaves outside. His hand sneaked under the pillow. Then he switched on the torch and instantly fired at a shadow; he sprang straight through the mosquito netting firing again as he jumped.

Livamada had vanished through a hole cut in the palm-lath floor.

Upon the clean yellow matting were drops of blood near a long white dagger. With shaking hand, Markham picked up the deadly thing. It was a skiver from the shin-bone of a man, needle pointed, the knobbed bone handle carved to the symbolic skull of a sorcerer. A wisp of human hair, damp from the sweat of a hand, was twisted around the haft.

"Things are jolly serious," whispered Markham. "I wish I had killed you, Livamada!"

The house-boys walked on stealthy feet next morning.

The plantation boys came quietly up for work much earlier. All eyes covertly sought Markham, watching what he would do. Quietly he ordered them to work, standing on the veranda until each squad walked away.

Then he got his rifle. He patted the cockatoo's head as he fastened its chain. "Don't look at me like that, old sport. It will be the last time you will wear the chain. I must chase the sorcerer now. He's slipped away by canoe, so you are perfectly safe, old bird. Don't you understand? If I do nothing, the boys will say I'm afraid, but if I go with a rifle looking for the dog he will keep hidden away over on the mainland. We must hold our prestige, Cocky."

But he never forgot the look in the eye of the bird! He trudged right across the island carefully examining its three villages. He knew he would not find his man. The villagers eyed him quietly, just watching. It was afternoon when he had searched the last village. His eye caught sight of Lala walking past the *Darimu* house. She gave him just one fleeting glance!

He left immediately, but when once in the *sac-sac* swamp he ran along the sodden path, his heart in his mouth, expecting every moment to see his home rolling up in smoke. But, after an hour's run, nothing had happened. He slowed his pace, breathing more easily. By now he could just see the tops of the plantation palms, with occasional glimpses of the water-ways. Climbing a gentle rise quite near the house he heard with surprise the sharp, clear rattle of an anchor chain. The *Aramia!*

He smiled, and walked on reassured. Everything was all right now. But he suddenly sprang forward and raced. Why was not Cocky calling for Cap'n Dick? His voice should have made the palms echo long ago!

As if in answer, a curdling screech rang through the palms. Markham raced. He flew out into the plantation and caught sight of Reynolds running up from the landing.

As Markham thundered through the back of the house Reynolds dashed up the front steps. Both men met on the front veranda, gazing down at the cockatoo, its wing broken, its head torn from its body.

MINERS AND MINER'S HOMESTEAD, BATAVIA RIVER
NORTHERN QUEENSLAND

THE KING'S COLOUR

THOUGH it seems laughable now, that wretched trip really was misery. I had worked a tin-mine in a lonely area of northern Queensland, and had "hung on" until the last shilling. Then the price of tin fell lamentably and there was nothing left to do but walk away. My companion was "Scandalous" Graham, the last wages man employed. It was some time since he had received any wages, but although a notorious "growler" he never mentioned the oversight. A well-known "hard case;" a shearers' cook during the shearing-season, his nickname "Scandalous" was earned by many an escapade.

We set out together for civilization. The third day was miserable, cold as a polar ice-chest. The hills appeared lifeless, and their granite boulders wet tombstones. The track wandered down slippery spurs, across flooded ravines, then up again into shrouded hills-apparently without end.

Scandalous Graham's boots squelched doggedly behind me. He clenched two chaff-bags across shivering shoulders; that and a heavy heart was all the swag he carried. Gone were his swaggering walk, his cocksure whistle; his aggressive face was now as pathetic as the droop in his bristly moustache.

I felt like Scandalous looked. One sodden blanket as swag, a battered billy-can, a pannikin of flour, a pinch of tea-and not a shilling in the world!

"How f-far now, Jack?" stuttered Scandalous.

"Dunno, Never travelled this track before."

"It's lost souls' track. I can hear 'em moanin' in the breeze. Su-sun's nearly down. Must be ashamed of itself. Don't believe these corpsy lookin' shadder mountains ever seen a proper sun anyway. Ugh! They reckon northern Queensland is so hot only n-niggers can live in it. Silly galoots! They orter import Eskimos, not Italians! "

We plodded on.

"Jack!" groaned Scandalous.

"What! What in heaven's name are you croaking at now?"

"Wish I *was* croaked," he moaned. "I'd be warm now sittin' on the hobs O' hell. Wh-what if we have to camp out to-night again? You with one blanket an' me under chaff-bags. An' a fistful of wet flour for supper. I could eat--"

"Shut up!" I snapped.

"Oh well, if I don't talk the cold'll freeze me tongue. Ugh! It's colder'n a barmaid's last night kiss. Say, Jack ?"

"What !"

"I won't never drink again!"

"Liar!"

" 'Struth I won't! Never no more. Just think of th' lovely quids I've done in! Think of the silk stockin's I've bought for the publicans' daughters! Nice warm stockin's too, Jack, with jazzy garters sportin' beads. We ain't even got socks! If only we had that--"

"For the love of Mike stop crying."

"The pot an' the kettle. W'y don't you boil over sometimes an' be human? I wish me pore feet wasn't so sore! Me pore corns is froze to me boots an' I can't feel 'em 'cept when I put me blasted foot down. I do wish-" I turned furiously – to stare! Away down a misty valley to our left stood a group of huts with friendly spirals of chimney smoke. I pointed.

"Watsonville!" yelled Scandalous. "Rooblooming-hooray! There's a heaven after all! An' it's right down there in them warm huts with lashins of tucker for two pore starvin' wanderers. Come along, Jack, me old icicle, we'll hit 'em up before dark. Ho, for the land O'billy-tea an' steamin' stew! An' they ain't bushmen if they don't hand pore Scandalous a nice warm blanket, p'raps two, an' a doss beside the fire with the old tom-cat!"

Enthusiastically he pushed on ahead quite forgetting the late state of his feet. We slithered down that slope on the heels of anticipation. Without doubt it was going to be an awful evening out in the open air. Those huts breathed of home.

Gingerly we stepped the stones across a frothing creek, then clawed up the clayey bank. It was sundown as we approached the huts. We were surprised to see a nondescript mob of half-clothed niggers shivering outside a humpy door. Their hunch-backed mongrels were the picture of misery; their crouching women more so.

We walked confidently towards the nearest hut and knocked. A scowling miner pulled the door ajar. We saw his mate bending over a frying-pan. Warmth and the scent of frying onions hit us in the face.

"Good evening," grinned Scandalous sociably, "hellish cold ain't it! What's all the niggers doing round the big hut?"

"Waiting for the government yearly blanket issue," answered the man surlily. "The policeman's come out from Herberton to issue them. He's there now!" He glowered darkly.

"By Caesar!" chuckled Scandalous. "Blankets! Why, my mate's only got a worn-out horse-rug an' I haven't got one at all! It's hellish cold too, freezes the heart out of a man O' nights. We've only got a bit of wet flour for tea too," he added expectantly.

"Well you can go down to the creek and cook it. There's plenty of wood and water down there!"

He slammed the door, grunting as he bolted it. Scandalous stared stupidly. My heart fell.

Night had come; wind moaned on the hill-sides; a drizzle of rain set in. Dumbfounded I stumbled towards the creek and with numbed fingers began gathering firewood. Scandalous came crawling down as I fumbled with the matches.

"Wh-what do you make of that?" he stuttered incredulously.

"We're evidently poison here," I answered. "For heaven's sake scratch about for some dry bark; you'd give a man the creeps shivering there like a drowned pup!"

We learned later that the Herberton miners had been harassed by tin-thieves. Naturally, the lonely few away out here at the Watsonville camp were taking no chances with a pair of strangers.

We coaxed a fire, put the billy on, then crouched miserably in the smoke.

A few coals glowed at last. I mixed up the doughy flour while Scandalous crouched with shivering arms to the damp blaze. His happy, devil-may-care spirits had evaporated with his anticipations. He was a live man dead.

"Wh-what do you think of it?" he whispered. "Tell me, have I f-frozen to death coming along this cursed track or am I truly alive an' are those men in that flea-bitten hut really Australians?"

"You're alive at present," I said grimly, "but you'll be frozen before dawn."

"My Gawd, Jack!" he wailed, "don't say we'll *have* to stay out all night!"

"You'll make a handsome corpse."

With stiff fingers I patted the dough into cakes, scraped out the blackened coals and laid the johnnies on to cook. As I lifted off the billy a keen wind blew over and through us. We gazed automatically upwind, or rather sniffed up. Into Scandalous's watery eyes dawned an intense longing.

"Johnny Walker!" he whispered incredulously. "Great snakes alive! In the hut where the policeman is."

"And that's our share of it," I said.

We gulped longingly as the whisky-scented wind, perfumed with frying onions and musical with boisterous laughter and clash of pannikins, floated down the creek.

"May I go hoppin' to hell!" observed Scandalous emphatically.

I stooped and turned the johnnies on "the coals. Scandalous humped down on the wet ground, anguished face in his hands.

"They call it a white man's country. They talk erbout socialism an' Christians an' mother's love an' Chris'mus. Even the niggers is goin' to have blankets! Me pore cold toes!"

Miserably we swallowed the charcoal encrusted cakes. The tea was sugarless.

Presently the door of the big hut was opened. A flood of warmth cheered out into the night. Three men stood outlined, one in the uniform of the mounted police.

"Hi!" he roared. "Line up, boys! Get your blankets, quick feller, then clear back to camp!"

At once the freezing niggers rushed the doorway, bucks, gins, piccaninnies, in a yabbering chorus.

"Silence!" roared the policeman. "Silence, or I'll keep the blankets and lock the whole lot of you up. Line up! Same way longa missionary, what time he teachem you singem hymn."

Scandalous threw off his coat and tugged at his boots.

"Pull me other b-- boot off q-quick!" he stuttered. "Quick! Me fingers can't undo the blasted laces!"

I bent to his boot. "Centipede in them, or a coal?"

"Neither," he snapped, "a blanket."

I stared. He burst a bootlace and swore luridly.

"Rub me feet with charcoal quick," he gasped. "I'll dress up nigger fashion an' get a blanket if I freeze in me dignity doin' it!"

I understood. He rubbed his face with charcoal while I hurriedly scraped his feet – and received no thanks. His corns were tender. The job finished, he jumped up, looking the question.

I was dubious, but Scandalous's hair is jet black, his eyebrows shaggy and fierce, his face strikingly ugly. With the layer of charcoal daubed on in such unscientific haste he did look like a nigger. In fact I couldn't help thinking he *ought* to have been a nigger. Possibly I looked the thought for the whites of his eyes protruded menacingly.

"You'll do," I agreed hurriedly. "Just look like that!"

He turned and limped away towards the niggers. "If any of them tread on his feet," I thought, "there'll be a row."

The policeman, with a native trooper standing by a big pile of government blankets, had the recipients fairly straightened out. I sauntered across to watch the fun.

My shadowy mate slouched through the squabbling gins and butted well up the front line alongside an overgrown buck whose brass plate proclaimed him king. The policeman shouted again for silence. From the anticipatory grin on several miners standing by, I guessed something was doing. I was sure of it when a mangy cur sidestepped behind Scandalous and suspiciously sniffed his feet.

"Listen, all feller you!" bawled the policeman. "Big feller King far away longa sea give him gubinmint big feller blanket gib it longa blackboy! Now you feller blackboy thank him big feller King. You sing him, 'God Save Him King.' Go ahn now! Alla same missionerly teachem you."

An agonized silence greeted this official announcement.

The mongrels ceased whimpering except the one that had just received Scandalous's heel in its ribs.

"Go ahn now!" roared the policeman. "Maybe I no give him you blanket, s'posem you no sing 'God Save Him King.' Go ahn now. Sing that feller song."

From the line of shivering niggers there quavered a mournful yowl. Such a woebegone rendering of our national anthem was surely never sung before. An overcome tyke sat back on its haunches and howled like a lost soul.

I peered among the shadowy group and sniggered at poor Scandalous, his mouth sagging open, his song droning through chattering teeth. He glared up at the king who was threateningly bending towards him. Suddenly the king roared, the anthem ceased.

"What dam' fella you?" howled the king. "My cli' me no plurry pool. You no plurry boy belonga me! What tribe you from, hey? You blurry yeller gohanna! You stealem our feller blanket, hey? Me show you – you blurry nigger tief!"

He pounced straight at Scandalous's throat. Both men splattered into the mud. Scandalous bounced up howling, to kick the king a resounding "bung" on the stomach, then wheeled and uppercut an open-mouthed nigger.

They mobbed him. Panting bucks, screaming gins, howling piccaninnies, snarling dogs. Scandalous catapulted from the bedlam and bolted with dogs snapping at his heels. I snatched a billet of wood and raced after. The mob rammed straight through the door of the next hut with a splintering crash, a swaying lamp, a thud of bodies, hysterical yells. I dashed inside with the mob and glimpsed the stupefied faces of two white men as they were violently up-ended on the floor.

Scandalous had dived under a bunk and secured a death grip. The king and a henchman grabbed each a leg and tugged in opposite directions. Scandalous howled in ear-splitting crescendo as the dogs scrambled in for their cut. I swung my waddy on the king's thick head, but his henchman sent me spinning. Both white men sprang to life and swung chairs. We cleared the hut but its simple furniture was wrecked. As the niggers were stampeding outwards they up-ended the policeman rushing in. We stood panting as he picked himself up.

"What in heaven's name is the matter?" he spluttered. I glanced down at the dishevelled bunk. A ferocious, filthy, piebald face glared up. "My heavens!" gasped the policeman. "What's that?"

"My mate," I apologized.

"Come out O' that!" thundered the policeman.

"Hide yer ugly mugs then," snarled Scandalous, "while I backs out; them-dorgs has chewed me pants off!"

He bumped his head crawling out and bounced to the centre of the floor raving. "Wot the blazes has it got ter do with you anyway! You big centipede! Chewin' whisky while men perish--"

"I'll --" roared the policeman, but he wheeled around on me. "Here you!" he ordered thickly, "out with it! What is the little game?"

"See here, constable," I replied with dignity, "keep your officiousness until it is called for. My mate and I just feel like trouble if your friends are inclined that way."

"Here, here!" snarled Scandalous, spitting on his hands.

"Eat 'em up, Jack! I'll bury ther corpses!"

"The position is this," I explained. "My mate dressed up nigger fashion because he wanted a blanket. We'll perish to-night without blankets. We're travelling from Stoney Creek to Herberton. We are hungry and footsore and not at all humorous. The hospitable owners of this hut shut the door in our faces this evening. Now you've got the strength of it and can go your hardest."

Scandalous encored heartily, then bent to tenderly feel behind. The policeman chuckled, the tin-scratchers grinned.

"I ain't no oil-paintin'," growled Scandalous sulkily.

"You sports will excuse my back. It's a gentleman compared to youse, anyway!"

He lifted a box to the fire, bent forward, arranged his bedraggled shirt-tail, seated himself carefully and stretched two skinny, charcoal-daubed legs to the warmth. He sighed – a sigh that talked.

A tin-scratcher reached for the billy-can. "You boys must be hungry," he remarked agreeably. One of the policeman's friends quietly left the hut. The officer turned to me:

"Do you know anything about tin-scratching?"

"Yes. That's what we are making towards Herberton for. But we are not known. We'll have a rough time battling without tucker and tools."

"I'm riding back tomorrow," he answered. "I'll call in at Jack and Newell's store and stand my word for tools and a month's provisions."

The door opened before I could thank him and in strode a miner with a half-empty bottle, two blankets, and a pair of dungaree pants.

"You boys might do with a warm up," he suggested amiably. "Looks like you had a rough time."

Scandalous twisted around. A delighted grin spread from ear to ear.

"I wanter pray," he cried. "I wanter sing--"

"Don't!" pleaded the policeman.

North Queensland 1890, gold prospectors using the cradle.

THE PIEBALD'S BELL

HARGREAVES cursed the truant horse as he followed it back along the dew-marked tracks. Dawn splashed a granite peak with crimson bars. The Rocky Range was still a wall of gloom. A colony of starlings had awakened and proceeded to arouse the whole bush-side. The scent of damp grass grew stronger with the slowly warming air. All nature was filled with the brooding loneliness of the far-out Australian bush.

Hargreaves was relieved that the rogue's tracks showed he was still hobbled. Otherwise he'd not stop until he had reached Coen, the isolated little mining-camp, where he was foaled, some ninety miles south down the peninsula. But this daily tracking was irksome.

Presently the horse-bell clanged jerkily in the distance ahead. The piebald was plunging southwards in between bites. Hargreaves quickened his steps and, now freed from the slowness of tracking, soon came up with the horse, cunningly planted among a clump of tea-trees. As the man spied its hiding-place the piebald gazed over its shoulder with a look brimful of resignation – for the time being.

"You dashed rogue," admonished the man as he slipped on the bridle, "you've given me another five-mile walk. I'll hobble you shorter to-night, and you'll carry the heaviest pack to-morrow!" But the good-humoured scold of the horse-lover smiled in his voice as he bent down to unbuckle the wet hobbles. Then springing on the unimpressed piebald he rode bare-back back to camp.

Before saddling up the packhorses, Hargreaves walked thoughtfully along the deep gully beside which he had camped. He fancied that gully. Its bedrock was of blue slate, crossed by bars; the wash of iron-stone boulders and quartz gave a hint of porphyry. It was dry except for the rock-hole which had given him water.

With a light prospecting pick he chipped at a pebble-filled crevice running along a bar. That crevice looked an ideal "catch" for gold. He determined to try a prospect, anyway. Handfuls of the gravel he threw in the dish, scraping deep into the crack with the long pickpoint. Presently he drew a sharp breath and peered into the crack: wedged there among the gravel was a glistening yellow speck. No need to wash a dish – the gully carried coarse gold!

The pick slid from Hargreaves's hands as he looked up at the sky and laughed with the birds. Not at any joke, nor yet for the joy of life, but simply because he had found gold.

He hurried back along the gully, chuckling aloud to walk it off. He was quite alone, and had found gold, virgin gold, heavy payable gold. The joy of discovery must be worked off before he could either think or work.

Back at the crevice he scraped it out with shaky hands, lifting the scanty sands into the dish with miserly care. Experience whispered that the crevice was a "natural catch," the dish would glisten yellow when he'd panned it off. Carefully he swirled the dish and as the water licked the gravel away his eyes smiled at the diminishing residues. Soon his waiting ear caught the scratch of something solid rolling on the dish bottom. His heart thumped excitedly again as the first yellow pellets peeped up. And the gully was his very own – he was alone in the wild bush.

He put the dish aside, laughed quietly into his hands as he lit the pipe, then clambered up the steep bank and strolled into the bush-dreaming and smiling as he walked. For two miles his brain rioted in gold. He saw it piling up, bags full of gleaming yellow gold. Tall grasses swished to his long strides; a black and yellow goanna ran hissing from his feet, as he came to a meandering line of tall trees. He walked right in amongst them and halted in fresh delight at the sight of water.

The very thing! Water to wash the dirt. It could be horse-packed to this creek and put through sluice-boxes. The "boys" and their horses could camp here, right handy to the golden gully. Abruptly he turned back towards the gully, intent on pegging a reward claim before hurrying back to the Coen to report.

At the gully he hesitated. To make certain, he'd try a few dishes all along the gully, then start for the Coen first thing tomorrow morning. No sense in starting a local rush if the gully was not rich enough to justify it.

That evening, when too dark to see the gold in the pannings, he boiled the billy, ravenously hungry, but not tired. The day had been far too short. After tea he smoked, staring at the fire, thinking clearly at last. He had proved the gully to be gold-bearing for a mile along its course. The head, just where two ravines junctioned, was by far the richest. Each ravine carried gold, and the rains of centuries had concentrated both deposits at the junction. It was only a small gully, but, judging by his dish prospects, he estimated £6000 of gold to be in the junction alone. About ten men's ground all told. The prospector was entitled to five men's ground. Ten men's ground! Five men's ground! That meant halving the gold. His share would be half! Above and below the ravines the gully was payable, but not nearly so rich as at the junction.

It was just a "golden gully" he had found, not a goldfield. Numbers of those gullies, easily worked out by a score or so of men, have been located in that wild peninsula. Just a "wet season" gully, but worth a quick few hundreds, with the possibility of a quick few: thousands each, to the first dozen men who get there.

Hargreaves's pipe cooled out. An owl hooted from the precipitous darkness astride the coastal range; a mate answered melodiously sombre in the distance. The stars glinted as a thousand specks of gold. The night was very still. The piebald's bell, night-softened, told that he was once more starting for the Coen. Hargreaves stared at the dulling fire.

For three weeks following, Hargreaves worked at stoning the gully: throwing the heavier stones out on the bank; breaking the rock-bars so that the water to come would have a fall clear of obstruction; clearing fallen timber from the gully-bed so that it should not obstruct the getaway of tailings. Finally he got the pick to work, loosening the gravel bed and throwing out the smaller stones. In another month the wet season would flood the gully with running water which would carry away the loosened gully gravel, leaving behind the heavier sands and the gold. Running water, if properly harnessed, will do the work of many men. Thus he would clean up a little fortune from this junction at the catchment of the two ravines. Himself! He had been living hard while prospecting these last three years without any luck, and he deserved the lion's share of what he had found. During the wet season he would clean up the cream of the gold that the junction contained, then report to the Coen. The boys there could have all the rest of the gully. He would just have time to cut the water-races and prepare the gully; then the storm waters would sluice away ground that otherwise would mean twelve solid months' toil with pick and shovel to shift. And he'd clean up £6000, not £3000. He had ample tucker-nine months' supply. And he had the bush to himself.

As usual, he awoke with the streak of dawn, hurried away after the piebald, then returned to camp and worked on into the gloom of night. The bush things listened to dull thuds and saw the moonlight shine on freshly-rooted stones being thrown up on to the banks from the gully bottom. At night, he would crawl into bunk and fall asleep dreaming of gold. His lean, drawn face lit up with a fierce but happy look, supremely content in the finding of his heart's desire.

One dawn, he was returning to camp with the persevering piebald – (he secretly enjoyed each morning trip now, seeking that ever truant horse. It gave him something to growl at. The days were far too busy, the nights too full of golden dreams to leave any room for grousing. Except for the piebald, the unaccustomed luxury would have been denied him) – and was happily admonishing him when he heard pick blows. Muffled, but distinct, regular and systematic, but certainly pick blows from the hidden depths of the gully. He dropped the piebald's bridle and stood quite still, fear-eyed, something clutching his heart.

The Coen boys had tracked him! They'd rushed the gully! He crept forward and peered down the steep banks at the junction, then sighed thankfully at seeing that the ground within his own pegs lay untouched. Walking quickly along the bank, anger gripped him, for around the first bend was a line of men, their backs bent, shovel blades flashing in the early sunlight. And around the following bends he heard the thud of picks. Chinamen!

"Get to hell out of this, you yellow swine!" Hargreaves roared along the bank, shaking his fists at the toilers who, without straightening their backs, gazed up impassively.

"What! You won't go! By hell!" He jumped down the bank but his foot turned on a loose stone and bounced him in a heap to the bottom. Furiously he rushed the two nearest Chinamen who immediately loped up the gully, gathering their comrades as they ran. They flew around the first bend, and Hargreaves turned panting on the men who watched impassively from behind.

They fled down the gully, pursued by the white man's flaming words of wrath. He turned once again, his boots crunching heavily in the loosened gravel, mad anger on his face as he heard from somewhere the pick thuds still vibrating without a pause. As he raged around the bend the shovel-men scattered before him, scaling the gully walls as the quickest escape. Hargreaves ignored them and, with clenched hands, advanced on the pick-swingers. One by one they dropped their tools and walked before him. He snatched up a pick and rushed.

They ran, their bare feet pattering upon the loose gully stones. With wind fast failing he chased them around the farther bend, where worked another line of patient shovel-men. The pick-men clambered the gully sides and disappeared. The shovel-men, one by one, dropped their tools and walked, then ran before him. He chased them until they, too, clambered the steep sides and the gully stretched empty before him. Drawing the painful breath of exhaustion he climbed the bank. He was near done.

He'd have a billy of tea before commencing work. He'd cleaned them all up, anyway.

Chinamen! Chinamen! Rushing a new gold find! Against the mining laws! How on earth had they located him? He'd thought he was all alone too!

While raking the campfire together he paused, listening as an animal might who has baffled the hounds only to hear their baying again. From the gully floated the dull, methodical blow of picks, the muffled scraping of shovels thrust through sand. Clenching a blazing fires tick he rushed down amongst the Chinamen. They scattered and scrambled up both banks like monkeys, to impassively watch the white man race down the gully. As he chased their comrades around the nearest bend, they quietly dropped back.

A mile down the gully Hargreaves gasped against a slate bar. He'd cleaned them up again! This was the limit of the gold run and there would be none of the yellow rats down farther. With head leaning gratefully against the cool stone, he strove to ease the fury within him. Curse it, his beating heart was mocking him as with the distant thump of pick blows.

With the easing of his breathing his ears tingled. It *was* pick blows. From away up the gully came softly. "Thud-thump, thud-thump."

Hargreaves walked slowly back, something like a sob at his throat.

The Chinamen this time scrambled partly up the banks, waited until he passed, then slipped down to work again. He walked to the very gully-head, then, laughing queerly at the work-sounds breaking out behind him, climbed the bank and strode grimly across to his camp. Grasping a cartridge-belt he returned. At the nearest man below he levelled the rifle and shouted, "Go quick! I shoot!"

All within the bend ceased working, looked up, then quietly bent to work. Hargreaves's finger eased on the trigger, a curiously baffled feeling choking his rage for along his rifle-sights the yellow digger swung his pick slowly, evenly. Hargreaves just simply couldn't be a murderer. Almost whimpering, he fired at a rock beside the toiling figure. The bullet flattened and its ricocheting fragments shrieked along the gully. Rapidly he fired and the tortured lead whizzed in the enclosed space. The Chinamen dropped their tools and fled. Smiling happily, the white man followed along the bank, firing down into the gully where between bends toiled figures. Once again he cleaned the gully up and laughed triumphantly as he gazed down at the rock on which he had leaned exhausted not an hour ago.

From away up towards the gully-head came the sound of picks at work.

Hargreaves toyed aimlessly with the rifle. He was beaten.

In the daytime now, he sat overlooking his claim, wishing for any Chinaman to put a pick within his ground. He knew he could shoot for claim-jumping – such was the unwritten law of gold. But the eighty yellow diggers never in any way interfered with the marked-off ground. It was ready loosened and stoned now, much of the hard earth broken up, nearly prepared for the thunderstorms to come and sweep the debris away.

The Chinamen waited for no storms. Discovery for them meant *finis*. Forty men picked, then shovelled away the loose wash; the remainder scraped the rock bottom as clean as a housewife sweeps the floor, and in baskets a string of them carried the dirt the two miles to Hargreaves's creek. He glanced towards the winding pad already worn by the loping feet. With tireless energy they were working up the gully, so as not to leave one ounce of gold behind. And when the wet did come, with the running water's aid they would sweep the remainder of the bed-rock as clean as a new pin, and disappear as silently as they had come. And the whites at the Coen would miss a good gully! Hargreaves did not dare to ride and warn them. He guessed what would happen to his own rich ground with eighty men working it day and night! He was helpless. The very gold held him so.

Came the distant clang of the bell of the piebald sneaking Coen-wards as usual. Hargreaves, sitting on the gully-bank, stiffened slowly while a thoughtful smile stole across his face. With a laughing cheeriness he strode to the camp, discarded the rifle, and, snatching a halter, set out after the horse. On the way he crossed a dry ravine that emptied into the big creek. He glanced around, noting curiously that the bank had been undermined. Close by was an abandoned camp littered with empty ginger jars.

He understood then. A couple of wandering Chinese fossickers must have been prospecting the ravine when he had found the gully. They had simply spied, then hurried away back to the Palmer River. From that old-time diggings their friends had gathered like hawks to the feast. Even in his anger Hargreaves admired that swift bush trek, over two hundred miles of wild bush, loaded with heavy baskets of rice, staking great hardship on a chance. They dared not follow the one bush track along the Overland Telegraph Line; had dodged even the very few rough station homesteads.

Hargreaves caught the piebald and, hurrying back to the camp, caught his own riding horse. He'd chase the piebald a good rousing start-off, anyway. Hitching both horses to a tree he slipped off the piebald's bell and disappeared within the tent where he wrote a note stating all that was occurring at the gully. Wrapping the note in canvas he lashed it to the tongue of the bell. It was protected as within a metal case. Smiling, he restrapped the bell around the piebald's neck.

The liberated horse would make straight for the Coen, be at once recognized, the dumb bell noticed and examined. He slipped the halter off the piebald and, saddling his own horse, slung the reins over its head to mount when suddenly his foot slipped from the stirrup-iron as sinewy yellow hands snatched the bridle-rein. Amazed, Hargreaves stared at the score of men who had leapt from nowhere. One dived inside the tent and slipped away with the rifle.

Hargreaves sprang again for the saddle but was jerked sprawling while the frightened horse was pulled aside and unsaddled. Hargreaves roared mockingly as the scared piebald lit out with tail mast-high, the freed saddlehorse galloping at its heels. Hargreaves punched and kicked and bit and scratched while ten men rolled atop of him. He was pommelled until his exhausted body felt a pulp. Through all his berserk rage he dumbly wondered that he could not struggle up. Somehow he had never realized that Chinamen possessed pugnacious strength the same as other men.

They left him there having proved who was master.

He could do anything he liked, so long as they could work the gully out without interference. He shaded his eyes from the sun and laughed.

A fortnight later, Hargreaves, from the gully-bank, watched the long blue ribbon of smoke that rose straight up from his galley fire. It was almost like a signal smoke.

Presently, in the distance, on to a razor-backed spur, there rode a horseman. He sat, clearly silhouetted, gazing far over that country of hills and winding creeks. Hargreaves hurried to the fire and stirred denser the column of smoke. And in answer saw that, in a canter, came riding over that distant spur an increasing file of horsemen.

As if holding the joke of a century, Hargreaves walked to the gully-bank and laughed down at the sweating men below.

Alluvial workings, North Queensland, 1920s.

THE MIRACLE

ANDIMERI liked toiling in the gardens. It was a man's work. He dug with his pointed wooden stick and loved the smell of the moist earth. The garden was the village pride, rich under the tropic sun with its sugar-cane and tobacco, its yams trellised on bamboo rails. The grunting laughter of the tribesmen drifted across the cultivation as they toiled half-hidden among broad-leafed banana plants. For Andimeri was a wild man of the swamps; and his tribe, in common with the majority along the Sepik, and unlike most other peoples of New Guinea, toil in the gardens while the women tend the fishing-nets and traps.

He had already done his lawful share of work, and warily now he straightened. One keen glance showed him the brown of the tribesmen's backs among the yellow-green banana-leaves. He snatched up his spear and vanished into the surrounding grass, grass that grows higher than dense fields of maize. Quickly, noiselessly, and in perfect confidence, he walked straight through the bending forest.

The flat lands of the Sepik carry miles upon miles of grass; often ten feet high, giant-stemmed and leafed; grass above a man's head, below his feet; grass for ever around and below his canoe.

Andimeri, being in love, smiled. He did not understand love, but he felt its primal urge. Now he was going to see the lady-he hoped she would not see *him!* If she did he would probably lose his head-and he valued that above all things. Every Sepik River native does. Only one thing does he prize almost as much, and that is some other man's head. For the most confirmed and numerous head-hunters in all the world live to-day in that country of the Middle and Upper Sepik, Mandated Territory of New Guinea. Twenty-six thousand have been censused, but there are as many again who have never seen a white man. At Ambunti, the farthest government station, some two hundred and thirty-five miles up the river, the edict has been boomed across the swamps that *all* head-hunting must cease. But what are four white men against the hereditary instincts of fifty thousand savages?

Andimeri hurried cautiously, his fierce eyes eager, his features handsome in their alertness. His bronzed body looked quite nice. But his hair, carefully oiled into long, dogtail wisps, was his pride. A treble row of shells plaited as a collar adorned his strong round throat. Powerfully built, as many of the Sepik men are, his chest and arms were developed to perfection by a life of water-work.

Though his body flaunted the patterned weals of tribal markings he did not wear the flying-fox skin, proud badge of the killer. Carrying a twelve-foot spear of limbon (black palm) he looked what he was, a perfect young savage.

He paused, sniffing, with a slight swaying movement of his head, seeing distance as through a vast, trembling latticework. Nothing but grass, grass, grass. Yet presently he smelt something – a pig. Quite definitely, though it was rooting a long way off. As Andimeri's nostrils dilated he smelt it was a boar; and of good eating age too. He pushed on, loath to leave that boar unslain.

But his eyes smiled to a quickened remembrance of other things as at the swamp edge he stepped into his canoe.

It was a trim little canoe, even though a white man would have sneered at it as a flimsy dug-out. Ten feet long, it had been shaped from a log of tough, light wood: burned, then chipped out with a stone tool until it was a buoyant shell. Andimeri's weight sent the stern perilously close to the water-line, but the bow rose so that when he dipped his long, broad-bladed paddle the tiny craft shot ahead, gliding over what would otherwise have been clogging grass.

If ever you are canoed across that spreading swamp the only clear water you will see will be in patches of a few acres encircled by floating islets of sac-sac. On almost every floating log will be the mud-grey, motionless form of a crocodile. Your canoe-man will again and again shoot through a lane of grass that brushes back against his face before the canoe spins out into another open-water space, often so small that it will hold only one log and one crocodile. While you are in the open, the blue sky will be brilliant, the hum of insects loud, and the birds noisily indignant as the natives paddle through their favourite feeding-grounds. Over all will be the harsh, sinister boom of a *garramut* – the huge slit gong, man-length, fashioned cunningly from the hollowed trunk of a tree. Fascinating, that sea of tall grass swamps; those big, hidden villages; those sudden "round waters" (lakes) blooming with pink and white waterlilies, the haunt of countless white herons and wild fowl and fascinating, too, that muffled throb of the *garramut*.

After an hour of miraculously swift travelling, Andimeri shot into a dense wall of *pit-pit* (tall wild cane). Straight on he went through that packed forest of stalks and leaves, a picture of human-kind triumphing over unfriendly nature. He stood with one leg planted firmly before the other, and, using the crescent-tipped blade, punted the canoe. This part of the journey was over shallow water, with grass too dense to allow of paddling.

As the raised nose of the vessel slid over the submerged grass it sharply poked a way through the standing stalks, a way which widened as the canoe followed, pushing aside two living walls whose swaying tops brushed easily off heaving shoulders, to rustle up close again behind the canoe. A white man would have been lost in that appalling tangle. But Andimeri needed no compass to go swiftly and straight to his objective: those animal-men have the homing instinct of the pigeon.

Presently Andimeri's eyes grew wary; he breathed almost fearfully; his heart hammered. He was drawing dangerously near to his beloved–and death! The fear of that makes the wild man's blood course madly. Crouching, he poled slowly forward, his ears noticeably projecting, his square-jawed face thrust out over his chest; his temple veins swelling-as he smelt, smelt, for men! Then crouching on his haunches he poled very slowly, the grass just gliding along the sides of the canoe, the leafy tops joining again with no rustle, no movement that could not have been made by the wind.

Andimeri halted, staring, listening, smelling. A million mosquitoes hummed about him unnoticed; from the distance came the hoarse call of a crane. The smells of soppy dankness, of mildewing leaves, the heavy scent of lilies, were unnoticed. Then with dilating nostrils he smelt man!

Presently came a distant laugh that, strangely enough, seemed to reassure him. It was a man's laugh, too, and was answered. Andimeri poled ever so gently. With the stealth of a crocodile's snout, his canoe prow poked out through the edge of the grass and stopped.

Before him was a *barrad*, a narrow, grass-lined channel with steep banks, lily-edged. On one side of it, but invisible now to the crouching man, was the big village of Magdimbo. He could just see the tops of its coconut and betel-nut palms and kapiak-trees silhouetted in the clear air. He shuddered at the grim gables of its huge *Tambaran* house, holder of four hundred skulls. If he stood upright he could see the village huts as they sprawled among the palms back from the *barrad* bank. On the opposite side were the gardens from which came men's voices, muffled by the vegetation.

Crouching low, Andimeri poled sharply forward, his heart racing, his eyes staring up at the high banks. He had run the gauntlet before under this gripping love-urge.

If only the children kept playing in the village! If only the men kept working in the gardens!

Andimeri flew along the *barrad*, poling with superb strength while crouching low in the canoe, every nerve tingling, ready at even the shadow of a man to wheel around and fly back for the grass. He hissed past the canoes drawn up on the channel banks, urging his craft to where ahead of him a wall of grass spanned the *barrad*. He slowed up so that he might enter carefully, then stopped when he was concealed, and with heaving chest looked back at his wake.

When the tell-tale ripples had quietened Andimeri laughed silently. Eagerly he poled forward again, his eyes dancing with expectation. Very gently he thrust his prow through the farthest side of this wall, and stopped, his face all delight. Before him spread broad open water, the surface massed with lily-leaves so large that on any one of them a baby might play – a water mat bright with blue and white lilies. It rang to the ceaseless whistling and quacking of wild ducks, and screeching of sulphur-crested cockatoos. Snow-white ospreys fished in the distance, while grey cranes looked solemnly on. The languorous scent of water-lilies was over all.

Scattered over this picturesque water-way were the canoes of the women. But Andimeri saw only one, not fifty yards ahead. In his happiest love-dreams he had never imagined such luck. She was alone, bending from the frail canoe to reach for a *kunda* vine rope lashed to a bamboo stake. A vivacious smile played about her pretty lips, girlish expectancy shone in her eyes as she hauled on the rope, perilously near to falling into her reflection.

Andimeri gazed entranced, envying the sun that kissed her rich brown skin. He could have laughed aloud with her as she drew in the trap of latticed cane. The flapping of the prisoned fish came to him, sharp and distinct.

He watched her with a longing that became a physical pain as she drew yet closer, tending the line of staked traps. If only he could pounce on her with one sure, sleep-giving blow and then steal away, regardless of the terror of his tribesmen as he brought her home! But too well he knew that in so doing he would outrage tribal laws, and the heads of the men of Chauash would decorate the *Tambaran* of their more numerous neighbours of Magdimbo.

So near and yet so far! If only he could become a great *luluai;* if only he could command many fighting men; if only he could canoe with pomp into this haughty people's village and see their headmen gaze on him in sullen fear!

He sighed and lapsed into deeper dreaming, for no power on earth could bring his dream true. But dreaming sweetened a little the bitterness of the impossibility.

He prayed to the great benevolent spirit, unrealizing that he prayed. Well he knew the devil spirits of the *Tambaran;* but apart from these there was (his mother had whispered it to him) some dim, mystic Spirit that breathed over the great swamps, some Spirit which, though never seen, actually loved men!

A distant call startled him to the present and to thoughts of his head. It was the call for the women to return and cook the men's evening meal. One thrust of the pole and he disappeared into the grass and back into the *barrad,* his heart in his mouth. One swift glance showed him that all was yet clear. He sped arrow-swift down the water-lane, his haste betraying him into momentarily standing upright.

A returning gardener saw only his head, but it was enough. A piercing cry echoed over the village. Throwing discretion to the wind, Andimeri put his frenzied strength on the pole and thrust with the speed of a great fear. Water hissed from his canoe prow as piercing calls echoed from village to gardens; men were running, children screaming.

Andimeri burst straight into the grass ahead which lashed his body as it swished together behind him. Far over the swamps boomed the *garramut* of Magdimbo. Again it boomed, again and again, monotonously and ceaselessly, calling its lean brown hounds to the man-hunt.

Sweat beaded from Andimeri as he sped on and on, gasping in mouthfuls of mosquitoes while the grass whined as he sped through and through.

Could they follow him right to the village? Would his love for a woman bring his kinsmen's heads to grin from the peaked gables of Magdimbo? In an agony of remorse he sped on. His wake would close up behind him but the wrack would accumulate in a thin, tell-tale line around the grass stalks.

He burst through the grass into open water, and stood paralysed with astonishment. Instinct at the last moment forced his arms down on the pole and he swerved with a side-on crash into a great canoe of a size and shape undreamed of. Brawny brown arms snatched him aboard and he lay inert, gazing up at men who took no notice of him, the setting sun gleaming on what he dimly realized were rifle-barrels.

A long canoe burst through the grass behind, followed instantly by another and another. The leading canoe grazed the bow of the pinnace, the second shot by the stern before the savage crews bent to their poles and, in a welter of tortured water and gurgling lily-leaves, swerved almost in their own length in a frantic dash back to the grass. From twenty throats arose a long-drawn, curdling howl. A fourth canoe, bursting from the grass like a violently turning crocodile, slowed down, then thrashed back into the grass and disappeared.

A sigh of disappointment came from the uniformed police. Colonel Woodman, District Officer at Ambunti (on the Upper Sepik), sitting in the stern of the pinnace, dressed in whites, with the glittering government badge in his helmet, watched with quiet satisfaction the perfect discipline of his own savages.

The pinnace flew the Australian blue ensign, a flag that is recognized as the limit of power by thirty thousand brown men on the Sepik. Andimeri gazed speechless at the constabulary in their white-covered caps, blue *lap-laps*, scarlet cummerbunds around their waists.

Sergeant Remuna grunted, then spoke sharply to Andimeri. Andimeri did not understand. He had never seen a white man before; these strange things about him might have fallen from the moon. But the sergeant had a way with him, and presently the half-caste Malay at the wheel swung the pinnace round and headed it through the grass towards Andimeri's village.

That night, snug within his mosquito-proof cabin, the D.O. made an entry in his diary:

17.8.19. "Whilst penetrating a *barrad* through the swamp country to the north of Magdimbo the sergeant reported that the beating of *garramuts*, started a few moments previously, indicated that the alarm for natives to assemble for fight was being sounded.

"Thinking that the exhaust from the pinnace, perhaps, had made known our presence and was the cause of the alarm I was about to tell the interpreters to call to the natives, when sudden shouting and the sound of racing canoes came from the direction of a *barrad* leading off the 'round water' the pinnace had just entered. I stopped the *Osprey* at the mouth of the *barrad*, and almost immediately a native, hotly pursued by several canoe-loads of natives, emerged from the *barrad*. His canoe, colliding with the pinnace, was swamped.

"The P/B's hauled the native, who was badly scared, aboard the pinnace as the pursuing natives, sighting the pinnace, hurriedly turned their canoes and disappeared the way they had come, paying no heed to the calls of the interpreters.

"Through these, the native who had been pulled aboard the pinnace was questioned. It was ascertained that his name was Andimeri and that he belonged to a village through the *sac-sac* swamps to the south.

"Endeavoured to get in touch with the natives of Magdimbo, but after negotiating the *barrad* for some distance, it became so narrow and choked with grass that it was impossible for the pinnace to proceed farther, and having no canoes available it was decided to return to the main river and continue up-stream, taking the native Andimeri with me. Intend to take him to Ambunti for a few months until he can learn to 'talk,' when he will be given a *tul-tul's* hat and used as a guide to establish friendly relations with the natives of his place and the surrounding villages."

THE SQUATTING DEVIL OF SAMARAI

YUSSUF was heartbroken. He had lost his only brother, stolen from his own ship. The lad had been steering by moonlight with Duppa. The others were below deck. There had come a sudden crash from the swinging boom, a scream and a thump as Duppa jumped straight down the companion-way.

After a second's silence Yussuf sprang up to the deck and instinctively snatched the tiller. But nothing was to be seen except the usual beauty of starlit waters spreading among dim islands. The deck was printed upon Yussuf's brain. It was exactly as usual! But Akran La, the little brother, was gone!

And now Yussuf brooded, a raging fury in his breast.

For he had lost his honour with his brother, because there was no human foe whose life he could take as recompense to the old father waiting back there at Macassar. And the Malay who loses his honour dies accursed.

Squatting astern in his scarlet *sarong,* Yussuf thought deeply while the crew crouched for'ard tremblingly awaiting the dawn. Big Duppa especially! For the Malay with tigerish fierceness had throttled the big fellow until his tongue had swelled and his lips flecked with foam.

But Duppa could tell him nothing-nothing that counted. He and the lad had been whispering of hazards of the sea and of the Hanuabada girls when something vague and dripping had reached from out the sea across the lugger's deck. It had coiled around Akran La and dragged him quite easily overboard. It had disappeared then. The lad had time only to scream once, chokingly, just as his head touched the water. Duppa remembered that the lad's teeth and eyes shone very white; but he did not know what the thing was, except that it was a devil, like the devil-horse in the Thursday Island pictures that poked out its long nose and, curling it, lifted a man high into the air. Only this devil had no tusks. But it had many noses-and terrible eyes! Duppa gibbered when he whispered of those eyes. Calling all his years of sea wisdom to aid him in solving the mystery, Yussuf sat in the cold light of dawn sharpening his knife.

My friend Billy Banner finds in life a quiet happiness, and a never-ceasing pleasure in its wonders. Now he was merry, for a little visitor at Port Moresby was grey-eyed and quite delightfully saucy and eager to absorb island lore during her wonderful holiday. And Billy, well Billy, where a pretty face is concerned cannot help being just a little sentimental. Billy at the party had promised her a pearl, a "dinkum tearstone" from a New Guinea pearl-oyster. Like other Sydney visitors, she vaguely imagined that pearls grew plentifully on the sea-shores. Then young Clapham, clerk at Burns Philp's, had jokingly asked Billy if he would snatch the pearl from the bottom of the Devil's Pool. Billy immediately promised this too, quite tickled at the idea. But several of the experienced men looked askance; and the girl was told all about the Devil's Pool.

If you know the Samarai waters, that is if you are interested in pearling, then you must have heard of the Devil's Pool. It is a great hole in the sea bed, a long way from the palm-girt island, in which dwells an old-man octopus of giant size and unguessable strength. Divers, so several assert, have seen an occasional one of these brutes along the Great Barrier Reef and in isolated spots in the Coral Sea. Such localities, once identified, are well and truly shunned by the fishing fleets, whether trochus men or hunters of pearl or *bêche-de-mer*. The Devil of Samarai, as this one was familiarly called by the older divers, was known because it had chosen its den in a bed of rich shell, and divers had seen it. A South Seas man and a Manila man had apparently seen it, too, but they never returned to tell. Since then no one had been down into the Pool to see. Some men pooh-poohed the tale. But the girl, genuinely alarmed, forbade Billy to risk his life.

Her plea decided him. What had begun as a joke he determined to carry through in earnest. Besides, there would be profit in it, for that particular area of the shell bed guarded by this alleged octopus would be quite unexploited. With rising interest he hoped an octopus, a big old-man one, would really be there. For Billy loved the uncommon aspects of life, and the underwater world had livened his imagination with fascinating glimpses of a life of which man has but a very faint conception. To seek a pearl in an octopus den, and to have that unique experience sweetened first by the smile and then by the fears of a pretty girl, promised an experience exceptionally piquant.

Probably a rich haul of shell awaited Billy; but as for a pearl-a diver may open five hundred shells and not find one! Billy knew all this. Still, the gods smile on the venturesome, and this was their chance. A pearl snatched from the Devil's Pool-perhaps in the sight of the old man himself! Billy smiled in delighted anticipation. He had quite a thrilling storehouse of memories against old age, and this anticipated adventure promised to be a gem.

But the men of the Coral Sea liked Billy. When the party broke up an old resident frowned upon him: "You won't be such a fool, Billy!" he urged.

Billy smiled cheerfully, "I'll get that pearl if I have to salt the octopus's tail."

"Mad!" said Moorehouse grimly. "You know that the beast has really been seen; you know that the deaths of several native divers are attributed to it. Give the girl a pearl from any old shell. She won't know the difference!"

"But *I* will," smiled Billy, thinking of his memories.

"She shall have the genuine article with the Octopus brand. Why, she will treasure that 'tear of the sea' all her life."

"She'll know quite a lot of tears if daddy-long-legs fastens hold of you," answered the resident grimly.

But Billy laughed and went whistling down to the water-way where the lugger lay with her nose turned inshore as if awaiting his coming.

It was a divinely bright day, showing the water clear for many fathoms deep. It would be almost clear as moonlight down below," mused Billy as the lugger glided along – why, even at ten fathoms a man should be able to see the sea things winking!"

It was slack tide when they lazed over Devil's Pool, with hardly a breath of wind. In the near distance a dirty grey lugger was drifting towards them, the Malay skipper sombrely watching the other craft's preparations. When Billy was getting into his clumsy dress the vessels had drifted so close that the crews of both were hallooing to one another across the water.

Billy idly wondered if big Yussuf the Malay would pluck up courage to dive in company. He rather wished Yussuf wouldn't; he wanted the grim chance of this dive all to himself.

Clumsily he waddled overside, clinging to the short ladder while the tender screwed his helmet down. Through the open vizor Billy took a final glance at the sky – he always liked to do that-then smiled and nodded, and the tender screwed the face-glass in. Billy waited for the "click-clack, click-clack" of the motor pump; then he regulated the rush of air by the valve screwed to his helmet. Finally he slung himself backwards and went down slowly in a radiant whirl of bubbles.

He slipped into green twilight that dimmed softly until it enveloped him in dull green gloom. He met the corals while still going down. Far out they stretched, vague and indistinct, enclosing him in a basin of battlemented shapes dangerous with black caverns, curtained plants drooping from purple ramparts that trellised an occasional flower like a white phosphorescent lily tiger-striped with yellow. But Billy wondered that he saw no sign of fish, bar the swarms of tiny coloured beauties that darted into the flower gardens at his monstrous approach.

He came to rest on a gravelly bottom carpeted with yellow sea-grass and was interested, because a large gravel patch surrounded by corals was unusual to him. Basin-like sponges pulsed dreamily among upright grasses that showed no slightest sway of their tops, so still was the tide.

He stood there awhile, his right hand at the helmet regulating the air-valve so that he was receiving exactly the supply of air to withstand the pressure upon him from without. Very important indeed is that little air-valve. By its aid the diver lives and works while down below, and continuously fights the sea as it ceaselessly strives to crush him with the weight of its varying depths. Then curiously he peered more closely about him, and chuckled happily at sight of black-lipped pearl. The shell was here right enough, poked away up among the crevices and bopeeping from the weedy bottom. It was only the snappiest glimpse of pearl that he caught, for they shut their tell-tale lips instinctively as he approached. Clumsily he walked ahead, side-stepping in grotesque fashion when sinking down to pick up a shell; straightening himself like a bulging automaton to drop each find into the network bag at his waist. So he manoeuvred on along a shelving bottom that sloped into deeper gloom.

Apparently the grey-eyed Sydney girl stood a real chance of getting her pearl. But where was the devil that guarded this breeding-hole in the sea? He felt like that school-day when he had stolen a farmer's watermelon in ticklish trepidation over the watch-dog that never appeared.

In quick time he had bagged thirty shells, an excellent pick-up. He signalled, and down came an empty bag en a cord ringed around the line. Billy detached his full bag and signalled it up, then plodded on full of enthusiasm. It would be stiff luck if this hole did not yield more than one pearl, provided he could work it undisturbed for a week. Whether or not, there were some tons of shell here which would pay handsomely, perhaps yield a trip to Sydney. Billy smiled, determined to find that pearl.

Suddenly Billy stood still. For a ledge had taken shape just ahead, and fronting it lay a vague rubbish heap of white things and yellow-carapaces of turtle, dugong skulls, and bones of monster fish. And the realization of what they meant thumped at his heart. With an almost breathless alertness he moved very slowly a few yards nearer.

And the nearer vision brought the dim things into surer relief. Billy stood again, staring at the tall brown stalks of sea-grass, staring at where they were freshly bowed down, and in horror saw among the fronds the shadowy body of a man. There was no mistaking that brownish-white form, dimly magnified by the water. He seemed so forlorn, that lone human in his nakedness, so quietly reclining at the bottom of the sea. Then a shadow thing appeared beyond Billy's face-glass as something moved from the outer gloom and, floating down, squatted on the ledge and glared at him.

The octopus was mesmeric in its hideousness. Its bag-like body roughly resembled a nuggety man shorn of legs and arms. Its tentacles, thick as elephants' trunks, were loosely looped before it, the snaky ends trailing down far over the ledge. Billy fearfully guessed that each might reach out thirty feet. He loathed the squat black belly of that thing, suggestive of enormous expansion.

Shrouded amongst the tentacles he glimpsed a horrid beak. But it was the eyes that held him! Big almost as saucers, and water-green, their phosphoric glare was terrifyingly powerful-diabolical as anything in the Pit.

As Billy shivered and watched, the thing visibly changed colour, its blackish-brown merging into the varied colours of the surrounding sea-plants. But its eyes!

Billy's hand moved and shut tight his air-escape valve while signalling "More air!" Instantly the full power from the pump above seethed into the suit and almost immediately it began to bulge from the added air; but with his guarded movement the beast had also moved. Imperceptible that movement as with an uncanny effect of effortlessness its tentacles wafted out and their ends looped lightly around crags above and to the side of Billy. Signalling to the tender above, he gripped a coral block to prevent the lift of the air-inflated suit from dragging him off the ocean floor, for his only chance now was a whirling escape. The suit ballooned out fast, giving him an isolated feeling of roominess, the leather and rubber stretching to the stiffness almost of steel. Soon his arms felt that they were being dragged out of their sockets. He hung on tenaciously, his body feather-light. As his fingers slipped from the anchoring coral he shot instantly upwards until brought up short as a tentacle of the Horror shot out and gripped the life-line.

Billy floundered in a desperate endeavour to keep his head and balance. Through the face-glass he saw what was coming – the body of the octopus clouding through mid-water. Stretched to their limit, two tentacles gripped the bottom, others coiled out towards him; while several, like tautened cables, clung to his life-line. In a flash he wondered whether the air inflating his suit could possibly tear the beast from its grip or would the tough leather burst first?

Frantically he snatched out his knife as a tentacle threatened his body; he knew he must prevent that or he was done. He screwed tight the air-valve which abandoned him to silence. Taking a last desperate chance he slashed through air-pipe and life-line and would have shot free but that a tentacle tip had fastened around the neck of his helmet. He glimpsed the quiver of the beast as the severed life-line had released him upwards. He slashed impotently at the coil around his neck-and another on the instant fastened around his arm.

Helplessly now he writhed, a prisoner within an airfilled suit. He wondered how long it would hold him to the bottom of the sea just like that other thing lying in the grass.

Through his face-glass he stared at the Thing as it retained a grip of the ledge while almost imperceptibly lashing itself around him. He felt the slow, steady heave as it overcame the buoyant resistance of the air-filled suit, all that air pressing up into his helmet, fighting to shoot to the surface. Very slowly he was dragged down feeling the tearing pressure of the air striving to force him up. His head was thundering, his mind a seething hope that he might die quickly of air-paralysis or anything – anything except of this beast.

Consciousness was slipping into madness when a beautiful bronzed form came speeding down from above, gliding swiftly down from green twilight into gloom. Into his roaring head came dimly some fancy of an angel.

Yussuf, with his loved knife between his teeth, made terribly sure to thoroughly avenge the little brother. He struck downwards from behind, slitting open the envelope of the creature with one long, dreadful gash.

Billy Banner, obscured in a dense cloud of foul black ink one second, the next was shooting up through the depths to burst through the surface and float like a grotesque balloon.

"Thank 'God!" cried the distracted tender. "Overboard with the dinghy quick!" he yelled to the crew boys.

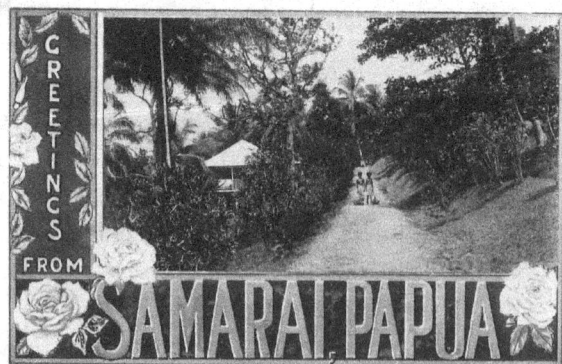

THE DEATH STONE

WARRIGAL felt peculiarly drowsy and stupid that morning. Dimly, his animal-like brain wondered why he was not out by the pleasant cooking-fires with the others of the tribe. How quiet they all were! No loud talk of the young men, no laughing chatter of the gins, no squeals from the piccaninnies.

His favourite hunting-dog, too, was not sleeping by his side!

Angrily Warrigal sat up. His fierce eyes instantly saw on the side nearest his heart, where his dog should have been lying, a little round, flat stone. The Death Stone!

For long breaths Warrigal sat staring in the gloom of his gunyah, a rugged black statue, midway between beast and man. His brain could grasp only one thing at a time. Some unknown enemy had "pointed the bone" at him. Then the spirits of the dead had brought the Death Stone to his side by night. And now – he must go away and die!

As in a daze, he crawled through the gunyah-opening, and stood upright in the new morning air. The birds were trilling with the sweetness of freshly awakened life; mists arose from the long, wet grass; the big Sun-god was peeping over the grey mountain range that hid the sea.

Mechanically, Warrigal grasped his spears and wommera, and walked slowly away towards the grey range which held the burial-ground of his people. From the tribesmen clustered around the cooking-fires came no sound of farewell, no sign, though all eyes watched him go. Only a young gin wept bitterly. But as Warrigal strode on with all the litheness gone from his sinewy legs, his mind was bitter only against his hunting-dog. It had not followed him!

When the Sun-god shone fiercely in his domed home Warrigal came to the base of an old grey mountain towering far above all else of the big, grey range. Around him lay in confusion fallen granite boulders often as large as the gunyahs the strange white men build. Far away towards the Sun-god's world, where the white-tufted eagle was circling, the grey boulders were piled in numbers like the sands of the sea. Here, in the days of old the gods of the earth and sky and stars had thrown stones at each other until, tired of their play, they had piled the stones in one mountain heap. Wandering white men call this gloomy landmark the Black Mountain, it lies in lonely majesty inland behind Cape Melville, in far northern Queensland. No trees, no vegetation grow on those boulders or in between. But on the flat summit, where lies a little loam, there cling stunted, gnarled trees, twisted and wrenched and tossed by the fierce winds of the sea, bent and bowed like the forlorn crosses on lone graves of white men.

Without hesitation, Warrigal began slowly to climb the mountain, choosing a zigzag course which picked out the interlocking boulders in such a way that a man could step from one broad surface up to another. Black men had climbed the grey mountain that way before some among white men had learned to hew a club out of stone. Warrigal never paused, but his steps grew slower, his heart sank lower as he climbed in the footsteps of the ghosts that had gone before.

At last he reached the wind-blown summit, and, standing there as the first man may have stood back in the mists of time, concentrated his gaze on the far-flung sea. He did not glance at the dwarfed trees. He knew what was there. Those hungry roots were deep in dust, brown, human dust. Around their twisted butts lay skulls of blackish-grey with little earth-coloured holes where air and rain and sun had bored through. There were many brown, and some a dirty grey-white, and others that glistened from the kiss of the sun; these last the eagles had picked clean, and the rain-storms had washed milky-white as they lay in their crude bed of sticks and twisted branches. Two were skeletons hanging downward, blown thus through the branches. Now, as the wind swayed them they kissed together in curious sound, like a snake rustling through dry grass. This was the burial-ground of his people.

Far below the foaming billows played along the Great Barrier Reef. The sea was life. And though he was soon to die Warrigal, like all things, wild or civilized, wanted to gaze on life to the last. He could see the squat shape of Nobel Island like a black toad close inshore, and far out, over rugged Cape Melville, the tall, needle-like peak of the largest of the Howick Group.

He climbed a little way down the mountain-lip, not daring to rest on the summit, for at night all the spirits of the dead people would play there. Warrigal shivered. He chose a gloomy, narrow-mouthed cavern whose rough walls were furred by the scraping past of rock-wallabies. The animal smell of this home of wild things pleased his nostrils. He squatted down with his back to the mountain summit, staring stonily out to sea – waiting.

Coming from the bowels of the mountain was the splash of running water among the piled-up boulders. Warrigal knew that the lilting gurgle among the deeper tones of this subterranean organ was really the laughter of spirits at play, awaiting the cloak of night before they came out to dance on the mountain-top.

When the long day sped, the Sun-god, sinking to sleep far behind the mountains, drew his blanket over the world. So came the hush hour when the live things of day retire and those of night get ready to prey over the earth. The wind died down until only the spume of its breath came with the softening boom of the rollers on the rocky shore below. Across the black sky a spreading net of stars twinkled brighter and brighter. With a sudden, stiff cat's-paw came the jangle of bones swaying from the branches of a tree.

The black man, motionless in the cavern, hunched his shoulders and hips so close that his body shrank by half. His mat of coarse hair shivered noticeably; he thrust a wrist in his open mouth to silence the snapping of his teeth. His livid, unseeing eyes glared out over the vast, slow-moving bosom of the sea. The spirits of the dead had come out to play.

A shriek rose from the summit, its fearful echoes rang through and through the honeycombed caverns. Again and yet again that laugh rang out. Then silence spread over the world until through the waiting moments there came the muffled beat of wings. The night hawk, sitting hunched up in the burial-trees, had called his mate for the evening meal.

Late on the third day Warrigal sensed his Death Spirit drawing very near. His instinct, razor-edged, felt it coming closer to touch him.

Noiselessly in the playing sunlight at the cavern's mouth stepped lissom Wy-wee, the young gin; like a spirit girl she came, her parted lips seemed breathless as the terror in her violet-black eyes. She gripped a freshly killed squirrel.

Long she gazed at the crouching man whose wild, fixed eyes stared past her over the sunlit sea. Then she knelt on the cold rock and edged up to him, beseeching his unseeing eyes, fondling her forehead against his, softly whispering his name. With tender hands she brushed his stiff, grizzled hair that was only a few days ago so healthy and black, but now a tangle of greying bristles.

Beseechingly Wy-wee held the squirrel to her man.

He moved not; he might almost be dead.

She glided from the cavern and ran upward towards the summit, jumping the rocks like a wallaby. In unspeakable terror she snatched dry sticks from beneath the grizzly trees, her fingers tingling from the dead things among the dead wood, then fled down the rocks back into the cavern. Shivering violently she bent over the sticks, rubbing two together with a twirling motion of marvellous rapidity. Soon they produced the faintest breath of smoke, then a stronger breath that grew a puff with warmth in it, then a quickly increasing spiral of hot smoke that burst into bright flame.

Deftly she arranged the fire and laid on it the squirrel.

The smell of singeing fur filled the cavern and drifted away through the open spaces between the rocks. As Wy-wee turned the tiny animal on the blazing coals an appetising odour of roast meat mingled with the incoming sea breeze. The Sun-god was sinking to rest. The cooking completed, Wy-wee invited Warrigal to the meat.

But he sat like a thing of stone. Tearing off a hindleg she pressed the warm flesh between her man's lips. It met only a line of set teeth.

Throwing the meat aside she sobbed on the chest of the doomed man.

The following noon three black shadows fell across the mouth of the cavern. Two of them, charm-painted, seized Wy-wee and dragged her screaming from the motionless Warrigal. Eurahah, the dreaded wizard-doctor of the tribe, stood a silent moment, gazing with snakelike eyes into the wild eyes of Warrigal, now fixed with the stare that comes just before the death-film. Satisfied, Eurahah glided from the cavern.

North Queensland Aboriginal, 1910 by Charles Kerry.

A SMILE FROM NEPTUNE

INTENSE excitement reigned at Dauan. The very palms whispered joy as they rustled above the village. Swift canoes shot out for Sabai and Boigu, to share the tidings of a great gift from the sea.

The "Gubinmint" on Sabai awoke next morning to find his subjects flown. Only the older school-children and the old people remained – and the very angry policeman. Even the native pastor was gone. The remnant shook uneasy heads to Authority's questions. Then Gubinmint stormed in vain on discovering that every canoe was missing. Marooned in his own village, the schoolmaster sought his glasses to uneasily spy on this latest prank of his grown-up children.

Not five miles away stood up Dauan, old-man mountain out of the sea. At that distance, among its shrubbery, grey houses clung like goats grazing upon its steep slopes; but the schoolmaster knew they were huge granite boulders reflecting back the sun. He focused the glasses on the tiny beach past the reef, that fronted the small village under the palms. The native school-house door was swinging idly; the village itself deserted; but the sparkling water-way over the reef was alive with craft. Grimly the Gubinmint noted its own big Sabai canoes amongst the vessels of Dauan; men, women and children massed on the outrigger platforms, while bounding towards them with a following breeze hulloaed the crowded canoes of Boigu.

"See what you can make of it, sergeant!" And the puzzled Gubinmint handed the glasses to the huge brown islander in khaki coat and blue lava-lava. That official's resentment increased the more as his local knowledge assured him he was missing something:

"Those mans find somethings," he declared emphatically. "They dive longa sea. Plenty jail wait longa them what time they come back – plenty build him road," he added grimly. With which verdict the powers to be had to abide in ill content.

While fishing out from the reef a secret of the sea had been unfolded to Baku, diving-boy of Dauan. He had located an old wreck, its ribs encrusted with the coral of a century. There rest many such in the Coral Sea, but this relic yielded treasure. For Baku had hitched an anchor rope to a rounded block of coral and with much labour, his comrades had hauled it up to the canoe deck. Careful chopping with the tomahawk had displayed musty wood intergrown with corals. With rising excitement, they had cut a hole in this wood and suddenly liberated an aroma fit for the very gods. It scented the air with a sweetness that tingled their deepest insides. Baku had smelt first, then screwed his face tight into the chopped coral and poked his tongue down the hole. His comrades gazed breathless as the face came up, unfolding its wrinkles in ecstasy to the rolling tongue. It bobbed down for more. Instant hubbub, while clawing hands lugged him away. Heads bumped in a rush to sample the hole.

It was Samsu who developed the brain-wave, Samsu who had once been to Thursday Island and drank "gingerbeerah" white man fashion. He pulled a bamboo from the canoe and thrust it down into the keg and sucked and sucked-until his comrades pulled him away and snatched the straw. For that old keg held a golden wine into which Neptune had lullabyed the dreams of a hundred years.

An hilarious, a joyous crew later sailed their canoe slap-dash up on to the very beach of Dauan. The villagers watched amazed while the sails flapped protestingly at the singing antics of the crew standing on their heads perilously out on the outrigger booms.

The village policeman walked to investigate; the native deacon followed, with the puzzled villagers crowding the rear.

It was Baku who with great cunning had urged the discoverers to leave just a sip for the policeman and deacon!

So now the three islands, men, women, and girls of Sabai, Boigu, and Dauan, dived for the gift of the sea. There were plenty of casks but treacherously hard to find, deep down in the sea, where the coral walls grew all over and through the old wreck. After much diving the boys would locate a cask; then four went down and with tomahawks and levers toiled to break it away from the coral's encircling arms. After two stupendous minutes they would rise with bursting lungs, but others were already swimming down to the task, while yet others were poised waiting on the canoes above. Women, those hefty island girls whose strength ofttimes puts a man to shame, helped enthusiastically.

And the sunlight echoed to rollicking fun and laughter, for was not all life a joy, made sweeter as they gazed across at lowlying Sabai and shrieked with merriment at Gubinmint's expense. For they had not defied Gubinmint; they had not done anything they were told not to do; they had merely gone avisiting to Dauan, and were not to know that Gubinmint might want a canoe to voyage across himself. After it was all over they would return quite innocently, and tell him all about the white man's ship. They knew he dearly loved to talk of the quiet old ships that sleep deep among the corals. They might even bring him a little of the entrancing firewater. They might!

And so, as the day wore on, they would prize away another keg and in triumph haul the shapeless coral lump to a canoe above. It would be left for all to see, lashed to the outrigger platform while they slipped below for more. For now the Council had decreed that no keg must be opened until they were all comfortable around the feast fires at night.

Wonderful feast nights those were. Marvellous singing, lovely dancing, the like had never been known before. The islanders became certain they were gods and goddesses. They rose to that height wherein they actually shrieked defiance to Gubinmint across the starlit water; the girls in particular making ribald statements as to his personal beauty and figure, encored by the rollicking laughter of the men, of Sabai particularly, as they recalled the wiping off of old scores against both Gubinmint and policeman. As lords presiding over the feasts, on the best village mats, sat solemnly the police of Dauan and Boigu, backed up by the island councillors. And due deference was accorded to their ordering of the proceedings, although they sat on a volcano, for nightly the old irreconcilables arose to the point of rattling their bows and shouting "to hell with the Gubinmint an' missionary an' whiteman." But the wine was never in quite sufficient quantities to finally force the tide into bloody revolution.

One evening, with three kegs grudgingly left in care of the police and deacons, the Sabai and Boigu peoples set off with low chuckles to their island homes to raid their own gardens, for Dauan could not indefinitely feed such a crowd.

The Boigu men were quite safe, for no white man lives on their island, but the Sabaites were uncertain of what awaited them. Very quietly at high tide they ran their canoes into the mangroves away from their own big village, then crept through the black mangroves and out on to the open grassy plain which is a swamp in the wet season. A million frogs croaked to the skies as they sneaked through the ankle-deep water. A line of shadows, they emerged through the tall grasses at the rear of the village, and melted into the gardens. Then what a grubbing in the dark for maniocs and yams; a hasty cutting of banana bunches and rummaging around for taro. Some eager shadows slipped amongst the silent houses, for what mother when so near her children would not dare to at least hear them breathe!

In his fine house all alone, Gubinmint slept, tired out with watching and wondering what it all meant. He was just one white man alone in the Coral Sea, with the destiny of three islands under his hands and hat, and a savage New Guinea coastline only a stone's throwaway.

So the village policeman alone watched in the shadow of the banana-trees, and grinned savagely while he listened and learned. Resentment flamed as two lads whispered laughingly under the very banana palm by which he stood. He let out and clouted Samsu on the ear, and threw his great weight on Goabar, while his bull voice roared for "Gubinmint!" In an instant the policeman was sent sprawling, for frantic fear lends unbelievable strength to the slightest of men.

Then arose a noise as of hurrying cattle as two hundred feet tore through the gardens. A pyjama-clad figure jumped straight out on to the school-house veranda, with starlight glistening along a rifle-barrel. Frightened children cried from the quiet houses. The policeman, his blood well up, thundered in pursuit, roaring his whereabouts to Gubinmint who raced manfully after, painfully handicapped by bare feet. At the forbidding blackness of the mangroves, the policeman halted. A stake had whizzed viciously past his ear. He listened to the crackling of mangrove-roots, to the pantings and the squelching of mud growing rapidly fainter. He realized that discretion would save him a broken head, so awaited in impotent rage until the ghostly Gubinmint should pluck the thorns from his feet and come limping up.

Back in the village, a crouching woman crooned over a child. She had recognized her laddie's voice and just could not leave him when he called, even though she knew it was only for a few heavenly days.

The others all got back to Dauan, flooding the waterway with song and laughter hysterically joyous. Midway out, they met the returning canoes of Boigu and their blended voices musically sweet made Gubinmint quite angry as he limped back along his lonely veranda.

The return of the commissariat was hailed with masked solemnity by the police and deacons and councillors of Dauan. The garden raiders were so exhilarated retailing their adventures that they did not notice that the guardians of the wine seemed incapable of rising from their mats to greet them, nor that the Dauanites listened smilingly though a trifle abashed.

However, the kegs were immediately attended to in a spirit of hilarious comradeship. Those wells of joy were full, but after the first one was emptied the commissariat raiders but doubtfully guessed that half the other two was water. However, day dawned bright and clear and happy with a guarded understanding amongst the visiting islanders that a closely representative watch would be kept on all kegs in future.

Clare was enjoying herself immensely. She had not been so happy for years and years. Her slender creamy form stood out distinctly against the strong brown and black figures of the island girls. Her hair too drew instant attention; it clouded to her waist, thick, quite straight, and jet black. The island girls' glory was beautiful but short and prettily frizzed in a million tiny curls. Clare's eyes were black, her nose and lips small. She smiled quite sweetly with this excitement and just loved to dive deep with the men. Of course, she could not stay down so long nor work so furiously as the deep-chested island girls, but she had all the excitement of plunging into the darkening gloom and peep-watching those bronze figures busily working amongst the wonder things of the sea. And strangely, she felt proud that this happiness from the sea was the gift of a white man's ship. She did not realize why.

Poor Clare! A half-caste aboriginal, she pined for her great open country around the Mapoon Mission station, so far away on the north-western Peninsula coast. Rama, while visiting on a pearling-lugger, had married her and carried her far to the little island in the sea. The island girls were quite nice to her; she knew they were sorry for her, that she had never borne a woman's pride. Little Clare, lonely exile. I saw her recently; the visiting missionary shook his head. Consumption!

But Clare was happy this bright day, and continually she swam down into the silence to spy the ghosts at work. And Baku and Samsu smiled at her, their smiles looking so friendly in the green twilight and strange, too, because their mouths could not open and no soul made any noise. They pointed once as if daring her to do something. She hastily glimpsed what appeared a blacker hole below this hole, for she was within the hold of the old ship. But she must have more breath, so she glided up like a white shadow dodging the purple corals.

She got her breath on the canoe above while mentally seeking courage to accept the challenge.

As the workers shot up from below she told them she would swim into the hole and they all, girls and men, laughingly dared her, never dreaming that she had the courage or the capability to do so. When their turn came again, she swam down, down, down between Baku and Samsu. The twilight clouded within the coral ship and her heart went faint at the little black opening below. But she swam straight on thinking to turn in the darkness below and then swim straight up through the misty water to triumph.

Both men snatched too late as they realized she had gone. They crouched on the edge of the den in agonized fear for they knew the demon that waited within. A gaping purple cavern opened before Clare, and surrounding it were rows of gleaming teeth. The sleepy giant groper that could have bitten her in halves never moved. She doubled in a frantic terror that caused her to miss the opening above. Something snatched down at her hair. She struggled away in agonized fear but a vice gripped her wrist and clung. She tugged and kicked and heard her heart hammering up through the blackness then opened her mouth to scream and all the sea roared in and her ears burst. Only when her struggles lessened could Baku and Samsu pull her out, then with bleeding noses and bulging eyes, they thrashed up with her to the sunlight above.

Warrior, Darnley Island 1921, by Frank Hurley.

THE CRUISE OF THE "GREYHOUND"

IT was lonely one afternoon as I sat dolefully on a log beside the Hughenden road. The billy and empty tuckerbags drooped against the swag. My pipe and pockets and belly were empty. Hopefully I watched a knight of the road slouching up the track.

The stranger, in old slouch hat, patched flannel, and trousers that had known much better days, looked like a depressed burglar. There was a hump on his shoulders, a scowl on his face; his shaggy brows and aggressive moustache were powdered with white dust. His defiant stare set me recalling faces when, with a startling oath, he booted his swag across the track, flopped heavily on the log, and entreated hoarsely:

"For Gawd's sake, mate, don't say you're out of tobacco!"

"What do you think I'm chewing an empty pipe for?" I inquired miserably.

"Hell an' fury!" he moaned. "Stony broke, tuckerbags busted, no smokes, corns on me trilbies, an' a thirst that'd swaller a brewery. *What* a life!"

"I'm in the same boat. You're not the only fool carrying an empty head and a heavy swag."

He thrust out a freckled paw and laughed enthusiastically.

"Shake, brother, shake! We pair right here. My birth certificate says 'Scandalous Graham.'"

I "shook" cordially. Every shearing-shed in New South Wales knows "Scandalous."

"I've seen you on Lightning Ridge," I said. "But you'd dodge the Devil himself in that layer of Queensland dust."

He thumped me delightedly:

"What! You from sunny Noo South too? That dear land where the old men never die and the girls never grow old ! We're blood brothers, lad. Innocents in a strange land. We'll boil the billy and make merry, for tomorrow we pad th' hoof."

"Righto," I agreed hopefully – "if you've got any tea?" His face fell.

"I always forget th' little things," he grimaced. "I'll tell you what. You're heading for Richmond, aren't you?"

"Yes."

"So'm I. We'll park our 'curses' here and hop into Hughenden; it's only a couple O' miles along the track. If I meet any shearer bloke, I'll sting him hard. If not, I'll pirate a cook in some man-fleecing pub in town, or I'm not th' sheik I was. That is," he compromised hastily, "if she's not a Chow."

"Great idea," I encouraged. "But I'm afraid I'll be no help; the ladies don't appreciate my personal ugliness at all."

"The conquest is mine," he winked. "The filly's not foaled that Scandalous can't rope in."

I thought he was the ugliest man in Queensland. "Then," he continued gaily, "we'll blow back here; feed up; an' before dawn be sailing down the Flinders first saloon for Richmond." He grinned hugely.

"I don't understand."

"You wouldn't. Now listen here. Half a mile back there's a Chow's humpy decoratin' th' river. He's got one of those sawn in half, red-iron tanks. It's down near the river-bank, away from the house in the middle of a turnip patch. He uses it for waterin' the garden. We'll borrer the tank, launch it, hop in, an' the streamlet will waft us down to Richmond. Like angels serenely floating down the stream of life!"

"H'm. But suppose it capsizes?"

"You can swim, can't you ?"

"Yes."

"Good. I can't. Now, look here. Would you rather trudge the seventy blazing miles to Richmond with empty tucker-bags, sore feet, an' the rags of your back flogging your tail-bone to a jelly in th' breeze-or would you sail down-river like a bloomin' tourist?"

"The gentleman act for me. Yours are the brains." Scandalous grinned amiably. "Righto! Here's where we light out for the sustenance. March on."

I attempted to hide the swag.

"Leave the 'curse' alone," he roared. If any crawler pinches it, he'll be the fool."

Seeing the sense in this, I hurried after him.

"Never pamper a swag, or the habit grows on you," advised Scandalous. "The 'curse' is the most parasitical thing in this parasitical world. No skirt alive can cling to a man with th' tenacity of a swag. You can generally shake a skirt off by getting blind paralytic on picture nights, but the drunker you behave to a swag, th' tighter it clings. Mine has clung so that it's sawed holes in my pink shoulder-blades."

Thus, much cheerier for mutual company, we neared Hughenden as the sun was sinking. I scouted hopefully on the town outskirts while Scandalous whistled ahead on his foraging expedition. Barely an hour later he returned, his face wreathed in smiles, a bulging sugar-bag over his shoulder. It held a cold shoulder of mutton, a loaf of bread, and some tea and sugar.

"I told her she looked only twenty-five," he grinned, "and had eyes like a gazelle I knew in Egypt. She'd have given me half th' pub if th' boss hadn't been so dashed suspicious."

"Forget her," I congratulated eagerly. "Let's hurry back and boil the billy. I'm famishing."

"Here, hold hard! We'll light up first." He halved a plug of Havelock.

"You're an angel, Scandalous," I exclaimed and meant it. "Where did you get the tobacco?"

"Pinched it from a drunk," he answered simply. "His matches, too. Dear old mum taught me never to do a thing by halves."

That evening meal was a taste of heaven to a friendless and famishing pair after a long, hard walk. Lying stretched on the brown grass afterward, gazing dreamily up at the stars, the soothing tobacco lulling me to sleep – it's a memory of stolen content.

Scandalous booted me before daylight. A billy steamed invitingly by the fire. Breakfast was spread on the log. A crow carked from the tree overhead.

"Hadn't we better save the tucker until tonight? There's just one decent meal left."

"God feeds the sparrows," replied Scandalous cheerfully. "You sit there an' watch me eat." He reached for the bread. I reached for the mutton, lively. In ten minutes even the crumbs were gone. "The ants has got stiff luck," murmured Scandalous as he wiped his mouth with the back of his hand.

Half an hour later, before dawn, we were stumbling over interminable cabbage rows, Scandalous leading the way, seeking the tank.

"If these Chinamen have dogs—" I ventured doubtfully.

"They have," assured Scandalous over his shoulder.

"They sooled 'em on to me and they'll sool 'em again if you speak so dashed loud!"

We stumbled on and presently located the tank, just the usual open-topped, square iron tank, but full of water. Scandalous swore softly as we vainly struggled to up-end it.

"Of course it had to be full," he growled, while struggling to shoulder it over. "If we was perishin' in a desert the dashed thing would be bone dry!"

"What if we turn the tap on?" I suggested.

"Of course!" snapped Scandalous. "Why didn't you do it before!"

We turned it full on, apprehensively waiting while dawn grew quickly and showed the Chinamen's house in the distance. Presently the tank was empty enough for us to tip it over. Even empty, it was a bit of a struggle to lift the tank over the crazy fence and manhandle it down the bank of the river.

"Get a couple of saplings, quick," panted Scandalous. "We'll need 'em to pole her off the mudbanks."

I grabbed two handy sticks from the fence, then boarded the craft -or tried to. Scandalous's clumsy scrambling embedded the tub in the mud, and I could not budge her.

Swearing fiercely, Scandalous tumbled out again, scraping a shin and the remnants of his temper against the rough edges. Pushing the clumsy thing and splashing out up to our knees, we eventually shoved it into deeper water. I clung to one side while Scandalous slung his legs over the other and jumped inboard – with a splash.

"Hell an' slaughter-houses," he yelled, "the blasted thing's sinking! She's sprung a leak. The swags are swimmin'."

I laughed. "Why, we've left the tap turned on." Scandalous flung muddy arms in the air and kicked the water in the boat. "Then turn it off!" he roared. "Standin' there gigglin' with th' tap turned on like a girl in a water-works! We'll have every dam' Chow in Hughenden tearin' down here in a minute!"

We worried the tub back to the bank, up-ended the water out of her, then pushed off again. She spun giddily as I scrambled in.

"She's a bit frisky," observed Scandalous amiably, "like all the uncertain sex."

The roosters were crowing and a dog barked up at the Chinamen's. A fair current in mid-stream speeded us up, at which Scandalous bawled a triumphant cock-crow to the rising sun. In boisterous answer the craft spun like a lopsided top, then clumsily reversed. We were travelling by degrees, our direction the plaything of the current.

"You balance the starboard an' I'll balance the port," ordered Scandalous importantly, "an' see if we can steady the *Greyhound* with the poles."

We steadied her a bit, though mostly starboard was the bows and port the stern. She joggled along for an hour, and we had just lit our pipes when an unforeseen problem in navigation claimed our attention. An over-grown gum had inconsiderately fallen out towards the centre of the stream.

"Of course it had to fall into th' water," growled Scandalous, "when it had all the air in th' world to grow up into!"

Now, there was sufficient room for a dreadnought to have passed, but the *Greyhound* made for that submerged tree with a vim and sauciness that told of set purpose. She hit it with a bang; sheered drunkenly off; collected her wind; then "bang!" again.

"Shove her off!" howled Scandalous. "She'll stave in an' we'll go to the bottom!"

"Aren't I shoving her!" I yelled. "How d'ya expect me to shove her back against this current?"

"Grab the branches an' pull her round the Hellfire Corner."

I grabbed a branch and pulled. The tub pulled too – backwards, as Scandalous was leaning forward. He grabbed my trousers just in time as the tank swirled dizzily.

The *Greyhound,* s pinning like a catherine-wheel, hit the log a terrific smash. As she shuddered on the recoil our heads banged the iron sides and we both dropped our steering-poles. Picking himself up, Scandalous yelled:

"Quick, quick! Lean our weight astern. If she only hits straight th' current might tilt her over!"

Luckily she did hit straight. The front part, relieved of weight, nosed skywards like a sick turtle. She slid on to the log and for one terrible second paused astride it. We sprang forward – so did the tank, and if we had not violently back-somersaulted it would have capsized then and there. She grated over the log to flop into deep water where, spinning round until tired, she floated into a backwash and grounded.

While we were getting fresh poles, the ugly face of Scandalous beamed.

"I've fathered a brain-wave," he declared in his bass voice. "See that leafy tree over there?"

"I saw it an hour ago."

"Yes, and that's about all you *did* see. Now, swing your lustrous orbs on it an' glimpse the rudder that's going to steer the *Greyhound* as straight as a parson's conscience! We'll trail a leafy bough astern and she'll waddle bows first then."

We tried it. With the butt of the branch as tiller-handle, jammed between a forked stick lashed down one side of the tank, she steered like a lame duck – lost a little in speed, but became as steady as a derelict.

Thereafter the day slipped uneventfully by into evening. We went while the going was good, for the sooner we sighted Richmond the sooner we would dine. It was awfully cramped, too, in that old tank. Ungraciously I wondered whether the long, dusty road might not have proved more pleasant after all.

"Glimpse the sky 'way up-river?" drawled Scandalous. "Um. Those clouds are saying rain," I guessed. "Never mind. We'll tie the rudder loosely and the current ought to keep the yacht in its course automatically, so to speak. If it doesn't, we'll only ground against a mudbank. But we should ha' painted the *Greyhound* with a skull and crossbones."

And he hoarsely bawled a pirates' song:

Fifteen men on the dead man's chest –
Yo-ho-ho, and a bottle of rum!

Presently he lapsed into silence. The stillness of everything was remarkable. Not a whisper from the trees as we passed; not one chirruping cricket. Seldom have I known a night so quiet. Finally Scandalous secured the rudder.

"It looks mighty threatening up-river, Jack," he said soberly. "Still, I'm going to bye-bye."

We huddled in opposite corners of the tank. I was acutely hungry, but in a matter of minutes Scandalous, his head sagging on hairy arms looped across his knees, was churning the tank into a hollow rumble of snores. Very soon I must have made a duet of it.

That dream was awful. The liner was in serious trouble. We might never reach New York. The cabin was suffocatingly dark, though the stars above twinkled like golden pinheads. The frightening thing about this storm was the absence of wind. No whistling from tortured cordage, no wild gusts shrieking along the silent decks. But the water gurgled against the ship's iron sides, lashing the straining plates with foam as it moaned past into the night. The frightened crew were struggling with the rudder as the ship was whirled around. It could only be a matter of minutes, possibly of seconds!

Frantically I pushed towards a port-hole.

Then certainty of death overwhelmed me. We were going to be rammed. A vessel was bearing down upon us, an irresistible thunderbolt from out the black night.

"Crash!" Flying legs and clawing arms; ears stunned with the tank's reverberations; cold water pouring down my neck! I sprang up and instinctively grasped the slippery branch that was grinding the tank under.

"Push her off from th' branches," I cried. "Quick! Shove – or we'll be dragged under!"

It was an uprooted tree in the swirl of a roaring tropical flood. Torrential rain at the river-head had rushed an avalanche of water down upon us.

Straining, panting, pushing, prodded by sloppy boughs, faces and arms scratched from the plunges of invisible branches, we succeeded at last in freeing the lopsided tank from the heaviest limb.

"Hadn't we better hang on ?" yelled Scandalous.

"We'll have something to cling to if the tank goes under!"

"No, no! Push her right off! This current will roll the tree over and over. For the love of Mike, push her off."

At our last gasp, with a scraping of unwilling boughs the big tree slipped by and a second later was lost in the gloom.

"Find the billy and bale for all you're worth – quick! I'll keep a look out."

But the eyes of man could hardly have seen the riverbanks that night, nor anything save the stars above and the ghostly white of hurrying foam. The air was one soft moan of unseen waters. It took Scandalous only five vigorous minutes to bale the tank.

"Thank God, she hasn't sprung a leak. What price our chances?"

"Evens!"

"Anything you like-only don't say your smokes are wet, like mine!"

Feeling inside the flannel, I drew out a little oilskin-enwrapped package.

Scandalous found his laugh again. Somehow everything seemed more cheerful with the old pipes going; even the *Greyhound* appeared to quieten down just a little, though its spinning was still sickening.

The anxiously awaited dawn showed us the river in rolling brown flood. We could only hold tight and trust to luck.

Three hours later, in a watery daylight, we sighted a tumbledown shack, a Chinamen's garden on the outskirts of Richmond. Two yellow men were standing by gazing at the river. Scandalous waved a sodden blanket and shouted lustily.

The men ran to a dinghy and with the rushing current behind them, quickly intercepted us and slung us a rope.

Then came the struggle. Those Chinamen lost sweat.

Scandalous was immensely exhilarated by the unusual sight; but I was scared that they might cut the rope and let us go. However, they hung to the job and a mile farther down-stream managed to tow us into a by-wash.

Scandalous immediately stepped ashore, his dirty face all smiles. I thought he was going to smother the exhausted Chinese with thanks. Instead, "Hi, John, I sellem you nicee tankee. New feller. No leakee !" he said.

"How muchee?" asked a Chinaman laconically.

"A quid."

The Chinamen bent te' their oars.

"How much you give?" roared Scandalous.

"Ten shillun."

"All right, she's yours. But you must chuck in breakfast. We welly hungly."

The Celestials debated a moment. "All li – suposem you helpee rowem backee, all li."

"Righto, it's a deal."

So we toiled in place of the winded Chinamen and battled back to the humpy. We landed the tank, and these careful Chinamen camouflaged her with a holey tarpaulin.

A little later, our insides warmly lined with curried rice, silver jingling in our pockets, and a cheerful whistle on the lips of Scandalous, we trudged down the broad brown road towards Richmond.

The Herald, a Missionary lugger of Torres Strait, in which Idriess cruised the Coral Sea.

THE BOOYA

"IF only we could find it!" exclaimed Rawlings for t he hundredth time. "It is worth millions!" He was walking the veranda, his face animated by desire. "What did you sayan ounce of radium was' worth?"

"Priceless," answered Musgrove. "There are only a few ounces in the world."

"And the Booya must weigh at least ten pounds!" broke in Rawlings. "A hundred and sixty ounces, worth --"

"Millions!" answered Musgrove. "Really billions, for it would supply light for the cities of the world; its energy is inexhaustible. Its rays might even vanquish disease!"

"Damn disease!" exclaimed Rawlings as he wheeled and gazed towards the massive bulk of Gelam. "Think of the money, the power! Two men owning the world's radium, selling it grain by grain, every nation bidding! And it is here – where? We have searched every cranny in the island; you have won the confidence even of the Zogo-le, and all we know is that it is here – somewhere!

The two men were searching for the Booya, the "spirit light" of the Eastern Group of Torres Strait islanders; a "sacred" stone which is alleged to throw off an unquenchable bluish-green light. There were in existence, according to tradition, three of these Booyas, one each held by the Zogo-les of Mer, of Eroob, and of Ugar islands.

When the first missionaries landed on the Eastern Group in Torres Strait they, with their South Sea henchmen, in perilous isolation and seeing nothing around them but crowds of head-hunters given over to idolatrous ways, burned the Zogo-houses and the Au-guds – huge idols these, of polished tortoise-shell – burned the divinatory skulls and masks and accessories of Zogo worship; destroyed the Zogo-grounds and the sacred shrines; discredited the priesthood of the Zogo-le, and wrought general havoc upon the religion of the islanders. But the keeper of the shrine's innermost secrets, the Booya of Mer, was buried in its deepest cave, its whereabouts a secret known only to the Zogo-le. These had made a vow with their spirit fathers to train their sons to the mysteries of the priesthood, so that, should Time overthrow the white man, their descendants would be able to recover the Booya and rehabilitate the religion of their race.

Of a substance perhaps stranger even than radium, the Booya was set within a socket held by a bamboo rod with various symbolic decorations done in shell, ochres, and bone. The composition of this setting was such that the rays were directed upward, to ascend from the main Zogo-house only on the occasion of an island victory, a calamity, or the death of the chief priest of the cult. The rays ascending in the form of a searchlight, were visible far across the Strait.

Of the very few white men who have had dealings with the Eastern Group, perhaps not six all told know of the Booya. The last of the Zogo-le describe emphatically and intriguingly the rays of light shed by this apparent stone. Nothing can stop the rays, they say; it will penetrate through stone and iron. Those ghostly rays will penetrate an iron ship and shine far out through the other side. When turned on to dugong and turtle the innermost secrets of their insides become visible but the creatures turn mad! The queerest of happenings are told, by those who should know, of the powers of these phantom rays. They have been so told to me, and in other ways to the "Wandering Missionary," MacFarlane, who for twenty years with sympathy and understanding has worked among these most interesting people and gained their deepest confidence. To the half-dozen men who have become convinced of the reality of the Booya, the only weak explanation we can guess is – radium.

I have heard the theory expounded that the Booya may originally have come from some lost civilization, possibly from a fleeing migration of that vanished people who have left those huge monuments on Easter Island or those more utterly vanished still, whose jungle covered ruins have been refound in the Solomons. The Torres Strait islanders say it was a highly-cultured people who in ages past brought the Booya to Mer.

Such are the shadowy facts concerning the Booya.

Now to the story of Rawlings and Musgrove, which you can believe or not, as you like. These two men had been, each by different methods, searching for years for the Booya of Mer.

Now Musgrove abruptly stood up. "Well," he declared, "only Gelam remains."

Musgrove was a big man, his hair iron-grey. His unsmiling face indicated the thinker as he stared towards the age-old volcano, the crater filled in centuries ago.

"What of it?" inquired Rawlings expectantly.

"Why," Musgrove explained, "the Booya is hidden in a cave. We have searched every cave. But the whole inside of Gelam must be hollow – we have never searched there!"

"I'm ready," exclaimed Rawlings.

They searched Gelam for weeks, working its wide miles of grass-grown surface for any trace of a cave. They examined especially its ravines; tangled places they are, long and steep and quiet. Rawlings searched with an eagerness turning to exasperation with failure. Musgrove searched eagerly, too, but methodically, patiently. They combed the hill of Zomar, the spurs of Upimagar; they roamed the slopes of Mekarnurnur and traced the ravines right back into Gelam. Finally, as a forlorn hope, they climbed down into the valley of Deaudupat, whose head is at the very base of the old volcanic mountain.

The valley soil is of porous ash; scattered palms peep from stunted scrub entangled by vines. A parched valley, grey and desolate, it is the site of the old taboo grounds – the home only of spirit hosts awaiting the return of the ancient worship.

After weeks of searching and hope deferred they located a scrub-clad depression somewhat cluttered with fallen rocks. Rawlings gazed up at the steep hill-side but could see no sign of a landslide which would account for those loose rocks. Might not they have been carried there, and earth filled in amongst them, and grass grown upon it! The very surmise set them working. Rawlings was filled with excitement as he tore out these rocks day after exhausting day. Strong man though he was, and even with Musgrove's help, those wedged rocks barred their progress for a week. Then he broke through into a cleft which clearly ran into the mountain itself. But how far?

They sweated, often lying on their sides, gouging in between the rocks, and eventually were able to crawl right into the cleft until the roof abruptly vanished, and the rock walls opened out into a tunnel. Standing in their torchlight, eager eyed, they stared questioningly at each other. They carefully ventured into the silence, Rawlings in trembling anticipation, Musgrove curbing his joy.

Presently Rawlings flashed his torch at a branch tunnel. "We could easily get lost," he said. "My heavens, wouldn't it be awful to be lost down here in the bowels of the earth!"

Musgrove chalked a directing arrow on the wall beside them.

"We will have to be very careful," he said quietly; "this old volcano may be a maze of galleries and pitfalls."

"I would never have thought of it," laughed Rawlings.

"Your talks with old Passi have borne good fruit. What would the old heathen say if he dreamed we had located their precious cave?"

"The question is, what would they do?"

Carefully watching their path they walked a winding quarter of a mile, drawing deeper in towards the heart of Gelam; they passed the black mouths of two more tunnels, and then their own widened to a chamber dangerous with numerous openings. They stopped, searching the black roof, flashing their torches on to clefts and twisted fissures in the towering walls. Not dug by the hand of man, these tunnels, but riven by nature when the mountain's volcanic fires were slowly sinking back into the earth!

"It's waste of time and energy rushing things," decided Musgrove finally. "We must plan our search; it has only just begun. God knows how many of these passages intersect the old volcano. We are in a labyrinth. If we get lost we perish. Don't walk so fast! I'll chalk a wall as we go along. Watch your feet, too, or you might drop into something."

Still impatiently, but now more cautiously, Rawlings moved on, straining his eyes, seeking a light.

The feeble torches merely gave the blackness emphasis: there was cavern after cavern encompassed by fantastic walls. Their torchlight was like a dim candle wavering in the Pit. Queer shapes seemed watching them, hunched-up rocks left by the cooling lava.

"We must return," Musgrove decided. "We have been hours in here, and my chalk is nearly done."

Rawlings swore impatiently; but they followed the chalk-line back and emerged, to Rawlings's amazement, into starlight.

"It means a systematic search," Musgrove said, "perhaps of weeks."

Then one day, deep in the belly of Gelam, Rawlings spied a faint blue mist stealing through a crevice near the roof a hundred feet up. Eerily stationary, it seemed to come from some deep inner chamber. Rawlings shouted excitedly as he climbed; the rock gave foothold in projections of twisted shapes until, at eighty feet above, the wall flattened into a broad ledge. He ran across to the crevice, and peered through on to a broad rock platform. Rawlings shouted the discovery and squeezed into the crevice.

Musgrove began climbing, his heart thumping violently, refusing to allow himself to believe that the search was successfully ended. He scrambled up on to the ledge, ran across it, and stepped through the crevice on to a platform flooded with a bluish light. Even the fissures in distant walls showed eerily plain. But his eyes were instantly attracted by a pillar of violet light rising from a circular pit, evidently the old volcano throat away down in the floor below.

Musgrove gazed astounded, more astounded still when his eyes followed the violet light upward and saw deep into the semi-transparent roof.

"Look!" he shouted, "the rays are penetrating the solid rock!"

But to his horror Rawlings took no notice; he was making towards the circular pit.

"Hold back, man!" he cried. "Don't go near the rays!" An excited face looked up.

"Nonsense!" Rawlings answered. "The Booya is down there. It's too late, anyway! We're bathed in the rays."

"That is only the reflection from the roof and chamber walls," called Musgrove urgently. "Look up, man; look up! The rays are piercing the very roof!"

"We can go to the edge, anyway!" Rawlings called back. "I'm near it, and the rays don't affect my eyes. It's the Booya, man – the Booya!"

"Wait for me!" called Musgrove insistently. "I'm coming … You fool," he cried as he scrambled nearer, "remember the legends of the Zogo-le! Even the priesthood suffered awful death if they came in direct contact with the rays!"

But Rawlings was now edging across the cavern floor.

A defiant laugh floated through the chamber as, like a fascinated child, he hesitated within yards only of the crater-lip, staring at the pillar of violet light.

Musgrove edged out towards him.

"My God, Rawlings!" he whispered, "it is beyond our comprehension. Something that has never been even imagined! Powers never dreamed of may exist there! Don't risk anything further!"

There was no glare, no sound, no smell; just a pillar of intense violet light. Rawlings tossed a pebble into the pit. It vanished noiselessly.

He turned a startled face to Musgrove. "How are we going to climb down?" he demanded. "It must be a frightful depth!"

Before Musgrove could stop him he had peered over the crater-lip.

Horror chilled Musgrove. The rays permeated that portion of the man's body leaning over the crater-lip. His bones were shadows within transparent jelly!

He turned back from the rays. His body appeared normal again, but his eyes blazed with violet fire. "The Booya is down there," he exclaimed tensely. "I could not see it – I could *feel* it! I saw nothing but violet! My brain is violet--"

Without warning he leapt straight at Musgrove, shrieking: "You shall look, too, Musgrove – you shall look!"

But Musgrove sprang aside and abruptly shot out his leg. As Rawlings crashed, Musgrove raced across the chamber and clambered up the wall.

At the top he glanced down, panting. His blood ran cold as two violet eyes blazed up from below. He scrambled over the flat top, crept through the crevice, then, gripping his torch, steeled himself for the perilous descent into the darkness beyond. He jumped the last ten feet to the bottom. Then he glanced up towards the crevice, and there, framed in the faint blue glow, he saw two violet eyes!

Musgrove trained his torch on the chalk-line as he started to run through the mile of winding passages.

He had not gone a tenth of the distance when footsteps pattered behind him. Wheeling around, his scalp tingled at sight of the living skeleton pursuing him. Its eyes like molten gold, its body jelly enclosing dark bones. And grotesque trousered legs.

Musgrove switched off his torch and ran, panic-stricken; he crashed against the wall to crawl frantically forward, then crouched still.

Rawlings groped towards him-that thing with the legs of a man, but the upper half a luminous framework with tiger's eyes, feeling its way with shadow fingers – a new thing in a world below the earth!

Musgrove pressed back against the wall, listening to that sibilant breath, hearing his own thumping heart, while Rawlings came groping past. Rawlings hesitated with his head cocked sideways, a hideous caricature of listening. He turned to grope back. Nearer he crept, feeling the wall with his bony claws, toeing it.

Stealthily Musgrove crept to the opposite wall.

Stealthily Rawlings crept across too, listening, groping. Yard by yard, Musgrove drew back as the luminous man came on. Time, sound, everything ceased in the concentrated effort to dodge this supernatural thing. At last he felt his spine pressing against the very platform wall and instantly imagined that to climb might mean salvation. Gropingly he began the ascent. But Rawlings began climbing, too, following in Musgrove's footsteps!

Musgrove reached the top of the wall, then waited, his back to the crevice. Rawlings ascended rather than climbed, a luminous shell arising from the gloom. But he did not come quite within reach of Musgrove's threatening foot. His glowing eyes searched the rock crannies, then deliberately he started to creep around by the right, chuckling as he passed: "Why, Musgrove, I see you, I have seen you *all* the time! Darkness for me no longer exists, neither of sight nor of mind. Be sensible, Musgrove; come and look into the rays with me!"

"By God, I won't!" gasped Musgrove as Rawlings sprang.

They fought as madmen fight. They tore at one another on the very brink of the platform; they kicked and clawed and howled as they rolled upon that ledge within the heart of Gelam, deep in its waiting silence. Musgrove stiffened as skeleton arms raised him bodily above the brink. But Rawlings threw him back on the ledge and laughed.

"Why, Musgrove, you are paralysed! I am only playing with you –

playing! Wait until you gaze into the rays! You will feel the strength of a hundred men. Then we can fight! Come!" He bent down and they fought towards the crevice, they fought through it out into the blue light, they struggled right to the very edge of the rock. But there the rays reclaimed Rawlings; he planted his foot on the panting man and stood gazing at the violet pillar, fascinated.

"The Booya is there," he whispered; "all alone, at the bottom of the earth."

"Go down and get it, Harry," whispered Musgrove, in desperate hope.

"I'm not as mad as that!" shrieked Rawlings, and laughed to the echoes. But his eyes gazed back to the violet pillar.

"I wonder," he whispered. "It draws me; it draws me!" He stepped to the edge of the wall, and began climbing down.

Musgrove rose to his knees. Rawlings was climbing with an uncanny ease and swiftness. He reached the bottom and walked straight across the floor to the funnel lip. Musgrove watched him peer over; farther, farther still! ... And then he was gone.

Musgrove sped as if from devils – sped, seeking the open air and daylight, terrified for his reason. He found himself running back along that mile of tunnel, laughing in an ecstasy of relief – and ran into a barrier of earth and rock raised at the tunnel end!

Dazedly he flashed the torch back along the wall. The chalk-line was there; he had come the right way. What in heaven – God! *fresh* earth –the natives had buried him in.

He cried aloud, clawing at the earth, snatching away the stones, throwing all behind him as an animal might claw. He shrieked aloud to Passi, Passi the descendant of the Zogo-le; cried to him of the kindnesses he had done the islanders, of the many times he had stood between them and the whites; of how he had tutored them, had taught them the values of pearl-shell, of trochus, of *bêche-de-mer*. And as he cried he dug ahead and flung the dirt behind him.

Then came a listening silence in which he broke down altogether.

They dragged Musgrove into the sunlight and laid him at the feet of Passi. He gazed up at the brown, wrinkled face, the black eyes that hid the thoughts of a savage and a knowledge at which civilization can but guess.

"White man," Passi said at last, "for long you have lived amongst us, a friend against the greed of your countrymen who are our present masters. Otherwise your tomb would have been Gelam. Know then that no white man may even touch the Booya, though they come in ships to get it. I only may reach it. It means my death, but first I can hand the knowledge of it to my unharmed son and then he may direct its madness on any number of men, any number of ships. White man, the Booya sent cities mad long before your countrymen were known. Forget the Booya, and go!"

And Musgrove went.

Passi, the Marmoose of Mer, with his drum.

THE BONES OF LEON CHANG

THE grave-digger leaned on the cemetery fence, waiting. And something was coming now – a Mr Yuan Tai; though as yet the planter of clay did not know this. He was morose; economic conditions made him so. Lights were bustling and winches rattling on the distant wharf, where the *Taiping* was loading up with pearl-shell. All Thursday Island slept, except the wharfies. They made hay while it was overtime, thought the grave-digger sorely. Mostly able-bodied men, even the few toughened booze kings among them showed no signs of dying. And the one probability intended to beat it to Darwin by the next boat.

The grave-digger lifted dejected eyes to the sky. It was a blaze of stars that tinted the water a delicate blue. The dark hills of Prince of Wales and Horn islands hemmed in the water as a crescent lake before the town. Still pearling-luggers dotted the water-way. The roofs below glinted to the palm-tops silhouetted above the water-front. All nature and even the works of man hushed, quietly beautiful. But the grave-digger's pockets were empty and financial emptiness drains beauty from the soul of man.

He thought hopefully of the hospital, nestling away below the guns on the fort. But the few patients there were convalescent. With a fellow feeling at another's difficulties, he wondered how the doctor was making a crust. Convention demanded that sawbones wear a white suit and pay his bills, but then he could charge a handful of guineas an operation, whereas the grave-digger only collected two pounds a knob on the failures – the crumbs from the rich man's table. And mighty few crumbs this year. The island was beastly healthy.

But births! Heavens, the doctor must be coining money through no effort of his own. The climate after all was on *his* side. Live and let live, the grave-digger gloomily told himself, did not apply to him.

Yuan Tai walked quietly up the deserted road leading to the cemetery hill. He stepped daintily, as a cat steps, and sipped to the dregs the expectation of his dreams: he was about to desecrate the bones of Leon Chang, his lifelong enemy. Never would those bones rest in the land of Chang's fathers, for Yuan would substitute the bones of a thief. And Leon Chang until the stars should dim would wander homeless in the heavenly sphere.

Gloatingly Yuan Tai lived over the years. The rivalry in youth, culminating in the love which brought the Lotus Flower. But not to Yuan Tai! And his heart had withered, for when a Chinaman really loves, he loves for all time.

Leon Chang had triumphantly planted the Lotus Flower in the New Land and Yuan Tai followed, as the weed follows the flower. On Thursday Island they had grown with the years as buyers of *bêche-de-mer* and tortoiseshell. But always it was Leon Chang who had forged just a little ahead; who had made bargains just a trifle shrewder; who gradually became the merchant. Perhaps the strength of Yuan Tai's mind being concentrated on his grievance, had lost him the race against Leon Chang.

Not that he still desired the Lotus Flower. By no means. She was ugly with the bearing of many children.

Either of his two younger wives was more desirable now than she. But Yuan Tai knew that after death would come the spirit life in which the Lotus Flower would blossom again to beauty in a youth that would never fade. As such he desired her forever. And time had made recompense. It had allowed him just enough: the spirit of his fathers had whispered him that *his* time was measured.

It was two years now since Leon Chang had died and his relatives were preparing by the law of the land to remove his bones to China.

The Chinese believe implicitly in earth to earth. A man's bones have been breathed into life by his native soil, and he must give them back to crumble in the Flowery Land and regive life to others yet unborn. Without this disintegration of the bone into the native elements from which it sprang, the soul wanders for ages lost. So Yuan Tai planned that after death had touched the brow of the Lotus Flower, she would awake to find Yuan Tai waiting to greet her and not Leon Chang.

"Good evening, Mr Bruce," greeted Yuan Tai suavely.

"Evening, Mr Tai," answered the grave-digger. "What if we get on the job while the going's good?"

"Proceed," nodded Yuan Tai.

The cemetery gate creaked as they turned forgetful backs on the town to walk down the hill upon a softly protesting path of grass. On the hillside to the left clung the white headstones of a Catholic group. The grave-digger glanced towards them grumpily. Catholics never die. He'd had a hole dug there ready for twelve months and it was still waiting. Altogether, five holes scattered indiscriminately, all ready for the planting, and no one to plant. On the little hill to the right leaned some Church of England graves, They were better: they died sometimes.

The men halted a moment at the small tin shed where the tools are kept, then went on along the pathway where rest a group of Japanese beneath their cemented beds of stone and leaning white posts charactered with Chinese black. But the Japs weren't much good. Some died in their diving-dress. (Even the sharks did a man out of a job!) And the live Japs went home to Japan.

The cemetery was all quiet beauty. Isolated from the town by small hills green with grass and trees, it sloped gently down to the grass-grown road by the dark mangroves lapped by the waters of Alpin Pass. A dear resting place for the wearied bodies of men. God's one spot where white and brown, black and yellow may dream in peace together.

But Yuan Tai was not wasting thought over peace to the dead. His philosophy knew no dead.

The peace of the cross-strewn hill-side had sweetened a little the economically embittered soul of the grave-digger. His mind felt rested. There was a tenner in this night's work; it was worth five plantings, and with no hard holes to dig. He merely had to keep his mouth shut. Which came naturally, for he lived amongst silent people.

They crossed over the deep drain that carries the rain-water to the sea. Here in a friendly group lay the "white" English and the "black" English, and farther on amongst the creepered trees rested the "white" Catholics and the "black" Catholics and the "browns and yellows." The grave-digger had a warm spot in his heart for them, for the converted people were the only ones who died on Sundays. That meant an extra ten bob.

Soon they were rustling among the pagans and the grave-digger wished them peace, for the devil claimed his own frequently. Of no particular religion or quite irreligious, just pure pagan or clinging to some grandfatherly cannibalistic rite, these cosmopolitan sleepers were the sheep without the fold that brought grist to the gravedigger's mill.

Unobtrusively poked into a protecting clump of grass was a stick, which marked the forlorn resting-place of Lo Ping, a thief. Here the grave-digger set to work. In shocked surprise the silence hushed to the sacrilegious ring of the pick. He grunted between tugs at the grass-roots, luxuriating amongst the stone mound. The shovel tinkled as he swept aside those clods of regret and the clattering was music to the fruiting passions of Yuan Tai. Soon the mound was levelled and the toiler settled to work. An old hole is easy to dig out. At five feet he thumped wood. His grunt rumbled as hollow as the sound. He worked cautiously then, for he was afraid of dead men's bones. He had known live ones who had lost their lives from a scratch.

"We'd better clear the other one," he growled, "an' swap 'em in the blanket. Leon Chang's got a good wooden box. This feller only sports packing-cases an' they're rotten."

"A good plan," agreed Yuan Tal, "I want 'Leon Chang' to appear exactly as his friends expect to find him."

"This hole is as slippery as th' road to hell," grumbled the grave-digger as he scraped the wet clay from his hands. Just in time, he checked himself from remarking that one Chink, dead or alive, was much like another.

Yuan Tai knew better. His countrymen would detect the fraud at any little mistake. But La Ping was the same build as Leon Chang; and no living man could identify either man's bones. La Ping's bones would return to China in the coffin of Leon Chang. A fish breached from the water below; the sound echoed from island to island.

They trailed through the grass to the English-Chinese section. Here Leon Chang's cross of white stood startlingly plain beneath a broad-leafed frangipani. The Christianized headstone loomed coldly impressive. An iron rail protected it. Shells and artificial flowers glinted steelily beneath the R.I.P. In an unobtrusive corner peeped a little Chinese vase mothering half-burnt joss sticks to scare away evil spirits. Tribute from the doubting soul of the Lotus Flower.

The grave-digger stepped over the rail and systematically laid the ornaments on one side. Time was short. He was sweating before his heaving shoulders worked below the surface level. Yuan Tai leaned over above and sweated also, but inwardly. His face gleamed sickly by the headstone, expressionless like most of the suave, well-educated Chinese, except that now his eyes betrayed the vengeance lust burning his mind and heart. To him, this was no sanctuary of the dead. There were no dead here. All was life. Death was a transition lasting minutes only. These graves were empty except for bones. But of life – spirit life – there was a fair abundance. Most had sped to other distant worlds. But there were laggards; those but recently born into the next life, curious and fearful over the transition and as yet not educated to their new environment. Leon Chang would certainly be here, anchored by the relics of his past. And his fear would be beyond measure at this inhuman desecration.

Yuan Tai gloried in the knowledge of the power he, a mortal, had over the spirit world. Through the material bones of Leon Chang he could torture a spirit member for ever; and it could not retaliate in this material world. He shivered over the grave, eager to gaze upon the bones of his enemy.

The hole grunted hollowly and the grave-digger leaned back and wiped a moist brow.

"Struck th' box; the job's about done," he murmured -then stared up aghast. Yuan Tai stared also and felt his stomach chill.

From the tombstone head glared eyes of liquid fire, round and unblinking, aflame with an awful vindictiveness.

With sobbing breath the grave-digger pulled himself together and threw a clod of earth, but the owl stared until the third clod, and then it only flapped to the frangipani-tree directly overhead. Yuan Tai thrashed the branch with the clay-daubed shovel, raining hysterical curses against all evil spirits in a screeching Chinese.

Agitatedly the grave-digger scraped clean the coffin-lid.

He was in a cold sweat.

"It's hell's own job," he muttered. "Don't know what's crawling over me. Here, Mr Tai," he whispered, "hand me that screwdriver. I feel as if someone's walkin' over me grave!"

Yuan Tai handed down the tool and listened to the clumsy efforts below. Presently the toiler handed up the lid.

"Now th' blanket," he whispered. "And you'd better hop down and give me a hand to bundle him into it. It will be a damn awkward job if you don't, because I've got the blooming creeps."

Without a word Yuan Tai lowered the blanket, then peered into the dark where lay his enemy. It was shrouded; but Yuan Tai gazed as if seeing beyond the Veil.

"For Gawd's sake!" stuttered the grave-digger. "What in heaven is b-bitin' you! Do you see a g-ghost?"

Yuan Tai sighed. Like a man overwhelmed he lowered his legs into the hole. He was sore afraid for he had seen the sockets below gleam with the eyes of the owl.

"Be careful!" cautioned the grave-digger, "this is a narrow grave. If you slip an' break your neck you'll be giving me another two quid," he joked feebly.

Yuan Tai did slip, quite suddenly. And a rib of Leon Chang sharply snapped beneath his falling weight. He wailed as he sprang from out the grave. The gravedigger was instantly beside him with his hair on end, his legs quivering, his mouth hesitating whether to howl or curse. Yuan Tai examined his thumb. A bead of blood welled upon it. He gazed as if seeing a vision within a crystal. Satisfied, he said calmly:

"Leave him alone, exactly as he is. Replace everything; also Lo Ping. Then dig a grave – for me."

He smiled at the grave-digger's face.

"But," burst out the man, "what silly rot! A tiny prick like that! The night's got on your nerves."

"It is a prick from the rib of Leon Chang," said Yuan Tai quietly. "I will die of blood-poisoning. Ah! You understand! Now listen! I will have time to set my affairs in order. I will give you an extra £10 for to-night's work, and another £5 to keep an eye on my grave, and when the time comes for my friends to lift my bones, you be answerable that they have never been tampered with. Swear fidelity by Leon Chang down there."

"I swear."

"Then that is all," nodded Yuan Tai. "I shall expect you in about three hours time." He turned and walked away. The grave-digger found his voice:

"Go straight to the doc, and get a serum injected against tetanus," he called.

"You remember to come to my shop and collect your money before it is too late," came back softly – "and bring your measuring tape."

The grave-digger grunted, then turned to his job. His nerve had come back. The economical barometer had risen to normal.

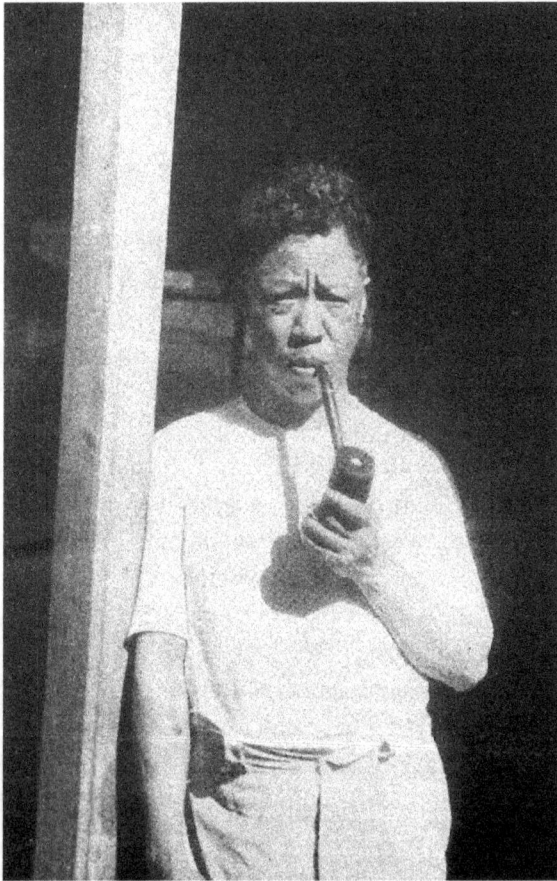

A meditative Oriental, Thursday Island 1925.

THE CALL OF THE PACK

MAN and beast glared threateningly into one another's eyes. Yet hardly a man. Midway between the two. For his tribe, who carry on the riddle of existence in the Bad Lands which fringe the western coast of Cape York Peninsula, are still in the Stone Age. Their greatest contribution to science is the jagged piece of quartz with which they operate on the young buck when initiating him into warrior-hood, and the sharp splinters of quartzite which form the wicked barbs of their war spears. Their simple cooking-utensils are of bark, their weapons of wood made hard by slow roasting in the fire.

Now Murooroo, initiated warrior of the tribe, with a broken leg and one arm crushed beneath a boulder, lay pinned in the dry gully-bed and glared back at cold, yellow eyes which stared into his.

Three dainty birds with fan-shaped, blue tail-feathers twittered busily in a honeysuckle bush, a black snake slithered gracefully over a grass tuft, insects hummed in the flower-scented air, and all the warm life of the great bush went serenely on.

Murooroo did not waste time in reviling his unskilfulness in stepping on the finely-poised boulder which had overbalanced and crashed with him to the gully bottom. His brain was not developed for such detailed thoughts. But it could reason the chances between life and death.

Could the dingo kill him? Could he kill the dingo?

His hunting-spears had fallen beyond his reach. He could use one leg and one arm. Was the dingo too cunning to come within reach so that he could suddenly sling leg or arm around it and sink his teeth deep into its hairy throat?

For a long, long hour the dingo glared at the black man. Through its baleful eyes its brain slowly calculated all the strength, all the weakness of the savage black pinned beneath the stone. Then, lifting its prick-eared head, it sniffed the air's message long and carefully. Satisfied, it edged a little closer to the black man, dropped on its belly, laid sharp head upon outstretched forepaws, and waited.

The hours slipped by. Over all was the afternoon silence of the bush, with a drongo calling far away. But intense listening could distinguish many things. The scratch on bark as a goanna clawed up a tree, the "thump! thump! thump!" of a passing wallaby among the bushes on the bank above, the hum of insects, the murmuring of countless leaves. Presently, soft black shadows enveloped the gully, a cooling breath came in the air.

The black man had boastfully left the hunting-party to kill big game by himself. They had laughed derisively as they went their way among the coolabah-trees. Now they would miss him at the campfires tonight, and anxious would be the talk of what could possibly have happened to him. There would be a clutching of spears and glaring out into the dark lest enemies had got him, enemies perhaps even now prowling around the gunyahs.

But fear of the spirits of the dead would keep them from looking for him, for the dead folk walk by night. At the first blush of the Sun-god, though, they would be on his tracks. Quickly they would find him – but only his gnawed bones would be left if the pack came!

Murooroo's gleaming eyes stared hard at the dingo's gaunt flanks. The gully shadowed into darkness and silence.

A light shone suddenly from the wild man's eyes. A pleasant, unfamiliar thrill ran through his body as from the birth of thought came slow understanding; and from understanding, hope.

The dingo's flanks were lean and hollow. The ribs stood out hard and taut, almost like those of a dead thing. It was famishing! But now it had made certain of its meal, it only had to wait. It would not call the pack now as the night wore on, for that would mean that it must fight for a small share of the meal.

If the crippled man could only keep it off him until dawn – until his friends came!

The dingo dragged on its belly a little closer. The black man bared gleaming teeth while a low, half-fearful, half-triumphant rumble came from deep down in his throat.

Far back in the gloom of the stunted timber a mongrel was loping over the earth, its nose to the ground, following tracks. Now and again it stopped short, the bristles from its mangy, scar-striped back rising stiffly erect, fangs gleaming in a noiseless snarl, its red-rimmed, burning eyes piercing the darkness ahead, to right and left, and behind. Then on again on noiseless pads, only to halt fearfully again at the scent of that something crossing the tracks. But it went on again, this mongrel, this survivor of cruel thrashings, this wild man's dog with the heart of gold, terrified now at the scent of its dingo enemy, it carried on, following its master's tracks.

To the gully-bank from where the rock had fallen the mongrel crawled upon its belly, head pressed to the ground, flaming eyes searching the blackness below. As it saw the back of the crouching dingo a shiver of fear raised the bristles on its neck and along the knobby backbone.

The dingo had crawled in a narrowing semicircle around the black man. Its instinct told it that the almost helpless savage would live long. But now the night was here, the man-thing's friends had not come, hunger gnawed fiercely at the dingo's lean flanks. The provoking odour of the meal so near, stirred its vitals.

Murooroo, twisting his neck as the beast crawled past him, knew it was getting on the boulder side, behind his head, where he could not use his good leg, where his good arm would be of the least possible use, and where he could not keep his eyes fixed upon its instant movement. One quick spring, one clash of teeth across his throat, and he was done. Reaching behind him he clawed a hole in the earth and lowered his head into it. This stretched back his neck. But he laid his claw-like hand across his throat and snarled defiance into the eyes of the dingo. Again he tingled with that strange, exultant feeling. Inch by inch the dingo crawled nearer and nearer. While down the creek-bank fifty feet behind it now crawled the mongrel, manoeuvring every inch as the dingo moved its body, quivering with the fear it dared not whimper.

For two hours the blazing eyes looked into the twisted eyes of the black man. For two hours the dingo had not moved. The mongrel, crouching close behind, drew in noiseless breath for the spring, as it sensed the stiffening of the dingo's tail, the tautening tendons of the hind-legs drawn in well under the bunching body.

The mongrel sprang a quarter-breath before the dingo, its fangs snapped at the dingo's back as both animals crashed on Murooroo's head. The surprised dingo leapt aside and vanished as if on wings of lightning.

The black man threw his arm around his hunting-dog and mouthed it and cried its name again and again. It licked his face and whimpered.

From the high bank the dingo looked back over its shoulder, then stopped, sharp nose in the air. To its twitching nostrils came no other scent of man or beast; only the crooning black man below with the mongrel shivering across his chest. For long the dingo watched, motionless. Then it sat slowly on its haunches, lifted its head to the starlit skies and howled. A long-drawn, mournful howl that swept many miles over the silent land to echo in distant rock-walled gorges, a melancholy howl that floated far over the low hills and down the scrubby creeks out on to the great open plains.

Murooroo, closing his eyes, lay back against the cold earth and shuddered.

It was the call of the pack.

A FISHER OF MAUBIAG

MISI, strolling happily along the beach with spear in hand, felt that life was beautiful, like the sunlight upon the sea and the scented air about the woods of Maubiag; though sometimes, he reflected, the flower-blue sky became overcast when the gods rumbled angrily and frightened the hearts of men.

Smiling, he stepped into the water and waded out chest-deep. Then he swam with the slow, easy stroke that makes the Torres Strait islander master of the water from sun-up to sun-down. He swam well out from shore, to the deep water which white men call Shark Passage. Here he trod water, treating it as if it were the land at command of his tireless feet, while he gazed upon the sea. It was as calm as the face of his little wife, crooning over baby Misi in the brown thatch home upon the palm-clad shore.

Deeply filling his lungs, Misi rolled like a porpoise, then swam down, down – an eerie and heroic figure in that queer underworld. His brown arms shot straight ahead, then swept to his sides – not fast – while his hands moved with the twisted motion of fins. Almost simultaneously, his legs spread sideways and back; then he shot straight down for quite a long time before his limbs moved again. Nursing his strength and air, his movements were rhythmic and slow, but his body sped down very fast.

Big-eyed fish darted from his approach; inquisitive ones circled and flashed up again behind him, their snouts coldly expressive of curiosity.

But these open-water fish were not his prey; they were too elusive. He sought the fish that lived in the reef, which here went down cliff-like to the unknown depths: a wall of coral festooned with plants and grasses, trees and flowers, and things indescribable of shape and sex, but of riotous life and colour.

His trained eyes spied within a crevice in some purple coral a wisp gently waving like a butterfly's wing. Easily, he kicked and turned on his side, his spear-arm poised with a grace unattainable above in the world of light and loud sounds and jerky movement.

He jabbed at the butterfly wing, and immediately felt the bamboo haft vibrate with the quivering of a pierced body. He pressed hard and felt the crunch as the prongs went through the fish and grated on the coral; then he kicked out and shot surfacewards, his spear held prongs uppermost, for thus every kick of the impaled fish planted it deeper on the prongs. When his head broke through the surface he drew deep breaths, keeping afloat without exertion.

Methodically he snapped the fish's neck between thumb and forefinger and threaded it on a strand of lawyer-cane twisted around his waist.

Then down he went again, and "fish-eyes" like vivid yellow pennies gazed out from a pulsing cabbage-plant as he shadowed past. This time he spied, jutting from under a ledge, the dreamily-moving tail of a red cod. He manoeuvred his spear, for when under water a bamboo haft unceasingly buoys upward and demands knack to train it into position. Then he jabbed hard and felt the prongs pierce through thick, firm flesh. The cod hardly flapped; its breed often will not struggle until they see the blue sky broadening above the water surface.

Again Misi darted up, quickly, yet with little apparent effort. He threaded his fish and gazed lazily at the sky while with porpoise-like grace he swam farther along the reef.

He flashed down this time on top of a giant coral-head enmeshed by jelly-like suckers of purple which coiled slowly upwards to suck him in.

But Misi was no scaly prey, so he contemptuously glided past the suckers and impaled an unwary parrot fish. A beautiful fish with scales of an intense blue. It struggled violently as Misi shot upwards and the water it thrashed flashed blue and green. So Misi dived and jabbed; and the Spirit of the Sea was kind. His string became threaded with fish until it would hold only one more. Proudly he surveyed the catch gleaming around his body. He would get the last one, and throw the full string at his girl-wife's feet. Once again the men of Moa, who already envied him his wife, would envy his fishing prowess.

He sped down, a splendid child of nature, and seemed to melt as the deeper waters received him within a coral garden walled by gigantic gnome-like things whose squat bodies housed drooping antennae, and among crimson bunches of fleshy life quivering with a million cells, and flowers of the sea of purple and white, orange and gold. Out from cracks in the gnome-things waved slender feelers like stalks of long brown grass. Tipping these, diamond eyes watched him piercingly, then blinked disconcertingly, only to shine again. One of the things kicked, like a misfiring torpedo, and its painted body shot back into the gloom. Misi rose quickly. He had dived down into a colony of crayfish, beautifully marked creatures as large as lobsters and with a powerful backward propelling motion of the tail. The smack of this tail, vibrating through the water for long distances, is a signal eagerly listened for by sharks; those within hearing swarm to the spot. For the shark loves crayfish as the schoolgirl loves ice-cream.

Misi breathed in the sweet air and deliberated. The island was quite a distance away; it was risky to venture below again; he had one more fish to get. But very likely no shark was within hearing of that tail-flip. He felt strong and brave, and the world was good. He would be acclaimed a great fisher in Moa if he secured a full string of fish from Shark Passage.

Breathing deeply, he dived and speared his fish far down within a coral chasm. Then something closed upon his leg. Instantly he realized the tingling of pins and needles as the snout nosed his skin. Without the slightest struggle he went down with the shark. At the merest tremble, he knew his leg would have been swept off. Those divers of the Strait know intimately the habits of the shark.

Gently Misi upended his spear, flicked it, and the impaled fish flashed slantingly down into the gloom, a wispy trail of blood marking its going. Instantly the shark released his leg and he glimpsed the baleful green of its phosphorescent eyes as it sped into the depths.

In that same moment Misi lost his spear. He shot upward, and when he reached the surface the hunting weapon was nowhere to be seen. He could not hesitate. His straining lungs gasped in air, he whinged with joy as with lightning strokes he swam for Maubiag, making little splash or sound. For the language of the sea is sound; water carries its vibratory messages as does the air.

Misi cast backward glances at each swing of his arms.

His exertions pumped blood from his leg. He could only just see the tell-tale trail, but he knew that the shark's wonderful organs of smell might pick up the faintest traces.

Then, two hundred yards behind, Misi saw the ripples and the fearful black fin. He swam with maniacal strength, but the fin creamed the water as the shark sighted its prey.

He had just time to turn and face the monster, swimming in a sitting position.

Like all its kind, ever uneasy of man and uneasier still at an unexpected mode of defence, the shark wavered before the steady eyes of Misi and glided past with an awful suggestion of strength. Misi turned his face with it and swam on. It swerved between him and the land, and he swam straight at it, and it glided around him. Again he faced about; again the shark charged, and again it slipped off sideways in face of his glaring opposition. Once more it circled, and this time Misi knew its coming charge meant the snatch of death.

A quick writhe, and it came at him. He whisked a fish before the gleaming snout as a boy flips a stone on a pool. The fish splashed and skidded across the surface in sparkling leaps. The shark wheeled and shot straight back; and Misi turned and swam for all he loved.

Quickly the shark came again. It circled only once; then it charged. Again, Misi threw the offering, and the shark wheeled back as if it had fully expected the fish.

Misi swam now with ebbing strength. His leg was bleeding fast. Maubiag was very close. He could see the shells upon the shore, it seemed that the little hills were reaching out their shadows to protect him.

The shark returned. He knew it would circle no more.

The fish he threw it gulped on the bounce and kept charging. He threw another, and plunged frantically, his eyes bulging and pain stabbing at heart and lungs.

The next fish he flung skidded sideways and gained several God-sent seconds on the momentarily puzzled shark. The next fish he threw at an opposite angle, and plunged forward in frantic hope as he saw he could almost touch bottom on the beach.

The shark, enjoying the play, speeded up its eager rushes. Misi whimpered like a baby as he threw the last fish and wailed the name of his little girl-wife.

He was speeding through shallow water now, but he wanted just one more fish.

As the shark sped back on its last triumphant rush Misi turned and plunged straight at it, his outstretched arms with the thumbs stretched out like tautened hooks. He screamed as the thumbs jabbed for the cruel green eyes and his twisting body was slung up in a whirl of water. But the shark sped blindly aside and in a moment Misi was floundering ashore. He ran, crying and laughing, leaving a red trail on the sands until he fell at the feet of his little wife.

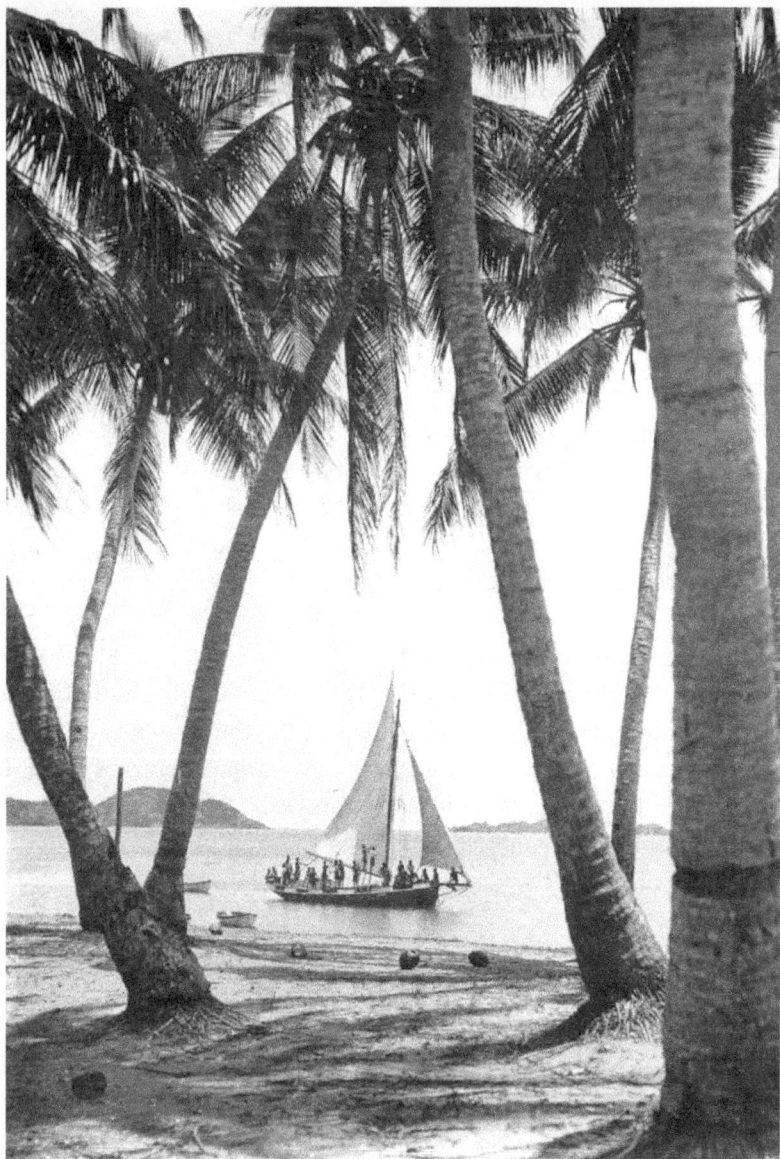

Sailing of Maubiag Island 1921, by Frank Hurley.

THE CITY OF SILENCE

BILLY BANNER stepped clumsily overside and down the short ladder; then through many pretty bubbles he slid down, down, down – and ungracefully landed in the mud.

"Missed," he smiled. Billy often spoke to himself when down below. He liked company, and a little conversation felt homely. He had finny company down there – their intentions were probably hostile. Of the sunlit world, all he had was the air in his diving-suit and the laughter in his heart.

He stood, planning out his way. The green twilight was exceptionally clear and seemed to focus upon Billy sagging in a sea of mud. "Like a waddling duck in a thunder-storm of silence," he mused.

Ahead, apparently far distant, though really very close, he spied a queer shadow. Cautiously he lumbered on then down to his belt sank silently. Instantly he tugged the life-line once, shut off the air-escape valve, and hummed, "Ta-ra-ra-boom-de-ay."

Billy had lived a long life down below-had lived it because he never got excited when death beckoned. So now he hummed an old-time song with submarine mud creeping to his armpits, and the air swelling out his suit; still hummed as he felt the steady pull on the line which lifted him from the sucking mass. As he shot up he unscrewed the air-escape valve to produce a whirl of bubbles while he tugged two short and two long strokes on the line. Gradually his ascent stopped as his dress subsided to normal. Then he made a loop in his life-line in which to sit, and tugged three times. The tender above, in accord with the signals, ran up the jib, and, raising the anchor just off the bottom, slowly moved ahead. And Billy, a suspended bundle of ugliness, was gently carried. forward over the sea-bottom, a fathom above the mud.

Eerily this monster drifted, who looked so much a part of the grim water-world and yet was not of it. He did not eye the bottom, for no pearl-shell lives on the mud. He watched the shadow taking form ahead, overwhelming in its magnified mightiness, and smiled cheerfully as he saw that the course of the lugger up above was going to bump him right into that shadow. After tugging twice and shaking the line once, he saw the trailing anchor subside into the mud. Tugging next four times he knew the lugger would not move until "talked to" again. Two tugs and a shake and down to the bottom he went, in front of one of the unknown wonders of the sea, maybe of the world.

A column of stone rose before Billy, probably sixty feet in height with a base seventy feet across. The top he knew to be flat and about six feet across, the whole composed of large, rounded stones. Along the coastline just out from Toori-toori (New Guinea) lay others of these columns. He liked to think of them as the "City of Silence."

Had the city been silent a thousand, or twenty thousand years? What human hands, dust very likely before the building of the Pyramids, had reared these towers? What manner of people these whose cities had been engulfed! Billy thought of Easter Island, with its mystery monuments; of the pottery dug from deep below the solid earth in New Guinea goldfields; of the super-men of wondrous powers and culture still hazily preserved in the legends of different island peoples. He lifted a leaden foot, put it upon a stone, hesitated, then, smiling delightedly, began climbing. This Silent City of his held a powerful appeal.

Between the stones grew sponges and weird marine things. Billy chuckled, for wherever sponges grow there also grow the fat pearl-shell. He glimpsed pearl, and smiled as it vanished like the tail of a firefly. He reached amongst the fernery and wrenched off a bashful shell, and chuckled again at a vanishing gleam higher amongst the rocks. He loved this game of hide-and-seek with the cunning oysters of the sea. They can hear, those big pearl-oysters, or feel the underwater vibration of a diver's foot-no man yet knows which. They rest with lip partly open, and the pearly gleam is like a smiling girl's teeth.

Billy's fingers closed around a shell the size of a dinnerplate, a heavy lump of indistinguishable stuff for seagrass grew upon it, and parasite shells. Billy wrenched it off and tucked it within his bag, while a dozen big shells, stowed among the rocks, hiding between the sponges and curtained by the grasses chuckled in their underwater language. For they had noted Billy's coming and discreetly shut their tell-tale mouths. Billy trod upon one, unaware of its presence. Up and up he climbed, waist-deep amongst the grass. Little fishes, sporting yellow stripes across their tails, peered inquisitively into his face-glass before fleeing in mistrust.

A rich rockery these pillars, fatly rewarding Billy's search! He packed the shell in a canvas bag, jamming the shell tight with a ponderous movement of his foot. He did not carry the net-work bag at the waist so often used. Presently he had twenty-five shells, exceedingly good work. He signalled and up slid the bag. Uncanny how quietly all things are done down below!

A dream sack came gliding down, and Billy was eager to repeat his harvest. He gripped a sponge that bulged against his thigh, and, leaning well back, peered through his side-glasses to spy around the pillar. A sea-snake darted from out the sponge, and its gleaming teeth snapped upon his corselet. Utterly surprised and in painful need of a dentist, the abashed thing back-somersaulted into the ferns. Billy chuckled and climbed on, while the expert tender above, by slow inch and inch, drew in the slack of the line and air-pipe on deck.

Then Billy stood, his hand upon a rock rounded by other hands. He had reached the top, very slow work against the water-pressure, though the physical body felt light owing to the compressed air within his suit. He gazed around, as from a peak he might look upon a city. Here he could see, only a short distance, through green twilight occasionally speckled by darting fishes.

He signalled again, and in reply could just distinguish the anchor gliding up through the green gloom ahead. Then twisting a loop in the life-line, he sat within it, and as the vessel gathered way he was lifted gently off the pillar and went slowly trailing through the sea, as serenely as if he was part of it.

By and by he distinguished stone and sea-grass, and signalled to down anchor and lower – a little manoeuvre which can be awkward for the diver if the tender on deck above is not thoroughly experienced.

Billy landed gently and peered over one of the blue mountains of the sea. Only the blue was not there, except in patches where walled rocks queerly reflected filtered sunlight from the sky above. A weird trick this reflected light played, far down in the murky green; for as invisible fish sped across one grass-grown crevice, they coloured to quick purple before vanishing again.

Chasms were there, too, falling right down through the dark water. Here stretched a sea-ledge miles long, caused by earth-torments when the world was young, which tore away the crust and left this jagged ledge.

To win more shell in safety Billy should drift back and prospect through the twilight waters over shallower and proved ground. But here, though obviously dangerous, what riches might he not find! Besides, he was of pioneer stock, and bubbling over with that wonder and curiosity which impels man onward into the unknown. In the precipitous clefts below, before the dull shadow green that defied vision but betrayed unguessable depths and things, he glimpsed vines trailing with phosphoric flowers and bulbous sponges, and intriguing shadow-phantoms.

He marked a phantom zigzag shading a guessed-at ridge down which he might walk, but, being a careful diver, he sought long and earnestly until he had discovered a way by which he could come back again, and believed he found it, though he could only return thus while the tide remained stationary. Then cautiously he began the descent of that narrow ridge, noting where apparently, away below, it ran back upon itself like a winding stair disappearing into a dark inner room.

Squeezing his sides were walls of water, while beyond and below were fantastic shapes which were huge rock masses and indistinguishable things. He got down by degrees, then turned with the winding stair directly under the ledge. Here it rose cliff-like before him; undermining it were caves, gaping black. And the water was much darker.

Billy adjusted his air-valve; the inflating air hissed into the suit, swelling it out with a steady strength against the increasing pressure of the water depth. When his air walls were strong enough to hold back the water walls he adjusted the air-valve to normal for breathing purposes, and stood, peering into the shadowed tangle. For the diver must keep his mind very clear when down below, must coolly calculate all chances before he ventures to move.

"It's like a gnomes' home in a pantomime," he chuckled, "with the sun gone down. I wonder if the gnome king is at home."

A fish, its broad side illuminated with shining pennies, and carrying a webbed sail folded into a groove along its back and a sword poking from an aggressive snout, dashed from the shadows. At its tail sped a long, shimmering, eel-like shape, gnashing sharp teeth. The sail-fish dodged, and the eel thing back-pedalled on Billy's face-glass and swirled below. Laughing at the amazement of the fishes, he trudged cautiously onward towards a haze of sponges.

In the darkening water Billy could distinguish shell, pin-points of light, but he studied the roof of the ledge under which he must go. He manoeuvred so that the lines would not foul in any jagged crevice, then ventured under the ledge, narrowing rapidly before him. There shell grew in such clumps that he had only to reach out and fill bag after bag.

Groping carefully forward, Billy presently stooped, but not in land fashion, for the chest weights would have toppled him over. A fine clump of shell beckoned just ahead, and he edged towards it inch by inch, eyes shining. His helmet scraped warningly on the sloping roof, and he sank back on his heels and edged forward crab fashion, with a pause to readjust the air-valve.

Again the helmet scraped. He stopped instantly, crouched still lower, and reached out his hand. The shells remained aggravatingly six inches from his finger-tips. He grew warm with eagerness. Creeping forward another two inches, he just tipped a shell. Another inch, and he pulled out a prize; then he relaxed his body, wrenched off a larger shell, and began placing shell after shell within the bag. Green and yellow sea-grasses flattened against his face-glass, but the shells were so thickly placed that his groping hand could feel them. The bag was filled, all but a last shell. Reaching to fit it within the bag he leaned the least trifle forward, and almost felt the sobbing sound that fastened around his helmet.

Billy remained as still as the grave. He was jammed fast at the bottom of the sea! Of the world above all that remained to him was the air in his suit. How sweet and distinct now was the smell of India-rubber coming down with the air from the motor-pumps above! But the weight of the sea and all in it were silently leagued against him.

Once more Billy began "Ta-ra-ra-boom-de-ay." He must drown this sense of fearful loneliness; he must not lose his head for a second. There lingered one faint hope. He thanked God that the tender above had been to the war: he understood Morse. Would he grasp impromptu signals now? Would superb seamanship do the rest? Would the way he was jammed and the ledge of rock reaching far out allow the job to be done without tearing away the air-pipe?

Still humming, he groped behind for a grip on the line, painfully pulled it until he felt it drawn taut, then began tugging out his predicament in long and short jerks.

Very slow the job was, very painful, and presently air-pressure in the cramped position forced slow, warm drops of blood from his nostrils. Already it was beginning to pain him to breathe; he felt his lungs panting as he had seen the panting of fish when drawn up into the air. His head was buzzing with a growing roar of new buzzes coming every moment. There was a pain coming in his bent spine too, but he was fighting to keep mentally calm. After a lifetime he thrilled. The line in his hand jerked back the message:

"Keep your tail up!"

He visualized the up-anchoring, the jib flying up and the steady manoeuvring of the lugger to gently sail straight out in a line with the slowly tautening life-line; then to crawl farther ahead, until the line was gently stretched to its limit, *away* from the ledge. Then the grim chances calculated before the tender took the fateful pull.

By the quivering strain on the line Billy's fingers wirelessed to his brain exactly what was happening above, he could *see* the lugger slowly creeping out on the open surface of the sea away behind him. His heart thumped painfully as he felt the life-line take up the strain, then pull slowly but hard around his chest. His ears rang and hummed as his helmet crunched, he felt the scraping pull on his hard-pressed toes. He hummed "Ta-ra-ra-boomde-ay," even while he felt himself being wrenched in halves by the straining of the line. It seemed that the world expanded when he was pulled out, but the rope instantly slackened and he was on the bottom of the sea signalling "Don't move!"

He lay there a while; then, rising with the life-line, he walked carefully out from under the ledge, gazed up to make sure that nothing was in the way of the air-pipe and life-line, then with the most thankful feeling in all the world, gave the signal to haul up.

On deck, when they unscrewed his face-glass, he was still humming "Ta-ra-ra-boom-de-ay."

Aboriginals taking sandalwood to the Mission at Spring Creek, far North Queensland 1922, by Ms EC Finger.

THE SANDALWOOD GETTERS

ON an ironwood rise close by the banks of the Kendal River lay the sandalwood camp. Stacked neatly in a long row were thirty tons of the precious wood which goes out of the far northern parts of Australia in its rough state, to be turned by the commercial Chinese into money.

Along the river-flats some fifty horses were feeding, their bells tinkling musically in the clear Peninsula air. The camp itself was a big tarpaulin stretched tightly on forked sticks, sheltering two serviceably made sapling bunks. Under the tarpaulin, too, were stacked the camp provisions, mostly bags of flour, sugar, two big panniers of tea, and cases of trade tobacco. Close by, in a row, were some forty pack-saddles and five riding-saddles.

Drying in the sun were long strips of salted beef. A score of crows, gossiping in the topmost branches of a huge she-oak on the river-bank, seemed hinting that that meat had never known a branding-iron.

Sitting eating by the open galley-fire were three aboriginal boys from the Coen tribe. Energetically punching a damper was Whistling Clancy, his carefree lips pursed in a merry tune as he rolled the sticky dough into shape.

Solemnly cleaning a Winchester repeater stood Long Toby, his brown beard freshly combed. His quiet face, with the quizzical twist of crow's-feet around his deep set grey eyes, told of the bush philosopher, of a nature that took things as they came, of the paddler of his own canoe.

Through the bush coming in on all sides of the camp were straggling tribesmen of the lower Kendal River myalls, each with a stick of freshly-cut sandalwood on his shoulder – some of the gins carrying two. Working thus for the white man because they craved that strange weed "bacca" and that instrument of priceless worth, the steel tomahawk.

As each "boy" brought in his wood he flung it down on a heap near the camp, then joined his comrades who formed a morose group of sullen humanity some little distance away.

Long Toby leisurely finished his rifle-cleaning, put the weapon handy against the foot of his bunk, then dished out to each buck and gin a pannikin of flour, half a stick of "trade" tobacco, and an allowance of tea and sugar.

As the aboriginals walked away to their camp across the river, Clancy, shovelling the red-hot coals on his damper, ceased his whistling to remark:

"The bucks are acting a bit nasty since you refused them that extra allowance of tobacco."

"Yes," drawled Toby, "if they got that they would have wanted more, and we haven't got it. We'll only want them a few more days until the wood is all in. Then your job will be packing it away to Port Stewart. I'll stay here and watch the camp and the main heap of wood."

"That'll be all plain sailing," said Clancy lightly. "But what do you think of that thieving swine who slipped his hand under my bunk last night! I thought he got away with nothing but a fright. He got something else, though."

"What?"

"The quinine."

Long Toby frowned just a little. Quinine, in the wide stretches of the fever country, can hold the balance between life and death.

"One of the most useful things in the world to us, was that jar of quinine tablets," he said slowly; "and about the most useless to a nigger. He'll eat 'em all at once. I wonder what sort of an ache he'll have by now!"

Clancy patted his rising damper cheerfully:

"It'll make his toes curl. I'll fetch some quinine back first trip from the Port. But, blow the fever. The price of wood is more important. Last we heard it was fetching: £45 per ton. That's old Ah Mow's price, Cooktown. That means: £1350 of the best, if the market hasn't fallen by the time we pack in. Allow: £400 for expenses, that means: £950 for the twelve months' work. Then heigh-ho for the city lights and the beaches, and the pretty bright eyes."

"Yes, and you'll track back to the Peninsula with a sore head, a still sorer heart, and a bundle of bobbed hair photographs."

Up the river-bank came a young gin, a plait of woven grass around her hips, a stick of sandalwood on her shoulder. As she threw down the stick a buck sprang from behind the piled heap and brought his wommera crashing fully upon her face. She fell in a sprawling heap, blood spurting from the flattened nose. The buck swung his wommera for another blow, to hold it poised as Long Toby shouted:

"Wantageree, hold!"

The buck glared over his shoulder, animal ferocity urging him to brain the woman, animal fear holding him back because of the "death fire" swinging on the white man's belt.

With leisurely strides Long Toby walked to the boy, and standing with legs wide apart, calmly filled his pipe.

"Why you strike Munya?" he asked carelessly.

"She slow," snarled the buck. "Me hungry. She dig no yam, no lily bulb. Next time she more quick!"

His gleaming teeth gritted as he glared down on the gin. Again Long Toby halted the threatening wommera.

"Wantageree, hold! Suppose you give Munya hiding! She no more work for me. Too sick. She no more get me wood. No good. Suppose I give you this," taking a pocket-knife from his pocket, "and flour longa your dinner. You let Munya go, eh! She get me more wood."

The bloodshot eyes gleamed at the pocket-knife, a prize indeed. The taut muscles of his arms relaxed, the wommera sank to his side. Stepping off the gin, he graciously agreed:

"Arright, s'posem you give him psugar, too!"

"Right," said Long Toby. "Come and get it."

He gave the black man his promised reward, then threw some Condy's crystals into a dish of water and carried it over to the dazed gin. The cartilage of her nose was hopelessly smashed, sand and tiny pebbles were glued to the pulpy mass that had been her face. Long Toby carried the trembling creature to the shade of an ironwood tree, laid her down, and dressed the wound.

"I would have shot the swine!" said Clancy in a thick voice. "What beasts they are!"

"If you'd shot and missed, he would have retaliated by killing the gin tonight. In either case the niggers would have got square by spearing us if possible – our horses, otherwise. As it is, everything is as you were, except for the pain of this poor little beggar. She's a plump little cuss!"

"Not bad – for a native," said Clancy approvingly. "Because you're actually going to see white girls within the next few months," smiled Toby, "you're growing fastidious. If you die in the city you'll want pansies on your grave."

"Better than a howling dingo," answered Clancy gaily. He strode towards the galley, cheerily whistling the "Wild Colonial Boy."

Five days later in the grey of dawn the horse-boys ran in the horses. The mob galloped to the camp, neighing and bucking, filling the cool bush air with a mad jangle of swaying bells. Around the galley-fire they propped with flying manes and lashing hoofs, frisky with the energy of a long spell on sweet grass.

Then came several hours saddling and loading up, the sandalwood being strapped to the pack-saddles, one bundle on each side, each bundle weighing one hundredweight. Thus forty horses took a load of four tons of wood.

The provision horses were packed; then Clancy, swinging practised leg over his saddle mare, laughed down at his mate.

"So long, old wire whiskers. I'll be back in a fortnight, with luck. Don't let the niggers run away with you."

"Never mind me," emphasized Toby, "but keep a sharp eye going through the Woorawilly country. That mob are a bit too fond of roast horse."

Clancy laughed, shook his bridle-reins and moved off whistling a cheery greeting to the brightness of the day.

Two of the aboriginal boys hurried up the straggling packhorses after Clancy, with their gleeful shouts plainly telling of their gladness to be moving out of hostile country.

Long Toby watched the team until it disappeared among the timber.

Then unobtrusively he observed Joe, the remaining Coen boy. Joe's eyes gazed longingly towards the timber, his ears drank in the lessening tinkle of a loosened horse-bell, the distant crack of a whip, the fading shouts of his comrades, the shrill, receding whistle of Clancy.

Down among their gunyahs, the wild tribe also stood listening. Then, when only the lonely. bush sounds came to their ears, they gazed up the ridge towards the white man's camp. Even the dingo mongrels were silent, as if sensing death.

At the evening meal Long Toby, with a pannikin of tea raised to his lips, halted the vessel. A cold, clammy hand seemed to touch his brow, cling there, then slowly, unwillingly fade away. Long Toby sipped thoughtfully. On the opposite side of the fire Joe, sullenly silent, ate his meal with lowered eyes, apprehensively listening to the murmur from the blacks' camp across the river.

With the quietness that came with the night, Long Toby felt his brow grow hot and cold in turns. He felt dull and feverish.

Deliberately he scraped out his pipe, knocked the carbon off on the log that Joe had just thrown on the fire, filled the pipe and lit it with a fire-stick. Standing up he stretched himself sleepily, then carried two filled water-buckets within the tarpaulin, arranging them under his bunk together with the remainder of the cooked beef and damper. A filled ammunition belt he laid under the coat which served as pillow, made sure that his rifle magazine was loaded, then turned in with clothes on and revolver still strapped to his belt.

Thoughtfully smoking, he stared unseeing at the twinkling stars that peeped in under the open tarpaulin, hardly conscious of the tinkling of horse-bells, of the lonely croaking of a mopoke.

The blackboy crouched beside the fire outside in the galley, but soon the night fear would drive him to crawl in under the tarpaulin and sleep beside the white boss lest a spear from out the dark should seek him. He was far away from his own tribal grounds. Therefore, he was an alien, and in danger of his life.

By midnight Long Toby was fighting against a raging attack of fever. In the small hours he was battling against delirium by will power, fighting too to keep his hot eyes open.

In the grey of dawn he lost count of things, but awoke later in a fit of shaking and clammy sweat. He glanced towards the galley-fire, from where the usual smoke did not come.

"Joe!" he called in a cracked, dry voice. Joe did not answer. Neither did he answer the second time. "He's gone: The rat and the sinking ship."

He lay back on the pillow, listening. But no silver-toned horse-bell came tinkling through the early morning air. He glanced at the saddle-rail. Both riding-saddles were in their accustomed place.

"He's walked," Toby thought; "the niggers must have speared the poor old neddies."

Reaching under the bunk, he filled a pannikin of water and drank greedily. Towards midday the fever attack recurred and, fight as he would, his throbbing brain took him far away in the world of delirium.

It was late afternoon when his wild dreams filled the tarpaulin camp with savages. In a mental struggle to regain consciousness, his wide open eyes gazed at the doorway.

As the delirium mists cleared he saw the crouched form of Mungaroo, the king, peering from behind the saddle-rail, while crouched by the firewood were the ochre-painted faces of others.

Still gabbling incoherently for time, Long Toby watched the spear hand of Mungaroo as it stealthily fitted a weapon to the wommera.

As the spear arm drew back to the poise, Toby's hand jerked up from his belt. But the bullet whistled high.

Instantly the blacks disappeared. Long Toby laughed grimly, and with shaking fingers recharged the fired chamber.

Towards sundown he became delirious again. It was midnight when he awoke to an overpowering, thickly scented odour. His eyes opened to a world of flame, the tea-trees on the river-bank towering high and milky white among rolling clouds of black smoke that drifted past the open tarpaulin. He lay still, imagining he was in a delirium hell. That sweetish, pungent scent recalled him to reality.

The sandalwood heap! He tried to crawl off the bunk, but a shivering attack warned him what was the use. He lay there, gazing at the rollicking flames fiercely fed by the oozing oil from the heated logs.

"There goes a cool thousand pounds in smoke," said he aloud. "Twelve months' hard toil. Clancy's city trip and his bright-eyed girl all gone up in smoke. And all because a mob of niggers think they've got a white man helpless. How the black devils are yelling!"

From the river-bank came a roaring of voices, with thud of stamping feet in unison to the sharp drumming of the gins. Long Toby's clammy fingers reached for the rifle:

"I suppose I'll have a visit tonight; I wish I was steady. I'd give a lot now for just one good dose of quinine!"

But the dawn came at last and they had not come. The camp sank to silence as Long Toby, weary-eyed and troubled, faced the fever of another day.

At nightfall he closed his eyes. That great heap of white ashes outside the tarpaulin made him heartsick. He was asleep instantly. Hours later he awoke, intensely alert. There had been no sound-nothing, only the danger instinct. His hand stole from his belt. There was a sharp "click" as the revolver hammer snapped back.

"Dommy, Dommy," came a terrified whisper. "Heaven!" he breathed, then in dialect whispered:

"That you, Munya?"

"A-i, me!"

"What you want?"

"Black man spear you soon feller."

"Oh, will he? Me shoot, quick feller!"

"You no shoot – no can see – black man throw plenty feller spear... Mungeroo tell him all together boy. Kill you easy feller."

"H'm! They'll sneak up in the dark, throw a volley through the tarpaulin, and I'm stuck as full of quills as a porcupine. Simple, but effective."

In the dialect, he whispered, "What you think, Munya. Why you come here?"

"You go 'way, Dommy. Quick feller!"

"Me no can go. Too much sick."

"Me carry you, longa big feller stone. You lie down. Black man no can see. Me carry water, tucker."

A ray of hope warmed the sick man's heart.

The "big feller stone" was a clump of granite boulders a little higher up the ridge. They would afford ideal cover from a spear attack. Besides, the position commanded the whole camp. A man with a repeating rifle among those boulders, if he only had food and water and yes, sleep! - might hold a tribe at bay. "Me no walk. Too sick. S'posem you can help me?" whispered Long Toby encouragingly.

"A-i!" whispered the gin eagerly.

Long Toby swung his legs over the bunk, but his knees gave way when his feet touched the ground. Try how he might he could not even crawl.

"It's going to be a tough go, my dark-eyed Juliet," he whispered. "I'm a heavy man, and you're an undersized little bundle of sinew and pluck. But we'll give it a go."

"What you say?" whispered Munya doubtfully. Long Toby smiled in the darkness.

"Me puttem plenty feller bullet longa bunk," he whispered. "You come back, gettem bullet, flour, beef, water longa bucket. You savvy?"

"A-i!"

"Right. Me try crawl first time." But he couldn't crawl. The black woman slipped her head and shoulders beneath his chest, gripped his arms, rose tensely to her feet, and bending double, staggered off. Long Toby's feet rustled through the grass. But the distance was not far, though the climb was stiff. Presently she sank down gasping among the black shadows of the boulders.

Long Toby rolled his weight off the bent back, and with a warm feeling in his heart gently patted the gin's clay-daubed hair.

"You're a little Australian, Munya," he whispered gratefully. "If I pull through, you shall have whatever is your heart's desire."

Her eyes gazed up like velvet stars at the tone of the words. And to Toby came understanding, with a queer, unhappy feeling in his throat.

Munya slipped away like a shadow, soon to return carrying two buckets of water. Another quick trip, and she returned loaded with a fifty of flour and a bag full of salt beef. The last trip she brought the spare cartridges, billy-cans, and a bundle of tobacco.

Toby smiled appreciatively. "I never thought of a smoke," he muttered, "blessed if I don't feel a bit better somehow.

"What for blackfeller no spearem me last night," he whispered.

"Plenty feller feast," answered Munya softly. "Roast 'em two feller horse."

Toby sighed. His old saddle-horse had been the faithful companion of years.

"Munya," he whispered, "you go now. Sneak back longa gunyah. Wantageree no can tell. When Clancy come, you talk longa him s'posem me killed. Clancy give you plenty feller everything."

But Munya hung her head.

"No go!" she mumbled stubbornly.

"Why?" asked Long Toby.

"By-em-bye' you sleep. Warrior throw spear. You die. Me stop longa you. You sleep, me look!"

Long Toby thought the matter out. It would be at least ten days before Clancy returned. In the meantime he must sleep and would require more water later on. If the fever proved stubborn he was bound to become delirious again at intervals, even if it did not settle him altogether.

"All right Munya," he decided slowly, "you stay. Let us count the odds," he murmured drowsily. "One sick white man with a rifle he can't hold steady. Plenty of good cover, enough tucker, ammunition, and nearly enough water. One black gin mostly all heart, with a little bit of head-piece chucked in. She'll go sentry, too, while I sleep. The odds against, are fever and niggers. Plenty of niggers and ten days to keep them off. The gin and I and luck might just do it. Maybe, maybe not."

His head, burning hot, sank down on folded arms. The ice-cold touch of a boulder against his temple was a soothing relief. He nestled his cheek against the cold stone. "I sleep. You watch," he whispered.

Sunrise came, splashing the tall range peaks with rosy light when Munya softly woke him. His head was erect in an instant, cool and clear. A smile shone from his anxious eyes. For a few hours at least, the fever had gone.

He glanced down the ridge, only now fading from the gloom of the lower country into the first grey tints of dawn. An excited, guttural yabbering came indistinctly from the sandalwood camp. As daylight brightened, Long Toby made out a swarm of shadows surging around the tarpaulin. They were raiding the tucker and camp-gear, shrieking in wild delight at each grand find from the white man's treasure boxes.

In another moment the sun rose over the ranges.

Long Toby breathed a little harder as he saw the hafts of many spears sticking through the tarpaulin.

The blacks quickly circled the sandalwood camp. Long Toby, squirming into a comfortable position, settled his rifle among the boulders.

An exultant cry came from a warrior as he cut the tracks. They crowded round him, yabbering in excited surprise as they read the signs of Munya's heavy imprint, pointing to where Toby's feet had dragged in the grass on either side. Then they surged up the ridge, eager, quick eyes to the ground.

"Here beginneth the fight!" murmured Toby.

He picked out Mungaroo, the king. His rifle-barrel, steady now in cool strong hands, covered the black man's body as with gleaming eyes bent to the tracks he came swiftly on at the head of his blood-eager tribe.

A hundred yards from the boulders he halted and, looking

triumphantly up, pointed his wommera towards the silent, shadow bathed rocks.

The sun shone coppery bright upon the grooved muscles of his oil-greased body.

As, with a piercing yell he came racing up the ridge fitting a spear to his wommera, Long Toby fired.

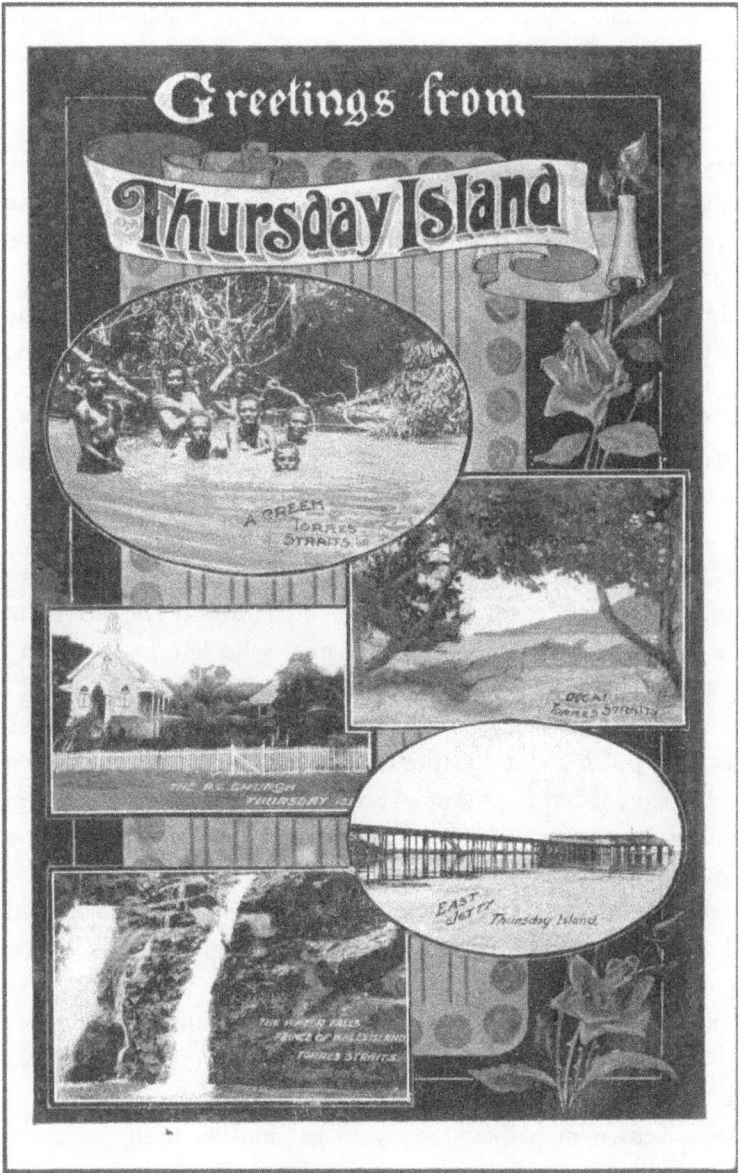

THE YELLOW LILLY

HERS was a haunting beauty, and her slow, lithe movements enhanced it. Her pale, cameo features were lit with sloe-black eyes. She was not yet eighteen; but very wary, very wise. They called her the "Yellow Lily," this calm half-caste Chinese, with her air of secret thought. She baffled us all.

She was the daughter of Huon Li Chang, buyer of pearl-shell, of trochus, tortoise-shell, and *bêche-de-mer*, and owner of a gambling joint famed as far as the China Sea. The passions aroused nightly in that gambling warren were not so suppressed as the longings of the Yellow Lily.

Thursday Island is Australia's gateway to the East, recognized so by all nations that seek the wealth of our Coral Sea. America has only become locally interested recently; but she "buys big." The rivalries of nations should not affect a little part-Chinee girl, but they have.

Night-time was the Lily's hour. Hazed in a cigarette smoke cloud, she glided from table to table, a tray of drinks in her hand, a flare of poinciana in her coal-black hair, quaint sandals tap-tap-tapping on the tiniest of feet. She wore a silken gown embroidered with a yellow dragon clawing down her back. That gown lisped intriguingly among the hoarse talk, the striking of matches, the clink of glasses. You could hear it come whispering along you sensed it. Men's eyes used to follow their desires.

But the Lily parried all their amorous advances with that slow, baffling smile. Her secret dream was a white man. Hungrily she desired to be the wife of one of the nice, white-clad men who live in the pretty bungalows, and keep aloof from the coloured life of the town.

I used to wonder how those gamblers breathed, for the tobacco-smoke would collect in a pulsing cloud just under the roof. As the night wore on it would grow heavy laden from the hot breaths, to come floating down in wisps, clouding the furrowed brows, bared chests, and sweat-glistening arms of those around the tables below.

The big store fronted the main street, but the gambling rooms opened out behind the store, and from them barred doors gave access to the tortuous lanes of Chinatown, which here led down to the waterfront.

When "the fleet" was in the money was big. From the pearling-fleet landed the smart Japanese captains, the divers and tenders. More than five hundred Japanese swell Thursday Island's population at the lay-up of the fleet. Keen brown men these, ready to gamble life itself, let alone money; only rivalled in recklessness by the less affluent Malays who played with veiled antagonism in Japanese company.

A sprinkling of whites was generally present, nomads mostly. Raynor was my pal, a wandering recruiter with a touch of the devil in his face. He had taken to me, because I was a wanderer too, I suppose, and did not ask unnecessary questions.

Assan Arrak these two years past had made fruitless love to the Lily, and one night I could see that he was feeling nasty about it. He was losing his cutter, too, at the largest poker table. That little vessel was all in the world that he owned. I could hear his teeth gritting like the fall of the pointed dice when whirled in the saucer.

But he didn't moan, just played on with a particularly nasty leer, emphasizing his grim brown face. He glanced up with a cynical smile every time the Lily glided past. He was one of those "nuggety" Malays, his brown arms bared in a white singlet, his heavily-muscled legs bulging from khaki trousers. His coarse hair was jet black, except where powdered a bit with silver.

"That's the Malay when he's going to do things," growled Raynor. "Nasty things. He's laughing inside at what is going to happen to someone. He'd kill his own father now if he stood in his way. He'd slit the throat of the Lily with pleasure. Malays feel like that when they're baulked."

"See old Chang watching Assan watching the Lily!"

"Yes, and see that grin on Assan's face as he turned back to the play – he's really playing for the Lily, and no one knows his cards."

"What are old Chang's cards?"

"The son of his partner in Shanghai, college educated in modern Chinese style. He's coming in the next *Taiping* to marry the Lily."

"And the Lily?"

"Plays a lone hand, seeks a white man as trumps. And here he comes!"

He stood there with some friends, smiling. Tall and straight, with fair wavy hair and a quite irresistible smile. As his inquisitive blue eyes met the Lily's liquid black ones, they brightened with boyish pleasure. She glided on, smiling, and the yellow dragon seemed to grip her slimness tighter.

"Phew!" said Raynor. "The Lily smiles! First sight, too!"

Latham was the American representative sent over by the Combine, or whatever they are, to try to corner all the T.I. pearl-shell.

"He'll find his job interesting," mused Raynor.

He did. Worked like a Trojan by day; put in as few social hours as he diplomatically could, and spent evenings at Chang's shop.

On heavy nights, near dawn was the signal for the tables to close down, and Latham's chance to make furious love to the Lily. Not that they were ever alone, but the crowd, dawdling out through the various getaways, arguing, growling, and laughing, with their thoughts obsessed by the gains and losses of the play, were intrigued by other things than the lovers down in the shadowed corner.

Chang said nothing, while seeing everything. He had no fear of Latham, for the Lily was never allowed outside the shop. As for any serious attachment – the father's strongest ally was the boy's white blood! It was Assan Arrak whom old Chang had to guard against most.

I used to wonder at the thoughts of the Lily as she served those pre-occupied tables, coming and going so quietly on her little sandalled feet, her eyes each evening greeting Latham's with a quick, fleeting smile. She moved so lithely in her silken gown and as she reached across the tables the dragon's writhing limbs tightened to embrace her. The vivid thing seemed alive, floating on her slimness. I suppose it was the dull lights, the heavy smoke, and her studied movements that helped the illusion. Latham used to stare at the dragon, too.

The crowd would sometimes joke a little in Japanese, Malay, or "lingo." But soon they would bend over their games again. A woman was a woman. Yes. But money was money! It was heaped before them on every table, wads of notes, piles of silver. They played at fever pitch till dawn.

"By Jove," prophesied Raynor one evening, "I believe the Lily wins. The very hopelessness of her chance is her strongest card. Latham, when he first came, would never have dreamed of marrying coloured blood and all that; but he will soon do anything to get her. Her smallest chance, yet her greatest, is to walk out of her father's shop in broad daylight and take Latham straight to the parson's. The unobtainable is hers – at the moment Latham falls."

"She is cutting it rather fine. The *Taiping* is due midday three days hence!" "Leaving Latham little time in which to choose," answered Raynor significantly. "Three days of indecision, with the final decision put off until the very last moment. And then – the China boy marries her the evening he arrives. Damned if he will, says Latham."

Latham's face certainly said so at that precise moment, for he was glaring towards the Lily serving Captain Osaka's table. The natty little Japanese was being conspicuously gallant, too.

"She is working on white psychology, plus galloping longing racing to a frustrated finale," puffed Raynor admiringly. "Clever little devil. I suppose her own white blood longs for the white people's life, but everything is against her: herself, environment, prejudice, not only of individuals, but the bitter prejudice of all colours. She'd make a great mother, too!"

"It will be a shock to the parents if she succeeds."

"A shock to both sides. Chang will be just as mad as old-man Latham; every bit of it."

Assan sat sprawled at his usual table, cynical disregard on his heathen face. Once I saw him glance across at young Latham, his jet black eyes all screwed up.

"Enjoying himself!" nodded Raynor. "Why?"

"Only he knows that! Like the Lily, he plays a lone hand. The cards will be on the table the day the *Taiping* berths. It's fascinating watching these little games. I've enjoyed them for years. I suppose it's part of what they call the 'spell of the East.'"

The evening before the *Taiping* arrived, Raynor and I lounged smoking on the veranda of the Grand. The pearling-fleet lay dimly at anchor, bobbing to a freshening breeze. Just across the water-way loomed the hills of Prince of Wales Island, largest in the Strait. The palms of Horn Island were a smudgy blotch.

Drifting almost to the beach with the tide came a smart looking cutter, the Papuan crew forward standing ready. The anchor rattled out to a hoarse command. Gloom was fast gathering into what promised to be a dark, ugly night.

"That is Assan's *Yellow Lily*," nodded Raynor with quick interest.

"She is Chang's now. Assan gambled her very last bolt to him last night. Chang takes the cutter over tomorrow, so Assan is anchoring her across at Chang's receiving-sheds. Which is sporty of Assan – but fishy."

"Why?"

"Well, anything might happen on a dark right. And why has he anchored her so close to the shore – in shallow water – on a presently falling tide?"

"He's too good a seaman to leave her to sit in the mud."

"Of course – therefore, he must intend to sail before the tide goes out – in Chang's boat!"

"What's doing?" I whispered.

"Come and we'll see," he invited eagerly. "I love watching these little intrigues – there's colour in them!" As we walked up to, then down the unlit street (electricity was only introduced recently) towards Chang's shop, Raynor said meaningly:

"The *Taiping* is due at 10 a.m. tomorrow!"

"If it were not for the aftermath, I could wish the Lily wins," I answered.

The dapper "modern" Chinese behind the counter of the big shop smiled and said: "I believe the *Taiping* is having a quick trip!" This was the "office" to walk right in. We did so, down through the back of the shop and into the rooms.

Latham was there already, looking smart and dean in his heavy white blazer, his face smiling and eager. The Lily was gliding among the fast-filling tables, cool and devilish enticing-looking. Once I caught her smile at Latham, a slow smile, pregnant with meaning. Her jet black hair was fringed over the creamy little forehead.

With the full coming of night, they drifted in until the tables were nearly filled, the devotees of fan-tan already clustered around the table with its square and numbers and heap of brass counting coins. Sink-I-loo and the six-sided dice were being heavily played when Captain Osaka with the air of an admiral, took his seat and carelessly placed a pile of £10 notes before him. As the poker tables filled, the night started in earnest. Bankers were calling the inevitable results: coins were clicking, dice rattling, while ever and anon a hush in the voices heralded the long-drawn "Ah!" as heads and shoulders arose from table after table but to bend again in fevered awaiting of the next result. A guttural curse, a gesture of disgust or fury, as play advanced and some highly-tensioned player lost his stake and nerve.

"Assan is late," peered Raynor. "I wonder what he is up to? Do you notice the smile of the Lily when she sneaks a sly glance at Latham? There, see that knowing reply in his eyes? I'll bet my lugger those two have arranged a surprise wedding for the coming bridegroom. What in the mischief can that Macassar ex-pirate be doing? Ah, here he is."

Assan came walking noiselessly down from the shop entrance, a half-smile on his reckless face. He took his stand behind a poker table, and coolly lit a cigarette. Smoking carelessly, he watched the play of the cards and coins while he really watched the Lily.

"Note his twisted grin when the Lily smiled at Latham," whispered Raynor. "Assan is enjoying himself."

It must have been three hours later that Raynor whispered warningly: "It's the turn of the tide-watch out for a storm!"

Almost as he spoke, Assan, as if fed up for the night, strolled casually down our end of the room toward a getaway door. The Lily, balancing a tray of glasses, was moving towards the end table. The Chinese guard turned to unlock the door at Assan's nod, while the Lily, coming up behind, paused for the Malay to step out of the way. As the guard held the door ajar Assan's fist shot out the contact was like a hammer blow – as the guard fell the Malay pivoted and, swinging his arms around the Lily, sprang out the door. Broken glasses tinkled shrilly as the door slammed.

Hardly a man realized what had happened as in the sudden hush Latham came raving down the room to fling himself at the door. We leant our weight to his.

"The cunning devil!" yelled Raynor. "It's fastened on the outside – he must have screwed a bolt on early." A yabber of tongues burst out as the crowd surged down to the door.

We shouldered our way back through them and out the front shop. We had the whole block to run before we could turn down a side street leading towards the waterfront.

"We'll never catch him," panted Raynor, "he's only got to run down the lane!"

Assan was running for all he was worth through the black night, down the slope to the beach. He had put the Lily to sleep by a blow on the jaw. He carried her slight weight easily. A nuggety Malay is "strong as a horse."

At the water's edge was his waiting dinghy. He laid the Lily in it, pushed off, and leapt in, panting as he seized the oars, calling hoarsely over his shoulder: "Up anchor! Up sail!" and the answering rattle of the winch was a guide in the night. As his powerful strokes shot him out to the hazy vessel, the pulley blocks creaked as the sail rattled up. He shot out an arm and, grasping the stern rail, heaved himself and the girl aboard, calling: "Up jib! Up fores'l!" With the girl in his arms, he bent low to climb down the little black companionway, while shadowy arms reached over the cutter's stern for the dinghy. The cutter was fast gathering way.

Assan groped into the tiny cabin, chuckling his hilarious triumph. Rather carefully, he laid the Lily on the bunk, his good old bunk, soon to be his bridal bunk. He struck a match to light the hurricane lamp, and gaped into the face of old Chang. Then he was stunned from behind.

The Lily married the China boy in the morning. She had to.

THE PEARLS OF GUNGADOOL

OLD BEN leaned by the hut door, enjoying the evening peace. The man suited the country. With a comfortably-built waistline, his face shone big and round and jovial. Good humour twinkled from the shrewd grey eyes that loved the scene around. It seemed fitting that a shock of white hair should crown that ruddy face and that the strength of youth should flow in the well-knit body.

Old Ben swore he was rich, for he possessed everything he wished. Within the strongly-built hut the storeroom was heavy with twelve months' supplies. The living-rooms smelled fresh and clean. The walls were hung with enormous buffalo-horns, each trophy a thrill. The rifle-rack gleamed with carefully-oiled weapons, and ammunition-cases were plentiful. What looked like neatly folded rugs on Ben's bunk were furs that would have been a glory in any show window. Outside were the outhouses, stored with buffalo-hides and salted meat. From the grassy plain behind the mangroves came the tinkle of horse-bells.

Enhancing this strip of the Territory coast are islands of irregular shape and lovely vegetation. Old Ben was the one white man in hundreds of square miles of country. He held undisputed sway – he and Gungadool.

Along the beach came laughing piccaninnies, naked as their smiling mothers. The youngsters halted a few yards away and challenged Ben to catch them. He winked prodigiously, and their laughing shrieks rang musically across the bay. But the gamest youngster amongst them dared not enter the hut, even though now was the time "Bin" had appointed for the distribution of damper. And so Ben treated the elders, who were also children, but dangerous. Thus far and no farther. Liking and respect, tinged with fear.

Only thus had old Ben lived long and heartily among these savages, in whose blood was the fighting-spirit of the Macassar proa men.

Later, in the cool of the night, the door opened and noiselessly shut. Old Ben nodded to the big savage who had squatted by the fire. It was Gungadool, the witchdoctor, a heathen who by sheer mentality working on hereditary superstition held in awed terror a country upon which roamed numerous tribes. By reason of his friendship with this man, old Ben did his work in peace.

A fine looking native, this Gungadool, his powerful physique overshadowed by an indefinable threat that made his glance feared more even than the strength of his arms. And now the scowl on his harsh face prepared Ben for unwelcome news.

"Cutter come soon. Leave Thursday Island." The deep voice boomed within the hut.

Ben sat down, handed Gungadool tobacco, and lit his own pipe. "You see him?" he queried in native lingo.

"Yah!"

Ben knew that Gungadool was instancing native telepathy, some queer power of second sight or mental messages that some among natives can attune to; a power that Ben had long since acknowledged but given up hopes of understanding. So he listened, believing but surprised, for no news had reached camp of a cutter cruising along the coast. And any vessel that might have come he would have expected from Darwin and the west, not from Thursday Island to the north-east.

"Kangaroo-rat man," boomed the voice. "No good!" Ben understood that the stranger would be a weedy man and, from the native point of view, undesirable.

"He seeks the weeping-stones of the sea," growled Gungadool. "He will steal them, if he cannot buy. He must not take the stones. They are mine. They are charmed. The voice of the sea whispers through them, and sings to me, and tells me many things. The kiss of the sea is upon them; I love them as a warrior loves his maid."

"What makes you certain The Rat knows you have the stones?" asked Ben quietly.

"Budgaree told, and the stones whispered to me. When Budgaree comes back to the tribe his feet shall go in the fire so that he shall never walk again."

The men smoked silently. Ben knew his aid was being asked under the unspoken pact between them.

"I expect you can fix the trouble yourself, Gungadool," he said at last. "But you can call on me for whatever help you wish. Only don't kill!"

Three weeks later distant signal smoke told the natives of the coming of a vessel; two days afterwards she anchored in the roadstead. Old Ben waited, for he knew that The Rat would visit him. He shook hands when the stranger came ashore, pained to think that he must regard the first white visitor in eight months as an enemy.

"Surprised to receive a visitor in this lonely paradise?" laughed The Rat.

"Not at all. I expected you."

"Nonsense! Not a soul knew, and not a boat passed me on the way."

"Yet I knew. And so did Gungadool."

"He's here, then?" whispered The Rat eagerly.

"Yes. Now listen: just for your own benefit. Gungadool told me three weeks ago of your leaving Thursday Island – and told me why."

"Why?"

"The pearls."

The Rat breathed deeply.

"By God," he sighed at last. "That's wonderful. Not a soul but myself and a nigger, Budgaree, knew where I was going or why. You have seen them, then – the pearls?" he asked eagerly.

"No. I did not even know of their existence until three weeks ago."

The Rat stared at the honest face, but he believed nothing. As if coming to a sudden decision he placed a hand on Old Ben's knee.

"Listen!" he said earnestly. "I'll take your word. I'll tell you all I know. If Budgaree's description is true, these pearls must be worth thousands. He tells me that years ago the tribe skittled a Malay pearler and murdered the entire crew. Gungadool's share of the spoil was a bottle of pearls, which the niggers, of course, valued less than a chew of tobacco. In those days the shell-beds were rich and easily worked, and those pearls may have represented a nine months' cruise, perhaps more. The way Budgaree describes their size and number just gives me palpitations. He told me the tale on condition that I'd ship him back to the tribe. He's been away three years and was sick for his homeland. But the nearer we got to the coast the more cold-footed he became. I knew he was only counting on the chance to desert and so get the trip out of me for nothing. So as soon as we came within swimming distance of land I trussed him like a fowl in the hold. I'm glad I know now the story of the pearls is true. I would have stripped his hide if he'd lied to me."

"Seems to me he's in between two fires," said Ben grimly.

"Why?"

"Because Gungadool promises to burn his feet off."

"Why?"

"Because he told you of the pearls."

The Rat stared.

"Telepathy," said Old Ben simply. "I assure you Gungadool knows everything about your movements, on any occasion when you plan anything dangerous against him. You don't understand what you are up against. Believe me, you have no earthly hope of getting those pearls."

"You won't come in with me?"

"No. And I warn you most solemnly, as white man to white man, not to make the attempt."

"Sure you don't want the sea stones for yourself?"

"They would be useless to me," replied Ben simply. "My life is here. I am contented. To fall foul of the natives would end me."

"But," argued The Rat in exasperation, "Couldn't I buy them? I've brought plenty of stores and trade!"

Ben slowly shook his head. "You're dead unlucky," he said quietly. "I don't blame you for seeking the pearls, but to Gungadool they are above price. He believes them charmed. Through them, he believes he can transmit, and get transmitted to him, messages portraying events that happen on the sea. He is a witch-doctor. I know him – and his power. And believe me, he would sacrifice his life before he would lose his charms. Take my advice. It represents forty years' experience. Give it up."

The Rat rose. The glint in his steel-grey eyes made his smile appear wry.

"No white man has ever bested me," he said quietly, "and no nigger is going to."

At dawn a skiff left the cutter and touched the beach just below Old Ben's hut. The Rat secured the boat to a mangrove stake then contemptuously kicked a native who crouched in the bows. "Tumble out," he growled. "Quick feller. Take me where him Gungadool camp. Quick feller now!"

The Rat tugged at a lashing and Budgaree staggered upright, eyes distorted with fear. He jumped as a revolver muzzle screwed between his naked ribs. He stepped off towards the mangroves, The Rat, walking behind, grasping the lashing which bound the aboriginal's arms. After a mile of winding in and out among the twisted roots they came out on to the forest country with its clearer walking among the fine big trees.

Miles away there jutted hills red-faced with cliffs, and in between splashed patches of green where the slanting rays kissed the forest grass. Three miles ahead stretched a sombre line of jungle, like a wall of dull green vegetation, and Budgaree made for this. Once only he appealed, talking in quick gutturals seeking vainly to explain danger, his eyes rolling as he sought to express fright and dismay. But The Rat savaged his head with the revolver butt until Budgaree stumbled on, so overcome between fears of the white devil and the black that his brain reeled.

A short hour brought them to the jungle. Its gloom enveloped them; it was cool in there; their footfalls were hushed on the leafy carpet. Budgaree whined once for he could not control his feelings, otherwise there was silence save for the coo of unseen pigeons, the dropping of seed-pods from the trees. The Rat's temper, on edge as it was with the need for caution, did not improve when he found it necessary to cut aside the vines that ever and again persisted in entangling the limbs and body of the bound Budgaree.

At last a screech of cockatoos foretold the lightening of this gloom-enshrouded place. Presently they came to the jungle edge and found that it clung around a tropical swamp that stretched indistinctly away. Water patches gleamed before them, interlaced with creepers above which towered giants of weeping-fig. Massed clumps of reeds and tangled grasses grew on many islets dense with the drooping leaves of pandanus palms. Unseen waterfowl fluted. Floating grass like green moss lay in still patches upon the moveless water. The air was deathly still and moist. The Rat gripped the lashing.

"Looks like the devil's bathing-pool, Budgaree," he grinned. "But if you've brought me here to drown, you're coming, too. Go ahead!"

To the black man's appealing lips The Rat screwed the cold revolver muzzle. Budgaree gasped and slid feet first into the water.

It was a slow wade from islet to islet, with water to the waist, their feet groping for the slimy logs below. From the disturbed bottom slowly arose many wisps of brown water growths like twisting twine. The Rat, peer as he might, could see only twenty yards ahead, for the tasselled grass clumps waved above his head.

They waded an hour; then, suddenly his heart leapt, for on an islet shrouded by pandanus palms there nestled a solitary, dome-shaped gunyah. The Rat forced a quicker path through the lotus-lilies and clambered up the bank, his breath halting at the rustling of the leaves. He sprang forward and thrust his revolver through the gunyah opening.

Utter silence; only his heart thumping. He drew back and peered, allowing the weak light to filter into the gunyah. But nothing was visible save Gungadool's charm bag lying beside the ashes of a still warm firm. The Rat snatched the smoke-grimed bag and upended it. Out rolled a medley of quartz crystals, lumps of ochre, human knuckle-bones, the dried claws of animals, a short cylinder of bamboo and what looked like a similar cylinder wrapped tightly in paper-bark fibre.

The Rat thrust his hand into the bag and withdrew something. Shuddering slightly, he dropped the smoke-dried hand of a child.

Hurriedly he untwisted the bamboo cylinder. Inside was a long, needle-pointed bone. Scornfully he threw the dreaded death-bone aside, and undid the paper-bark wrappings. His eyes bulged at the sight of glass, he scrambled from the gunyah and tore off the wrapper. His hands trembled violently as with face alight he howled like a mad thing. The bottle of pearls! He hugged the treasure and danced. The sharp crackling of pandanus leaves was the only accompaniment to his song. He looked round. Budgaree was gone! No matter – damn Budgaree. He had the pearls!

Thankful for a sailor's training, he re-entered the swamp, steering a course for the coast by compass. He waded hard, his dread being that he might not get through the jungle patch before sunset.

At length The Rat splashed from the swamp edge and, in smiling relief took a careful bearing, then plunged into the jungle. He would have run had speed been possible within that tangled labyrinth. He must keep a cool head too as to his course, for among that timber he had to sight the compass every few yards. How awful to get "bushed" in a ghostly hole like this! For the first time in his seaman's life he realized what the word bushed might mean. And the farther he penetrated into the gloom, the oftener he glanced behind. How easily they could spear him now! What if Gungadool were tracking him?

The Rat cursed softly, angrier in that he felt sure a panther tread was behind. He could *feel* it! To have gone under while securing the pearls would have been all in the game. Now that he really possessed them, death wore a harder aspect. He scurried on with ears, eyes, and muscles astrain. He pulled himself together, forcing his mind to make him steer the straightest, the swiftest possible course.

At last he emerged into the open forest and sighed with relief at the glorious strength of the sun. Hardly late afternoon, in the jungle all had been twilight. He broke into a steady run and the fresh air against his mouth tasted like an elixir of life.

Nearing the mangroves The Rat smelt the tang of the sea. He dared not waste time examining his booty. He would gloat over the pearls in the safety of the cabin when the cutter was under way. How glad he would be to see the last of this coast. A hawk screeched behind him as he plunged into the mangroves.

The sun was low down when The Rat emerged and greeted the sea with a laugh. One searching glance showed him the cutter lying peacefully at anchor three miles away. And there was the dinghy not a quarter mile away. To think that in this his first attempt, left alone in the bush, he had emerged at a point so close to his objective. 'Walking smartly down the beach he saw that the dinghy was floating inshore with the tide. Floating! Strange! He had tied it so securely too. He frowned, he knew what he would have said to a deck-hand guilty of similar carelessness. But his luck was still in, the dinghy had floated down towards him anyway.

He ran along the crinkly beach, thanking his lucky stars for so many favours. The dinghy floated in barely two feet of water, slowly drawing inshore.

The Rat took off his boots, for the dinghy had grounded on a mud patch. He was fastidious and hated boots full of mud, with his toes squelching inside. He waded out, whistling at the coolness of the water.

He reached for the dinghy – and went down suddenly and noiselessly, as if sinking in a depth of paste. He tried to spring back, but sank deeper. With horror he felt the mud ooze up over his knees; lower down it squeezed up through his clawing toes, dragging at his struggling feet with a quiet, terrible weight.

The Rat realized instantly what had happened. On portions of the Territory coast are patches of quicksand and a pale-blue mud, fine as sifted flour-and bottomless. He struggled and the mud quaked in a caressing grip upwards towards his thighs. Half sobbing, he hung his body outwards, but began sinking this way too. His clawing arms were mud laden but he must not lose his head, even if all the rest went down.

A canoe shot out from the mangroves, and a shout died in The Rat's throat. Budgaree was paddling, and the big nigger with the bloodshot eyes must be Gungadool. The Rat thrust the bottle under water and felt icy sick as the mud crept above his thighs. He strained his head above water. The natives watched silently. The Rat sought their eyes and knew that entreaty was useless. He took a great breath and roared a prolonged shout straight out over the water. It had to be a steady shout, for even with the expansion of his lungs he felt the mud grip tighter. He shouted again and yet again.

The mud had slid its warm arms around his stomach before Old Ben, with all the tribe running behind him, came racing along the beach. He harangued Gungadool, then shouted to the sickly-smiling Rat.

"The game is up, old chap. Hand the pearls over, and agree to give Gungadool half the supplies on your cutter It is the smallest price I can get for your life, and time is very short."

The Rat reached up the bottle to the darkening sky. "I will take it with me then," he snarled.

"Don't be an ass," called Ben. "Don't you understand I am utterly helpless? I can't reach you in time, no matter how I tried. The only chance to save you now is for Gungadool to reach you a pole from the canoe. And Gungadool has the canoe'!"

"The dinghy!" shrieked The Rat. "I would sink before I reached it."

The Rat glared wildly around; Gungadool stared impassively from the canoe. The natives stared silently from the beach, sulky hate in their eyes. He felt the mud sucking up under his armpits.

"Give in," called Ben. "You are euchred. In half an hour the mangrove worms will begin boring your flesh. And make no mistake, those natives will recover the pearls just the same."

The Rat's neck was kinking. He opened his mouth in defiance, but a splutter of salt water slipped between his lips. He nodded surrender.

Pearl sorting on Thursday Island, 1920s by Frank Hurley.

Native houses on the Fly River,1914, by Frank Pryke.

"AND GOD GAVE MAN DOMINION"

THE sun was sinking; the communal-house, though built high on piles, was already half-cloaked in gloom. The people, squatting in family groups on the limbon floor, still gobbled their food. From outside came a weird droning which would soon fill the barn-like building. Even so the smoking fires on the clay hearths would hold the mosquitoes in check until night enveloped all.

Lying upon the floor were long, caterpillar-like things, resembling pythons of the mammoth age – sleeping-baskets of finely-woven cane; most of them were fashioned long enough to shelter a family with each person lying head to feet. Leering from the shadowed walls were man-sized masks of terrifying aspect. Horrid weapons were stacked everywhere.

Men, women, and children – all were listening, as they ever do. They listen subconsciously, as we breathe. They listen for news!

It is always coming to them, though a white man often would not recognize it. It comes, faint sometimes as a sigh in the wind, from all directions, day and night, moaning over vast areas of water and grass; it throbs; comes as a tremor diminishing into distance; comes from the invisible mountains, from the unmeasured swamps. At other times its reverberations, harsh and sinister, boom out their message over village after village.

The *garramuts* speak--the giant *garramuts* of the Middle Sepik. By the tone these people know from which village a *garramut* booms; they read its message of fighting, of dancing, of initiation rites or festal ceremonies – of matters which interest the tens of thousands of savage men who listen day and night on the Middle and Upper Sepik, waters of mystery. Even that hated, dreaded supernatural creature, the white man; that curse which with ever increasing authority is endeavouring to stop head-hunting, cannot creep up the great brown river without every stone-age village receiving a warning. And from the river villages the news is passed across the swamps to those villages lying out amongst the grasses that the white man has never yet seen.

Suddenly, with one accord, these in their communal house rushed to the platform beyond the entrance. Kumunga leapt there first, his eyes shining, his mouth drinking in the news. For this that they heard now was the news that the Sepik loves, this news that came in deep, sinister tones.

It was the knell of death; it told of the taking of heads. At Parambei, only eight miles away, their warriors had just brought in five heads!

As Kumunga listened, his broad, savage face was transformed, his habitual scowl vanished. He listened breathlessly, with a child-like eagerness lighting his face.

A strong man this, young Kumunga, but not blooded yet. In tremulous sympathy his big chest rose to each roll of the *garramut*. His arms, big with their swelling shoulder muscles, hung to his flanks, where the big palmed hands clenched and relaxed to the rhythm of the *garramut*. His body was strength personified enlivened now by the blood-lust gleaming from his eyes. He looked what he was, a wild man of the swamps, scenting blood.

As the village listened clouds of mosquitoes rose from the grass and mud-pools beneath the houses. Many of the villagers, desirous of the last throb of the news, clung to the platform, thrashing their bodies with their millet-like reed whisks. A young girl peered covertly, reading Kumunga's face. She measured his proportions. She gloried in his strength, but she breathed deeper yet to the fierce lust in his eyes. Soon he would wear the flying-fox skin! With a wild beating at her heart she gloated on her hope.

The crowd crept back into the house. Kumunga only remained staring into the night. The mosquitoes had come, had taken over the whole earth. The families made wild rushes in the dark. Fathers called to laggard mothers, for it is the mother with her suckling babe who crawls into the sleeping-basket first. She creeps right to the end, closely followed by the man, who butts her with his head if she be unduly slow. After the man his eldest son. The last to crawl in is responsible for folding the end under; and the spirits help him should the father wake in the night to the torture of being eaten alive!

Kumunga could not bear the pests a moment longer.

On noiseless feet he padded across to Warminga's cubicle. Hanging up here was a loin-covering, a flying-fox skin. Kumunga stroked it with tingling fingers. For this was the emblem of a head-hunter, the sign for all to see that he who wore it had taken the head of a man.

An altercation arose from Kumusa's sleeping-basket.

Growling as he brushed his pest-bitten body, Kumunga gave the night entirely to the mosquitoes, and groped through the darkness to his own sleeping-basket. For each young man possesses a basket of his own.

Furious grew the row from Kumusa's corner, where the man's angry growlings were overridden by the screaming vituperation of Shabungun, his ten-year-old daughter.

Eager to be first into the family shelter her brothers had pulled her out by the legs and left to her the responsibility of closing up the basket; and before she had recovered her balance the family pig had rushed in. Shabungun was now struggling to pull him out by the hind-legs while he kicked and squealed his protests. Her brothers and sisters meanwhile were kicking down the length of the basket as their father was kicking at his family from its higher reaches, and roaring because the hungry mosquitoes were swarming in upon him.

The frenzied child had the pig almost out of the basket when with a practised kick it sent her flying amongst the cooking-pots whilst it scrambled up the basket over the bodies of the younger boys until it shoved its snout hard up against the eldest brother.

With a scream of anger Shabungun picked herself up and writhed her skinny body far up the basket. The cunning pig, lying snug, had hunched his legs tightly under his body. The girl did not attempt to grip them within those tight-packed quarters. She clawed over her struggling brothers and howled as she wormed her head underneath the beast; then turning up her mouth she fastened her terrible teeth in his groin.

Immediately the house rang to a crescendo of piercing squeals. The girl held on despite the family kicks until the pig, feeling that no relief would come by staying there, began to back out, his squeals made more piercing as the child quickened his decision with vicious bites and tugs. Men snarled through their baskets demanding peace; youths howled advice to Shabungun's brothers to kick her out; above all, Kumusa the father, roared the unmentionable things he would do to his daughter should she cripple his pig.

The long sleeping-basket convulsed itself to the centre of the floor like a gigantic serpent in travail; it collided with the family-basket of Kambam, and then bedlam broke loose.

But Shabungun ejected her pig and, giving it a parting bite, dived into the end of the basket and drew the opening close. Making a ball of her body she took in silence the kicks coming to her from the brothers, who were receiving theirs from the brothers higher up, who collected theirs from the father, who was receiving his share in abuse from all quarters of the great barn. Then vigorously the family set to work at killing the mosquitoes that had swarmed into the basket during the brawl. Until that was accomplished there could be no sleep.

Of course, the fault was with Kumusa's wife. She *would* have babies. Other families had room enough for their pigs to sleep with them. But Kumusa's basket was not made to hold the world!

At last sleep won, even the grunts of a disconsolate pig died down as it snuggled in between two baskets for warmth.

But Kumunga lay awake. His mind saw only the flying-fox skin. What honour must be the portion of a man who earned the right to wear the skin! He stretched his great arms against the basket in an agony of self-pity that he who was so strong had not yet been given the chance to kill a man.

With the morning came the exhilaration of a new day, bringing with it a mystic breath that was the sighing of breezes over many miles of water-grown grasses. After all the families had eaten, the women trooped away in laughing gossip to the fishing-nets, while the men strolled with guffaw and mimic spear-throwing to the gardens, as is the custom on the Middle Sepik. But Kumunga's garden-plot was well tended, and being free of ceremonial duties he idled out past the gardens, glorying animal-like in the sunshine among the betel-nut palms, his feet warming to the ground, his eyes gazing across the golden grass that rippled into distance.

At the swamp edge he untethered his canoe, thrust with the paddle and shot away through the grass-choked water. The impatience of youth, the urge to prove himself a man, filled him with a passion to measure his strength against something, anything!

He put his weight on the paddle making the tiny vessel cut through the grass and shoot out on to open water speckled dull green with lily-leaves. Grassy islets floated there, some with trees growing from their silt-covered mass of matted roots and decaying vegetation. Twice he jabbed savagely at the rough-tipped snout of a crocodile as it rose from the lily-leaves. He lived so close to the animal kingdom that he knew just where to strike to hurt. He jabbed again and laughed as a tail thrashed up from the water while he shot his canoe well out of the way of vengeance.

From distant Parambei came the boom of *garramuts;* Kumunga listened with envy and desire. The village was calling its people to the ceremonial dances accorded the victors in yesterday's hunt.

Kumunga dared not venture near that village of more cultured people – they would have his head in a twinkling. With sulky lip he poled his canoe slowly forward. He could not understand what was amiss. He felt man enough to hug the world. Yet it had no place for him. Miserably he poled on, his prow rasping gently over the broad lily-leaves. Gliding around a root-girded islet, his eyes fell on a slab of grey in the sunlight.

Now, crocodiles swarm in those mighty water-ways. They are as familiar as pigs and babies to the swamp men, who trap them, kill and eat them – and, occasionally, are killed and eaten by them. Kumunga dragged on his pole, snaking the canoe behind the sleeping creature.

Kumunga measured its length, his heart quickening.

Was he man enough to tackle the thing, alone; with his hands?

The crocodile was seven feet long. Kumunga looked at the ridged back, the serrated tail, the short stubby legs, the long tapering snout.

Drawing a great breath he shot the canoe forward, then with a flying leap he straddled the beast and gripped its pointed snout, wrenching the upper jaw with a sideways twist that locked the snout under his left armpit, while his left arm strained to dislocate the lower jaw. His legs were dug deep in the mud under the beast's belly, his knees drawn hard in behind its forelegs.

For a moment the saurian lay motionless, its eyes creased; then as its back collapsed its tail was thrown up in shocked agony. Frantically it scratched mud, struggling to gain leverage, frantically it lashed with its tail to smash this thing that was breaking it. But as Kumunga wrenched the snout backwards the tail vainly thrashed the mud while its forepaws harmlessly clawed mid-air.

Kumunga thrilled to the struggle as the coarse body strained between his gripping knees. Bunching his great muscles, he thrust and heaved, mingling his breath with the streaming breath of the beast. Its belly rumbled to Kumunga's ecstasy as he forced wide open the slobbering throat that all the sky might fall in. Mud spattered the grass and mingled with the water as the crocodile writhed to turn and rush into the stream. But the man-animal pressing down its back pulled against its jaws all the harder while its forepaws and hind-legs and tail vainly clawed and thrashed for leverage: it roared like a stricken bull as its lower jaw was wrenched from its socket.

Then Kumunga sprang clear, laughing as the thing writhed towards the water and a lingering death. Leaping to the canoe he seized his limbon spear and rammed it down the gaping throat. Filled with a singing pride such as but few civilized men may experience, he raced to collect the tribe that they should witness this sign of his manhood.

THE CASTAWAY

THE castaway was so happy that he nearly slipped into the sea; his gingery beard fairly rippled with smiles. He sang – and laughed at the noise; he shouted just to hear his voice echo among those trees. Yes, trees on the mainland! His ragged shirt and pants were held together by threaded vines; his tangled hair kept the sun from his eyes but not the smiles. Standing with feet wide apart on the logs he whistled a jazz tune of long ago. He was not a big man, but he made a noise like a giant. The sun shone and the water sparkled; he was nearly home at last.

Home! The northern Australian coast. White and golden sandhills, mountains in the distance, a beach ahead beckoning. He could distinguish the very trunks of the trees, the paper-barks snow white against the gums.

Perhaps the nearest white man lived hundreds of miles away; but this was the mainland, the Australian coast!

He pirouetted from log to log of the raft; he wished he could dance. It was a small raft, but he was mighty proud of it. He petted the logs with his feet. They were mangrove saplings really, cross-sected by poles lashed together with fibre rope he had made of coconut husk. The sail was his pride, a plaited mat of strips of coconut-leaves. He had woven many a lonely night into the making of that sail and now it had carried him across the Coral Sea right home. He chuckled at his commissariat. Yams and dried fish and shellfish neatly bundled in coconut-leaves against storm or spray. A big "cargo" too of golden-brown coconuts, drink for the gods, the reservoir all held together within a crate of sticks. Why, he could have voyaged a week longer!

But fate had been kind at last; had given him a light following wind; had made the tides always set in the right direction, and sent no cross-currents to whirl him away back out to sea. Yes, he was proud of his raft. It was great to be a man, a lord of creation, great to be able to plan out and do things; why he had even beaten the sea! His face changed at that thought, he gazed swiftly around as if guilty of sacrilege, almost as if he feared the voice of a taskmaster.

But the sea was a sunlit lake sparkling with good humour. Some joy, though, had been taken from the man, he gazed longingly towards the shore, wishing, praying it would quickly come closer. The gentle breeze on his cheek fanned by in a playful puff. The sail creaked, the raft gurgled, water bubbled up over his toes. He stood again with waving arms and laughed. The breeze livened. Heavens! in half an hour he would step ashore.

He wheeled around to a rumbling snort that suggested a giant in trouble. And so it was. A column of water spouted skyward, he could hear it falling like a fountain. Waves broke back from a slate-coloured bulk as a tail like a rearing stallion lunged down with a thunder-clap that echoed past him to the land.

"A whale," he cried aloud, "attacked by killers!'

He stared curiously as that massive disturbance forged away on another tack seeking sanctuary from the tigers of the sea. And hawks of the air too, for a ravening flock of sea-birds were screeching and swooping and pecking right on top of that surging mass.

"I hope the poor beggar gets away," murmured the castaway sympathetically. "It would be wretched to die on a beautiful day like this. By jove, he's travelling some! They're tearing him to pieces, poor old boy. How he rolls! I believe he's nearly done. There, he's gone now-sounded. I hope he manages to dodge 'em down under."

He watched awhile the birds swiftly flying in a twisted cloud that followed the course of the whale below. Birds were raining from the sky to the anticipated feast; their raucous screechings dispelled the peace of the day.

The castaway turned again to the land; he could see the stones upon the beach; counted some aloud; there were tufts of grass farther back too. His nut-brown face was very likeable, but no one was there to see that laughing excitement.

"I believe there are flowers on the trees," he called to space. "There will be bees buzzing among them and a butterfly or two." He would have danced this time for sure, had there not been danger of loosening the lashings that held the timbers together.

A volleyed screeching hoarse with excitement seemed thrown through the sky to swirl directly above him in hissing wing-beats that fanned his very face. He turned fear-stricken, his heart painful from presentiment.

Right behind him the water blackened as a cloud rose up from below and the whale broke the surface with tumultuous splashings. Its fog-horn gasp wheezed before it spouted hesitantly like the choked pipe of a bore. The castaway threw up his arms and wailed to the sky:

"Oh God, me the only man in the whole wide sea and a whale must run me down!"

With a terrifying, rolling momentum the great bulk swayed around to forge straight towards the raft. Perhaps in its agony and despair its small brain felt towards the raft as a drowning man feels towards a straw. A pack of killer-whales were at its throat; several thirty-foot lengths of stark murder streaked like black torpedoes to the white gut below. The water hissed to their tiger ferocity; it boiled from their powerful flippers as they' darted and snapped at the smaller lower jaw of the whale. As its mighty head surged aside they missed again and again to flash in at the towering body and tear out mouthfuls of blubber. The horrified castaway shivered to the clash of teeth, the hoarse rumblings from the whale, the thunder of flukes and leaping crash of tails.

A flash of blue streaked the wavelets as a twelve-foot swordfish buried its sword in the whale, to wrench free with a convulsive tail kick that. plunged it away to wheel again and charge in a berserk fury, ceaselessly repeated. There was a frightful menace in the very movement of that thing flinging itself again and again at the whale.

The castaway snatched at his slithering coconuts; then dropped the crate to grab the logs lest the heaving force them apart. They groaned as a rollicking wave took them broadside on, and he nearly stood on his head as the raft rose up. His ears were stunned by the shrieking birds swooping to snatch a beak of blubber from the living prey. Thunder slapped the water to echo and re-echo along the tree-girt shore.

"Thresher sharks and all!" cried the castaway as he slapped his knees in helpless despair. "Every demon in the sea all on to the one whale, and the whale on me!"

He snatched up his rude paddle and slapped, the water shouting "Shoo! Shoo! Shoo!" at the tiny agonized eye of the whale as its rounded bulk rolled aside, pressed in the very nick of time by the killers at its jaw. The castaway clung with knees and hands and feet as his vessel rose to buck and plunge in a veritable storm at sea. He lost three coconuts; he bumped his head when he jammed his toe; his mouth was choking with water and his heart with despair.

The sun glinted on oily ribbons where gaping strips of blubber had been torn from the slate-grey hide of the whale. It was only fifty feet long, but the castaway gazed up its glistening bulk as at a dreadnought. Its back humped ominously, then the great tail heaved up to thunder down in a water-spout that drenched the raft.

The rush of the thresher sharks nearly paralysed him; the cold, dead expression in their eyes froze his heart. Their terrible flails of tails swung up and hurtled down with blows that tore strips from the whale and clapped away to the shore.

The tortured leviathan writhed and forged right around the raft until out of a tidal wave, with titanic action, it threw its bulk clear of the water and fell like a shuddering ship, to crush these maniacs that were tearing it piece by piece.

The castaway clung petrified to his rocking vessel staring helplessly at the froth-red water through which half-glimpsed streaks of ferocity sped and thrashed and snapped.

It was the whale drawing their fury like a magnet that saved him, but in this maelstrom accidents might happen, and now again the whale was turning towards the raft as if irresistibly impelled. The demons at his throat seemed fully to realize that attraction and fought to drive him off lest his hope save him. With the white patch above his eyes emphasizing his devilry, a killer charged and rammed his tiger-toothed jaws into the glum, closed mouth of the whale, then catapulted on his own body to straighten out with a frightful leverage that obtained a crunching grip on the leviathan's lower jaw.

Instantly the attendant killers rushed in to the vantage, their teeth clashing like steel traps that sickened the heart of the castaway. Desperately on hands and knees he strove to hold his craft together. One killer among the furies at the whale's jaw was squeezed out of a grip, so twisting his body into a gigantic spring he straightened and hurtled up into the air to land "thump!" on the whale's back, tearing out a mouthful of blubber as he slithered back into the sea. The whale's head writhed up in a last monstrous shaking, the killers clinging like tigers as the castaway clung to his raft. There came a grinding dislocation as of bone, a snapping, a thundering of dukes and flails, hiss of flying spray as the whale groaned down, his lower jaw sagging. The fury of the thresher sharks became frenzy, the swordfish a livid streak careless whether it rammed friend or foe. Frantic gulls swooped headlong down to crash into the mat sail, one swished full "smack!" on the castaway's ear and overboard he went, but was aboard again with a shriek. He had lost all his coconuts, all his fish and his yams; now his logs were creaking and groaning and falling apart, two were bobbing away astern. He clung with fingers and legs and toes and tried to save the wobbling mast while he howled in helpless despair at the combat around. But it had ended when the leviathan's small under-jaw hung limply down, making the castaway feel sick as the whale looked, for he stared into a meaty cavern packed now with fiends tearing out the whale's tongue.

The castaway frantically paddled his crippled craft out of the storm, skirting the nose of the dying whale through a blood-foamed sea ringing with clashing noises and submarine groanings that mingled with the sucking sobs of tearing blubber.

With two more timbers trailing askew and his sail at a rakish angle the castaway paddled as if Satan were reaching towards him. He paddled harder still, with eyes bulging from their sockets, as the sea far around appeared dotted with fins travelling at a terrific pace.

Sharks came from everywhere, and like the demons they are tore and fought in the maddened swirl washing the whale, not only sharks, but the sea from shore and back on the sea-ward side was streaked with fins and ripples and foam as shoals of great fish raced to the feast. Air and sea was thick with ravening greed.

The castaway glanced once back at that frothing maelstrom, but his hair stood on end, and he paddled for the shore.

PEARLING BOATS, THURSDAY ISLAND.

The Divers Graveyard, off Darnley Island.

THE ENDLESS MYSTERY

ON the lake-like sea both luggers had drawn almost dangerously close together. Perhaps impelled by that unknown power which will attract driftwood to driftwood; probably the tide was the influence.

"Fate!" mused Heywood. "Like human life drifting goodness knows where."

He was sitting on the hatchway smoking. His eyes scanned the white posts on a grassy hill-side.

"The Divers' Graveyard. Alive to-day, dead to-night. I wonder if the dead really do die – finish!"

The tender, whistling cheerily amidships, was overhauling the diving-gear preparatory to the afternoon drift. The crew squatted on the deck opening shell. With the deft twist of their knives they laughed hilariously at carefree island jokes. The bluff slopes of Darnley Island near by stood up out of the sea, the white posts of the Divers' Graveyard plain on the hill-side.

Both luggers were drifting in dangerous waters debarred by law for that reason on the hill. The bottom around Darnley is notorious for its deep holes, which mean pressure and paralysis to the luckless or unwary. But the shell in patches is rich, and these divers were prepared to defy the law of man and sea and take a risk.

At a hail from the companion lugger Heywood waved in response. The vessel was manned by Japanese, whose diver invited him to dive in company.

Clothed in thick woollens against cold, they helped Heywood into the clumsy diving-dress, adjusting corslet and weights and big domed helmet with seriousness and care. Cumbersomely he climbed overside and clung to the ladder, waiting while a similar monster took to the water from the companion vessel.

Heywood nodded to the tender, who started the air-supply pumps. Heywood's face, deep in the helmet and framed by that little round hole, looked like a schoolboy's. By ear and nostril he gauged the working of the pumps, pumps that were to supply him with air. Satisfied, he nodded "O.K." The tender screwed on the face-glass. Heywood felt as isolated as a caterpillar in a cocoon. From his prison he gazed with more than usual longing on the old familiar world. He regulated his air-valve to the forced stream of air, his fingers tuned to a delicate nicety, allowing in just sufficient air for his bodily requirements and to fill his suit so that he would sink with a speed as nearly as possible controlled by himself. Satisfied he was master of his air and movements he nodded "O.K.," then slipped into the water with a backward motion, slowly sinking to a stream of bubbles. "Like entering into another world," he thought. "These dreaming fancies are persistent today."

The water was crystal clear; the sunlight reflected upon it from that intense blue sky characteristic of Torres Strait. Under such conditions, visibility is extended under-below to a distance and depth perhaps unknown in other seas.

He slipped down fairly fast through yellow-green water that darkened into blue-green at ten fathoms; then he descended more slowly. Through the side-glass he watched his companion descending "like a bloated spider," he mused. "I hope he doesn't get his web entangled with mine; we're drawing jolly close together." The life-lines and air-pipes loomed like hazy threads sagging down from above.

Gradually the "spider" faded away as increasing depth blurred vision. At twenty fathoms, Heywood was gazing anxiously for bottom, descending very slowly, increasing by manipulating the air-valve the air-pressure within his suit to press back the increasing external water-pressure, an inhaling the ever greater quantities of air clamoured for by his system.

At twenty-five fathoms, there formed below him a dull, brownish-yellow blanket. Like a blurred shadow it appeared to grow wavering upwards. He landed gently and gladly on this sandy bottom, then moved forward, lightly pressed by the tide, his fingers making the demanded air adjustments so that his body could live, and move, and think. He walked slowly now in shadow land where dwell silence and blurry things.

The pearl-oyster does not thrive on sand, so Heywood moved continually forward, searching the shadow bottom. peering through his face- and side-glasses at the shadows around. The deathly silence was accentuated by the far-off beat of the pumps, thumping hazily down through the air-pipe like the heart-beats of some far-away giant. Occasionally the heart-beats had unregisterable sounds, funny unguessable whispers that sobbed in mysteriously. For, when under great pressures, sound and brain, sight and thought, movement and blood and nerves alter their vitality and meaning in a manner unrealized by us above.

A shadow apparently on the bottom grew eerily defined into coiling strands of shadow serpents that was really sea-grass, with a vague patch behind it that merged into darkness. Heywood smiled relief; for a diver dislikes a drift wherein he sees nothing but wasted time and sand.

To his left presently loomed a shadow pyramid that was a hillock under the sea. Heywood drifted in amongst the grass patches and found himself walking down a sloping incline with snake-like grasses coiling to his thighs. Cumbersomely he moved his great boots ahead. Inside the suit, though, he could move quite easily; he felt very light too for he was moving in air. But to carry that big suit about, under the great water-pressure, necessitated slow, methodical movement.

Then loomed a threatening shadow that grew into a gigantic diver, becoming smaller but still magnified as the men approached each other. Like mammoth crabs they sidled closer. They stood, their domed heads thrust back as they peered up at the hazy droop of the lines reassuringly free from danger of entangling. The Jap sidled close and edged his helmet against Heywood's.

But Heywood heard only an indecipherable volleying of noises like word-sounds rumbling in a canister. Heywood shook his head. The small, brown face behind the face-glass smiled, nodding understandingly, and edged back into largeness again. Pressed by the tide, both grotesque shapes moved on into the shadow depths keenly peering at the rockeries gay with sea-cabbages large as wheelbarrows; at the coral ledges draped with reddish manes of sea-maids' hair; at the terraces of half-leaf, half animal-like growth in their hideous, their beautiful shapes, their weird mottling, their often ravishing colours; at the crawly things frighteningly suggestive of vindictive life.

The pearl is often the hidden flower in such under-sea gardens, the pearl that round one tiny grain of sand in an oyster's belly, grows and grows and finally kills the life within the mother shell.

Fearfully those groping shadows halted, bracing back against the tide, the Jap with upthrust arm, Heywood's heart dangerously beating as they pressed back from a ledge overhanging a "hole."

The deep-sea diver dreads falling into a hole in the bottom of the sea!

As nearly blind beings would, they peered down into that thick grey-green while edging back from its darker mystery. Probably, below them stretched a valley with its black cliffs and abysmal chasms terrifying in their invisible dangers, so unlike mountain valleys in the world above the sea.

Each had reached for his life-line to signal hauling in of the slack and each had stepped hard back against the tide-too late! That grass ledge that could stand the weight of unknown tons of water but not of two small men from a world regulated by other laws, collapsed, and out, over, and down they swept into depths of greatly increased pressure, their oxygen-inflamed minds overwhelmed with a horror that drowned the precious seconds in which reason might perhaps have saved them. The helmets bumped and those inside realized rather than heard a medley of sound never tuned to any sound on earth above.

Instinctive fingers closed their air-escape valves, seeking an inrush of air to force back the water-pressure now rapidly enclosing them in a "squeeze" of death. It was all over, even as the tenders above snatched the slipping life-lines and felt them fast. Down below Heywood sagged open-mouthed to the compressed air, his body convulsively straightening as the suit slowly filled out; he wondered (how he battled to overpower the wonder that races an oxygen-filled mind to a deathly exhilaration) whether he had "got the air" in time to prevent the "squeeze" giving him paralysis. He would not know until he got on top-on top!

A tugging at the life-line prompted him to tug "Haul up!" and he was drawn strongly up, only to be held back as if by a definite hand from the sea. He grated against the Jap's face-glass, the man's face was just coming down (he had been squeezed up into the helmet), his eyes protruded like fishes' eyes, blood dripped from his nostrils. Heywood's ears buzzed to indecipherable sounds from the grating helmets as his life-line reluctantly slackened. He gazed at what he was gripping as though he was facing a ghost – he was gripping the limb of a tree!

He read dawning horror in the Jap's magnified eyes slowly regaining reason. Both divers were entangled in the branches of a sea tree. Around them like pictures seen in a storm-cloud were the ebony limbs of weird trees – they had fallen among a forest of them. Heywood closed his eyes; deliberately dismissed thought; and with iron will concentrated on manipulating his air-valve until he felt his body and suit adjusted to the increased pressures of air and water. Then he forced his mind to realize that the excess of oxygen it was consuming would drive him thought-mad unless he could calm his reason. Only when master of his exhilarated mentality did he allow his eyes to open and thoughts to form.

Apprehensively he gazed on those sleek black branches.

He had seen the sea trees before, as branchless saplings, their tops bending to the tide; had inquisitively gripped a sapling and felt it grow rigid as a bar of steel. He had stolen on one as it swayed apparently alive as no ordinary tree is alive. Its short bunch of roots gripped a coral block. He had raised his leaden-soled boot and kicked the roots heavily, the sudden jar detaching the sapling. But had he touched it first, with finger-tips even, it would have quivered rigid and past a man's strength to bend. The largest sapling he had yet seen was not more than twenty feet high. He remembered the ebony walking sticks, the rings and bracelets the Torres Strait islanders carve from them.

But these were trees! Peering down he could distinguish a definite black trunk. Sleek black limbs, tapering thinly out, leafless, they sinuously swayed with the tide, bending as if to a caress. But the branches of Heywood's tree stretched rigid, the life-lines entangled between them as in a vice. "Like a spider pinched in his broken web," thought Heywood as the sluggishly struggling Japanese sprawled between the branches.

He was badly "squeezed;" he had failed to adjust his air-pressure with the immediate speed of Heywood. As he regained self-control he stared through the face-glass with eyes that expressed the fatalism of his race. For other divers have been caught in a sea-tree forest!

Heywood's vision was limited to peering space only through a soup-like grey that melted in gloom. He looked up, gazing farther to where the life-lines and air-pipes vanished in liquid less dense.

Questioningly the Jap's life-line tautened. Heywood watched with beating heart, knowing as the line took the strain that the lugger above had come about with her engine set just to beat the tide. How they must be staring down, up there, unable to help two fellow-men only a few yards out of sight, but in another element!

As the Japanese felt the pull he stared up. Heywood realized how he must be feeling, but his own heart pained as the limbs twisted across and his companion's life-line bulged tighter together in resistance to the strain. The slow, steady pull came within danger of tearing the line from the suit. Then the bloated grey spider sagged pathetically down again.

Just nothing could be done. They could not cut their lines and chance floating up "on the air." There remained the faintest hope that when the tide turned, strongly, those living limbs might release of their own accord. But if so, that would be-hours!

Heywood closed his eyes. In a flash (for the brain sees at vision speed when under that pressure) he realized that he was thirty-five fathoms down, possibly more-over extreme depth. On the extremely rare occasions when a man worked at that depth, he was allowed only fifteen minutes below, which meant half an hour at least to haul him up, necessitating six halts at varying upward depths to decompress the nitrogen out of his veins. One hour down would mean three hours upward journeying before they dared haul him right to the surface. Heavens! How many hours would he wait down here? They might require a day to haul him up. Would he be alive? If so, would his blood burst in nitrogen bubbles immediately they took the helmet off? He checked the thoughts with all the love of life that was in him and gazed at the swollen Jap, gazed into the mass around imperceptibly darkening, gazed at those hard black branches. "The grip of fate"-his thought felt aloof from his bodily feelings.

"Nothing can break those black bands, set here at the bottom of the sea to catch us. They grip as if this job was their mission in life." Heywood felt sorry for the Japanese, looking so helplessly monstrous, but since it was inevitable he was glad of his company. He was so close, and yet he might have been in the moon for all the help he could give.

The silence was appalling. He had no notion of time; a minute might be an hour. So utterly strange to lose the faculty of comprehending time! Unnoticeably, the greyish gloom turned to night.

"My God, sundown! For three hours a man's veins have been inflated with nitrogen! Anyway, I won't be able to see those eyes staring from the face-glass." He grew calm with the calmness of despair. Then all was black. Never had Heywood seen such pearls as shot up from the Jap's air-escape valve. A streak of effervescing green fringed with inexpressible beautiful bubbles flashed past.

"Fish. Phosphorus !"

Then everything turned purple-black. Heywood's heart choked as around him sublime beauty massed in pearl-streaked light, iridescent with orange, whirled upward like a glittering comet.

"The Jap is dead!" he breathed. " Left me alone! Plunged his knife through his suit and let out the air!"

For long, Heywood swayed in his suit. Then he groped for the life-line to tug and let them know above. Besides, the answering tugs would help dispel this ghastly loneliness. But he could not raise his arm. He knew then that he too, was dying; in a sublimely detached way he felt it was of little consequence. Queerly, far, far away he could still hear the throbbing hush of the pump. Fancy them still sending air down to him! The smell, too, of motor-oil came elusively down with each sobbing breath. Fancy smelling engine-oil, down here in the pitch night of the sea!

Then the black velvet surrounding him grew pin-pricked with gold that glowed to a million million points of softly floating light, greens and reds and yellows glowing and fading and floating. A trail of orange shot through the pin-pricks chased by vicious sprays of fire. And gradually a ghostly effulgence spread, through which Heywood found it more of an effort to peer than through solid green water. He gazed at the tree-branches now glowing green with phosphorescent light. As he gazed, the two limbs locked across the Jap's lines slowly slackened. "The devils!" thought Heywood. "They know that he is dead!"

But there came a questioning tug on the life-line and the limbs instantly tautened together. How long afterwards Heywood would never know, but stealthily the limbs eased apart; spread aside; their ends curved outwards to revel in the tide, and the Japanese slid away.

They felt the difference in the line, those men crouched waiting on the lugger-deck, for they immediately began to haul up the line. Heywood smiled pityingly. The Jap's body was crushed, dress and all squeezed by the water pressure right up into the corslet and helmet.

He watched that shapeless thing fade upward. "1 wonder whether water-pressure up the pipe beat the air forced down and told them?" he mused. "Otherwise they will take twelve, sixteen hours to haul up a dead man. It is queer how little they know, and they only two hundred feet or so away!"

Heywood had gradually lost all bodily feeling. His mind felt now the dominant ego definitely drawing away, isolating itself as if it possessed a body independently its own. And he felt inexpressibly comforted. Patiently and with certitude he waited a change as inevitable as night and day.

A monster fish glided between the branches, its scales distinct as shimmering jewels, its great eyes iridescent as an opal. And its way through the living phosphorescence sprayed fire. A much smaller fish, with two dainty bells of light drooping before its nose, darted towards Heywood's glass and peered. He smiled at the expression of snub-nosed alarm:

"Don't be scared, ugly fish. Things are not what they seem."

They buried Heywood, up on the grassy slope in the Divers' Graveyard, side by side with the Japanese.

Thursday Island jetty, 1922 postcard.

THE VANISHING DREAM

THE gentlest of breezes played over the island, whispering among the hilly undergrowth, trilling louder in the tremble of the broad palm-leaves upon the shore, crooning with the waves that played the tinkling shells upon the little beach.

The capricious Barrier Sea stretched far beyond the horizon. And up from that horizon, set in the blackest of velvet cushions, were the golden pinheads of the stars. Surely they had life! For when you gazed long at them they would twinkle back and smile as if in quiet understanding. Other worlds almost as unknowable as the tranquil thoughts of the man gazing serenely up. He also lived in a world of his own; for no man disputed his possession of this tiny island, which he shared with the birds of the air and the food-seeking fishes that ravaged its coral-bound shores. The red fire lighting up the rugged, sunburnt face suggested insinuatingly that this little world of his was good.

His gaze dropped presently to the line of the sea. Half-consciously he stretched out a hand towards the fire, just as a thinking man does to the quiet sympathy of the dog that sits understandingly by his side.

"To think," he spoke softly into the listening night, "that in places like this is the heaven men dream of finding only after death! It's a shame they waste their hearts away in the struggle, while all the time there are plenty of similar heavens going begging in real life, peaceful stepping-stones to the life ever after."

He was a beachcomber, with the island his kingdom, freedom his life. The countless fish that swarmed the reef provided his meat. The little cultivation patch; which grew things almost by itself, gave him sweet "buks," taro, and pumpkins. Papaw-trees, bird-sown, painted the brown hillsides. The banana plot bowed its stalks under the weight of fat fruit, and shady mango-trees, magnificent in spreading limb and heavy, dark green foliage, were speckled thickly with their luscious orange-gold harvest.

Springs between the little hills gurgled out their sweet drinking-water for him and the other life of the island.

For the rest, should he want it, he had the largesse of the sea at his door; for from among the corals and from the sand and mud and seaweed bottoms came *bêche-de-mer* and trochus-shell and venturesome pearl-oysters. At low tides in the shallow water, when his mind and body needed occupation, he gathered these gifts of the sea and cleaned and smoke-dried and cured each as it necessitated, and stored them away until the little pile of slugs and shell mounted to a ton or so. Then he would signal to a passing lugger and trade with the skipper, or else consign the shell to Thursday Island, and in three months' time (maybe six) a lugger passing that way would drop him his supply of civilized things. He could do without these things, which to him represented civilization and drudgery. But the very sight of these "necessaries" gave him a pleasurable thrill of independence.

The man arose, eyes half-closed. "And to think that tomorrow – any day – I may chance to pickup an oyster with a pearl rivalling Cleopatra's gem! And I don't want it. Not in the least! Blow the pearl, civilization, everything else but the croon of the sea on the reef, the sun, everlasting peace, and sleep!"

The days were hot, even for summer. The granite boulders that had long ago thundered down from the hillsides to meet their ever-encroaching enemy the sea, shimmered oily-grey under the fierce rays.

"Too hot to last," muttered the beachcomber; "there's a storm brewing."

He was walking easily along the rippling sea-edge, naked but for a cloth *sarong*. He needed no hat, for his hair was profusely thick, the eyebrows bushy and jutting. In one hand he carried a four-pronged fish-spear. In the *sarong* a sheath-knife. Nothing else. He whistled as he walked.

The tide was out, leaving isolated the coral creeks and pools and the tardy fish. In the pools waved slow, queer-coloured things that were neither fish nor plant; on the clear sands of the bottom were slow-moving shells of mottled beauty, and fish of rainbow hues darted from gloomy coral caverns into the brightness of clear water.

All life, ravaging life, living to its very full up to the last, an ecstasy of killing, eating, breeding!

The iron-brown man waded out into shallow water, careful of his feet against the needle-pointed corals. Then he swam, in slow motion lazing out to deeper water where now and again he floated with face thrust just into the water, so that he could spy the bottom. Occasionally he swam easily down, and sought amongst the ledges and sea-plants. After one such dive he came up with a big pearl-oyster. Swimming back to the reef, he there surveyed the shell with a slow, appraising smile.

"You're a beauty, Black Lip, and big enough to house my last night's dream-pearl that would he the envy of all the white-throated women in the world. And, incidentally, make me rich. But just in case you bear the phantom pearl and so would spoil the beauty of the day, and of the days to come – I won't open you." He threw the shell well upon the reef above high tide.

Walking on along the reef, he swung back quickly, for emerging from an underwater cavity he had glimpsed the long feelers of a lobster scouting to cross a sand-pool to the feeding-ground of the farther coral.

Lying hidden, the man waited until the big green shellfish showed nearly midway across the sandy bottom. Then jumping erect, he swung his arm high and lunged down. A squirt of water hissed from the descending spear, and the haft wobbled drunkenly as the transfixed lobster made violent efforts to escape. Securing his squirming prize, the man threw it up on the reef and walked on.

A barely-seen ripple wavered the mirror-like surface of a large pool. The man's arm was instantly poised. Then the long spear, slightly aquiver, shot far out. Only a trained eye would have detected a fish swimming there; only a trained arm could have swung the spear so certainly. The man calmly waited while the big bream, swimming frantically but ever bearing over, swam its life out in the coral-bound pool. Up rose the wooden haft; up, up; over the long haft leaned; now the white of the fish's belly showed; it was swimming in ever-narrowing circles on its side. The man watched the struggle. Time did not count. And the quiet satisfaction of the necessary meat for the day was his. At last, plunging in, he brought the still impaled fish out on to the reef.

Walking leisurely back with his catch the turning tide washed across his feet. Some distance out floated a something on the incoming water. The man watched it curiously, then stopped. What was it? Not a box from some passing ship; not a clump of seaweed. The skin of some native-killed animal, perhaps? No! Just *what* was it?

He sat on the sand, and waited. The sea-mother sometimes brings strange gifts to her nomads of the Barrier seas.

With the ever-strengthening ripples of the gathering tide the something floated a little faster; presently it came bobbing over the lip of the reef with the quickening waters and floated into the shallows.

The man, purposely delaying to satisfy his whetted curiosity, threw his warmth-loving arms to the kiss of the sun, stretched luxuriously, then splashed out across the reef. He stared, a queer feeling at his heart. It was so big he had not dreamt it could possibly be *that*. With childlike eagerness, as if afraid yet dazzled by the bare possibility, he splashed out at the run, bent over, and gazed. A questioning bewilderment drew his lips into a low whistle. Then he straightened suddenly, threw back his head and laughed. The gulls wheeled a little faster in their ceaseless flight, several swooped down to shriek with him. The man gripped the something in two brown-muscled arms, swayed it above his head and dashed it into the water, laughing strangely. Picking it up he turned and splashed back to the shore, face a-shine.

He examined it with almost wolfish eagerness. It was a big blob of stuff, in colour a slate-grey, except where on one side was glued a fist-sized lump of duller, blackish-grey stuff. In this latter were embedded two little black beaks of cuttlefish!

"Ambergris! By heavens, ambergris!"

The gulls, now swooping low overhead, wheeled yet faster and screamed in a chorus of shrill cries. Keen fishers themselves, instinct told them this man-thing had found a prize.

"Yes," he shouted, "ambergris! By heavens, best grey and it must weigh nearly a hundred pounds. All ambergris! It's a fortune."

Stooping, he put sniffing nose to the strange, unappetizing-looking blackish-grey piece. It smelt musky, almost a trifle sweetish. He pushed his fingernail into it easily, he rubbed a piece between his warm fingers and it softened like pitch. The big grey mass was harder, though he could press his finger-nails into it too, and when squeezed a while between his fingers a fragment grew softer and a bit blackish. It also smelt musky.

Laughing in uncontrollable excitement he grasped the big lump and hurried along the shore back to the hut. Once more he shouted up to the gulls: "Yes, ambergris! Good stuff and a great lump. I can hardly carry it! A little fortune!"

At the hut he put it down carefully; then ran up the nearest hill. From its grass-lined summit he stared straight out over the sheet of glass-like water. Miles away, its mains'l flapping like a broken-winged gull, lay an almost becalmed lugger.

"It's Thursday Island Coleman. I could tell the cut of that craft if she was but the size of a woman's thimble. My luck is all coming in one great lump. He mightn't have passed this way for months."

A signal beacon of dried bushes stood on the summit.

He struck a match. A sheet of flame leaped from the sun-heated wood. He tore down green branches and piled them on in such a way that a black column of smoke rose steadily into the sky. He laughed as he worked.

Night cloaked the island in a sullen, waiting calm. Beside the cheerful fire sat the man, one brown hand fondling the ambergris. He broke off a speck and piercing it with a splinter held it to the blaze. It melted like sealing-wax, then burnt, and its smoke smelt something like burning rubber. Eagerly he tried his most certain test:

"I'll try it on the grey," he whispered, "not on the little adhering piece of poor black stuff!"

He heated a wire prong from his fish-spear, then pressed it into the stuff. A brownish-black stuff like dirty pitch began to bubble up around the wire. He pulled it out and touched the melted stuff with his fingers; it stuck like little threads of pitch to his fingers. He held the wire in the fire and the stuff on it broke into flame; then blew it out and smelt the rubber-tainted smoke:

"There's not the slightest doubt. Now we'll see what John Chinaman says." He scraped a little into a pannikin of boiling tea. The stuff melted immediately. "John Chinaman says him welly good amberglis," he chuckled. "First-class quality, and last time I heard its value was worth £36 an ounce. A hundred pounds at £6 an ounce? £9600!"

He stared into the fire, then turned his face slowly until his dream-clouded eyes gazed towards the south. The fire burnt slowly out.

The man sighed almost wearily and cupped a slow hand under his chin.

"By heavens!" he whispered, "what gave me that thought? A woman's white shoulders! A good woman, too, with the breath of heaven upon her hair. Just one real woman to spend the money on and make happy!"

His hands clenched on the ambergris. He laughed softly, then jumped up and strode off through the night to walk the beach and dream till dawn.

Dawn broke. A disk of burnished gold came straight up out of the east and poised atop of the water. Then it leapt a foot. You could almost swear that an unseen hand was pushing it up. The sky shimmered into waves of quicksilver. Below it a long, broadening path of orange-gold danced away upon the water. The disk climbed straight up, and the silver sky changed into a fan of leaping red. A bird called among the trees; a mate sleepily answered; a fish plopped in the dark water. Then long, crimson rays darted straight forward and tipped the white coral reef with bands of growing scarlet; a sheen glinted from the palm-branches. The dawn had come.

"It's going to be a scorcher," said the man with folded arms on the beach. "Coleman won't reach here to-day at this rate. I wish the calm would break." The palm-leaves sighed lingeringly and a cool breeze kissed the man's face.

He laughed in quiet delight.

"Nothing can go wrong. See, there's a white horse!

And there's another and another!" He walked quickly up the hill. A long way out, right under the sun, a lugger stood towards the island, its crimson mains'l no larger than the puffed breast of a gull.

"She'll be no time with this breeze," said the man busily.

"It's growing stronger and stronger every minute. I'll have breakfast for the sake of keeping my racing mind occupied, collect my few things and have everything ready. By that time, she will be close in."

He dawdled happily over breakfast. It was luxurious to think that, though already monarch of all he surveyed, he was now about to set forth with a magic wand to conquer a new world. Not able to keep still a moment, he set about packing his few things.

Presently from the hut he could distinguish the lugger's sail, still a long way off but growing fast under a spanking breeze.

"I'll make sure she *is* heading for the island," he decided suddenly. "I'll have everything ready to hop into the dinghy. Coleman wouldn't like to be kept waiting. It's dangerous near the reef for a lugger when the tide is out. And it's coming in now!"

Gripping the ambergris he strode down to the beach and placed it on top of a boulder well above high-water mark, then brought along his swag, dropped it by the rock, then hurried up the hill. At the summit the breeze did not blow quite so strongly against his face. Half an hour later it had completely died away, leaving the lugger helpless a few miles from the island, the sea a pool of reflected light, the air hot and still.

The man gazed disappointedly. His bare arm touched a granite rock. He drew his arm away quickly.

"The rocks are as hot as fire already," he murmured.

"Burn a man. I'll keep the smoke going; I must do *something*."

The day passed slowly into sweltering afternoon before a dinghy put off from the lugger. They had nearly four miles to row. As they came over the reef the man ran down the hill to the beach. He laughed agreeably as the sweating black boys grinned a greeting. The dinghy crunched on the shells. Coleman stepped out, wiping a glistening brow.

"Goo' day, Cap'n Kidd! By hell, it's hot! If there's not a young hurricane inside of twenty-four hours I'm a Dutchman. How are you doing? I thought at the least you must have been dying by the amount of smoke you sent up. But you've got a million-pound smile aboard. Doing well?"

"Wonderful! Ambergris!"

"What!"

Coleman looked quizzically at the excited man whose grey eyes were shining so.

The beachcomber laughed amusedly. "It's all right I'm not crazy yet. But what price is ambergris?" He dwelt eagerly on the reply.

"Six pounds an ounce last time I heard," answered Coleman with quick interest.

"Come and – look! I've got the biggest lump you've ever seen! Washed ashore! And not out of jonah's whale either. It weighs nearly a hundred-weight. A gift from the good old sea!"

"My heavens!" breathed Coleman. "Why, that's – that's nearly ten thousand pounds man! Are you sure?"

"Positive!"

Their feet crunched faster over the shingles. The beachcomber laughed boisterously. Coleman was breathing hard.

"Where is it? At the hut?"

"No. I brought it down the beach when the breeze was blowing so as to be ready to hop into the boat. Here it--"

Coleman eagerly looked, stared; then a quick catch stilled his breath as he glanced sideways at the man.

The big granite boulder, its contained heat, almost a furnace in itself even without the pitiless rays of the sun pouring down upon it, was covered with a fast-vanishing film of sweet-smelling grease.

Torres Strait Islanders preparing *bêche-de-mer*, 1908.

THE WHITE WITCH

JUST eighteen months ago, Rothschild cabled le Strange.

A German had staggered into Port Moresby dying of fever complicated by arrow-wounds. He raved of a wonderful orchid growing in the seven-thousand-foot level up in the Owen Stanley range, above Dinawa, but down in the valley death swamps. Hence the cable: £1000 if we brought in one specimen, £500 for each additional prize, with a fancy prize for anything else new we might stumble across.

We started inland from Delana, le Strange, the leader; Long Harry, a sunburned northern Queenslander; young Matkins, just an ordinary Australian lad; and myself. Eight of le Strange's proved "boys" for armed guard, interpreters, and part carriers. For other help we must, as usual, hire carriers from village to village.

Le Strange had worked the outskirts of this particular orchid region before, but no one had dreamt of wonder blossoms in the death swamps. Those morasses are the breeding-grounds of the malarial mosquito, of ague and fevers in virulent forms. So, while in Moresby, le Strange had done some hard thinking – as a man would preparatory to dropping into a valley of death.

We trailed first through low lands until the climb began up through the eucalypt belt. In sight of Bioto Creek, meandering like a silver. wire between its dense mangroves, we glimpsed the Nicoro niggers watching from their hill of bright, red clay. At a thousand feet we struck Epa surrounded by forest and tangled undergrowth. The village trails closed in about here, wandering downhill and across valley and uphill again interminably, with the towering form of Mount Yule in the Papuan Alps mistily ahead.

We had a palaver at Epa with Mavai, before he would supply us carriers to go ahead. The old ex-cannibal is the usual Papuan sorcerer, and, as he has widespread influence over the local tribes, le Strange wished to keep sweet with him, if only for the safeguard of leaving our line of retreat open. Mavai is an over-broad six-footer, carrying a cicatrized chest and a war-club like a tree-butt. He had only ten wives, and was touchy for his dignity, explaining almost tearfully that but for a setback in a recent raid he'd have had at least fifteen.

However, we squared the crafty heathen with an extra ration of trade, secured thirty fresh carriers, and moved on again. The carrier trouble became worse as we passed through tribe after tribe.

We climbed steadily to Ekeiki, then through: Dinawa, slowly hacking through the jungle when the native paths petered out. As usual, it rained almost daily, and the scrub-itch got in its burning work as we brushed among the dripping leaves. Presently we were struggling among the Papuan razor-backs – climbing precariously along the humped spur tops, which are often a bare three feet wide, with precipices faulting sheer from each side, and growing deeper, darker, and nastier the higher we climbed. The brooding silence was accentuated by the "drip, drip, drip," from the foliage, and the occasional "wauk, wauk," of the bird of paradise.

After skirting the Delana precipice, we still climbed, now winding in and out between overhanging boulders of enormous size, like warts clinging to a giant's nose. What mysterious force glued them to the mountain side, the good Lord only knows. After climbing Madui we passed by the Aculama, hurrying in frothing foam far below. The nigger villages we passed through treated us to a sulky neutrality, for our well-armed party commanded respect.

After Dinawa we still climbed and climbed. Day after day. Often at starting we would mark a point a stone's throw across a valley; it meant a solid day's walking, hacking, slipping, sliding, climbing, before we camped there. Finally, we rose to the seven-thousand-foot level, a moonlight-like country of mist-wreathed mountain-caps above, and deep, mist-wraithed valleys below. A sea of peaks; its spray the mist-clouds which rose and floated above and below and all around.

We built a permanent camp dose by a stockaded village. The natives were a good-looking class of nigger; lithe and straight, bronze-coloured; the men clad in less than seemed necessary, the women with a cheerfully inquisitive smile and the short grass *rami*. They built us a home on piles about twelve feet above the ground, get-at-able only by shinning up a shaky ladderway. Fuka-lala was the chief wizard of this village. He was a withered bundle of wickedness, but knew his business; so le Strange was quick to square him.

It was while the bucks were shoving up the house frame-work, and the women carrying along the palm-sheaves, that we got the shock of our lives. By Caesar! She was a lovely girl, enhanced by such a setting. Her skin was lily white and seductively warm-looking; her figure slim and curving; her hair the usual Papuan mop, only less of it, the colour a glinting brown. Her cheeks were pink and the little bow lips just crying to be kissed; her eyes blue and innocently mischievous. A dog's-tooth necklace, stained crimson, looked startling against her milk-white flesh.

We stared. She dropped her palm bundle, gazed wonderingly at the first white men she had ever seen, and smiled in shy fear. Then her eyes challenged Matkins's. He flushed, and slowly she followed suit; an entrancing blush, the first of her life, I'll swear. Then she turned and hurried away, a little white queen in niggerland. Long Harry drew a longer breath.

"Am I in dreamland?" he demanded. "Who is she?" asked Matkins, eagerly.

"Gin, of course," said Long Harry. Then he looked at the boy curiously: "Albino," he said.

Matkins was puzzled, so Harry explained:

"A Papuan girl in a white skin. An Albino. A freak of nature."

"A white girl who'll have black babies," broke in le Strange abruptly, and we went on with our unpacking.

That night there was a pow-wow in the village. The Albino girl handled the star act, and immediately that we learned she was "Fi-fi," we understood things. A very occasional tribe among some mountain tribes have a girl witch-doctor, but she is strictly limited to one branch of the business. Fi-fi had the power of receiving messages from the god of war. Thus, on the night in question, the bucks were much disturbed by a rumoured raid from their fightable neighbours. Fi-fi was isolated in a little "charm house" to commune with the spirit warriors while outside, old Fuka-lala danced himself into hysterics, imploring the war spirit to give Fi-fi a message; the complete tribe, in a frightened circle, awaited the message of good or evil import. When Fuka-lala had just about winded himself and was getting mad about it, Fi-fi spoke – I grinned at the mysteriously assumed voice. It appears that the war-spirit told her the raiders would not dare to attack while the white men were living by the village. At which the tribe grew cheerful, and looked on us with a much more friendly eye.

Some of these Fi-fis grow very cunning, and, like the big witch-doctors, use the natives' credulity to feather their own nests. We learned later that our Fi-fi had already padded herself a nest of eiderdown.

Days passed by while we located likely swamps in the valleys, several so dizzily far down that the nigger guides resolutely refused to venture. Not even Papuans could live there, they swore. The fevers and malarial mosquitoes would quickly kill anything living. Besides, the most implacable devil-spirits in all Papua dwelt there.

We weren't scared of spooks, but didn't like the other things; so looked to le Strange, as the thinker. He set the whole tribe to making long coils of strong fibre rope, at which the natives are experts. He picked out the most promising swamp area within reach of the camp. Along a ticklish razor-back overlooking it, a track was cut – the only possible approach.

The rope coils and needful things were carried there.

So one fairly bright day, leaving Long Harry and a guard at the camp, we took Matkins and two "boys" with us to the point of the descent. We didn't want the quick-witted niggers pelting arrows and rocks from above. Papua is a land of opportunity.

Indistinctly below floated the unhealthy-looking cloudmist over the big swamp. We halted and peered down at a devil's scenery. An unguessable depth of green gloom, a scent of damp vegetation, jungle upon jagged razorbacks, and crags and peaks peeping from veils of mist. Hitching one end of the rope to a tree we slithered the big coil down until it caught against a bush. Le Strange and I stripped, then laced ourselves into the "armourplate." This was a loosely-fitting suit of waterproof canvas with glove-like arm-pieces. Over the head was a canvas helmet with a broad glass eye-piece and an arrangement for breathing-purposes. We pulled on boots, slung a bandolier over our shoulders containing automatic, sheath-knife, and small steel tomahawk. Le Strange had a compass. We were taking as few risks as possible.

Le Strange went first. We clambered down clinging to rope and bushes for close on a thousand feet before penetrating the cloud-mist. Then it was like crawling through muggy steam. Couldn't see each other five yards away. I had an anxious feeling that I didn't want to lose sight of le Strange, although he looked a magnified goblin dropping into the nether regions. We crawled through the cloud, and craning necks over shoulders saw three hundred feet below a broad table of palm-tops, swamp trees, and clinging vegetation melting into further mists. The cap of the swamp!

Just above us swayed the vapour cloud. Around us a death-like silence. We floundered down and squashed the soggy mosses at the swamp edge. Working to arrangement, we walked a short distance apart. Not far! We were in a dull twilight, and each must be on hand to hurry to the other's assistance should anything unforeseen occur. Being separated a little made our field of vision all the wider, and thus we could cover more ground.

Le Strange set his compass for a shadowy tree ahead.

Then we waded in. We could distinguish half the water surface. Stagnant pools, black from vegetable acids. In reality all was water and tree-trunks. The green patches floating between black pools were leaves of water-plants. Immediately we touched water billions of mosquitoes rose in one vibrating cloud and I blessed le Strange's foresight, and wondered that the German had not left his picked bones in his swamp. He must have anticipated le Strange's idea, for a rhinoceros could not have lived in that blood-sucking inferno.

We carried on. I was watching le Strange, he closely watching his compass bearings, for, although going very slowly the vapourly mist soon shut us out of sight of the "land," down which we had come. To be lost in that swamp! Ugh! A man's brain wouldn't stand it long, anyway. We stared up at the curious looking trees, quite unlike the sun-kissed trees on dry land. Somehow they reminded me of a fungus growth in a misty, closed-in pickle-bottle. But palms there were in plenty; and now and again I glimpsed the slender beauty that le Strange had carefully pointed out to me in lesser swamps.

Soon the water oozed above our knees. Somehow this water wasn't like other water; it didn't chuckle and gurgle and sparkle and swirl as we lifted our feet; it just filled silently in, and the decayed vegetation slowly waved together in inky masses that wouldn't sink. When up to our waists, the water felt much heavier, and a clammy gloom shut us in. I waded closer towards le Strange as the slimy tree-trunks grew thicker; mazes of water vines sucked at our legs. I was wondering apprehensively whether crocodiles could possibly be so high up until I remembered that there was no game for them to live on. It was the sort of place where one would expect to meet lizards of the pterodactyl age. Presently the water grew thin sheets of iridescent oily stuff that seemed to suck upwards as we moved. The feeling of everything was beastly.

The roar of the mosquitoes, though dimmed by the headpiece, was nerve-racking. And the humming masses against the eye-glass made me ward off, again and again, with quick, jerking arm the low-hanging tree cables that I momentarily imagined were snakes. Le Strange appeared a monstrosity as he cautiously waded on.

And yet in that festering unhealthiness there were beautiful things that grew on the tree-tops in riotous colours and festooned the crooked branches like rainbow garlands. Flowers of purple and gold, scarlet and yellow, and chains of waxy white blooms.

We kept wading slowly on, with a tingling foot out-thrust for invisible holes. Silent hours passed, and it was time for us to turn back.

We waded off at an angle, and shortly after turned straight again so as not to cover the same ground. It was getting loweringly dark away down there in the belly of the world. We tried to push on faster, but couldn't. I wondered what would happen if le Strange dropped the compass into this black corruption. It would necessitate tree to tree sighting then, with a chance of having to camp in a tree until daylight. Ugh! How the black waters clung to our legs!

I saw it! Its dream-like beauty dazzled me. In a muffled shout I attracted le Strange. He ploughed through the water-vines, and together we gazed up the tapering palm. Clinging to its tip among a blotch of milky-green leaves was the orchid. Four whip-like stems looped gracefully down, each tip flourishing a cup-like flower with gleaming petals of orange and black. From each cream heart floated a tendril of pure white, tasselled with gold. Its loveliness gave a compensating thrill for such a life as ours.

As we returned le Strange blazed the trees. We were taking no chances of being unable to re-locate the flower. It was too late to attempt reaching it now.

We had gone barely twenty yards when le Strange exultantly shouted, with up-pointed arm. There trailed another of those wonderful flowers. Their beauty so fascinated us that we never thought of the £1500 we had earned that day until hours later just as we were turning into bunk.

Even then le Strange was only planning how he could get the flowers out of the swamp.

Back at the swamp edge, there floated down to us the ghostly echo of our boys far up on top. The mountain Papuans have a remarkable power of throwing their voices. These ceased as we jerked the rope.

It was quite dark when we reached the top. Matkins looked happily sheepish. Beside him sat Fi-fi, She smiled very friendlily at me, and a little appealingly at le Strange. He was the one she was frightened of, though he was the very one she had no occasion to fear. Matkins had been teaching her English, he volunteered.

We spelled a few days before going down after the orchids; so as to give the fever as little chance as possible we saturated ourselves with pure, germ-killing fresh air. It meant long hours of ticklish work in that slimy water before we would get the delicate flowers to the top. And we would secure others if we possibly could. Le Strange always gave his Yankee employer a fair deal. That's why he got such good prices when he did succeed, I suppose.

Meanwhile Matkins had developed a theory. He delivered it one night at the camp, while the niggers were all sitting round laughing and joking with our interpreters, Fuka-lala squatting silent and wise-looking.

We listened to Matkins. He was in deadly earnest.

He spoke in that decided sulky tone a boy uses when he's certain of a thing and knows you will contradict, but intends to be as stubborn as he can. Lovely Fi-fi sat very close, gazing pleadingly at us in turn because she knew Romeo was barracking for her, and she badly wanted our sympathy. I wondered how the village bucks took her plainly shown preference for the white man; no doubt she had bluffed them with her spirit powers.

Matkins declared Fi-fi was a white girl. He was certain of it. He waited for the contradiction that did not come, then went on all the more doggedly because of the speaking silence. He didn't know anything about albinos, he said, and didn't care. Fi-fi was a white girl! She'd been captured when a baby from white settlers during a raid on the coast, and had afterwards grown up with the tribe. Or else she'd been captured from shipwrecked people, and her friends eaten, as had happened to people before. He didn't know which, and didn't care. He was going to take Fi-fi back with him. She was his orchid. We could have the rest. He didn't care a damn: he was going to marry her.

We looked at Fi-fi with an added interest. Of course, we were positive the girl was an albino, even though old Fuka-lala refused to point us out her parents. Matkins was only a boy in violent love. With this tropical setting, where everything that lives is passionate, we could easily understand it. As the girl flushed under our searching gaze, we felt a bit puzzled. Her skin was absolutely cleanly white. There was not the slightest trace of blotches as on most albinos, not even freckles. Her hair, too, was of a golden brown that any white girl might envy. And her eyes – there was not the slightest trace of pink about them; they were blue. Albinos occasionally have blue eyes, but a sort of dead blue hard to describe. Fi-fi's eyes were an orchid blue, merry and bright.

At last le Strange spoke. Quite nicely he explained to the boy all that it meant. Matkins stared at the fire.

The girl put an arm around him and smiled up into his sullen eyes. Le Strange ceased speaking. It was no use.

Three days afterwards we secured the orchids. Handled them for what they were-flowers that men had had to risk their lives to get. A week later we found another one. That was all. It was too much like tempting providence. The mother swamp guards her gems with ghastly care.

That particular country on the higher ground is splendid orchid country. We got some great flowers, and could have collected more. But we were anxious to get our three beauties to Port Moresby; besides, le Strange scented trouble over Fi-fi.

The boy was determined. So was she. He'd offered Fuka-lala all his earthly possessions, even to his share in the three orchids. Fuka-lala had contemptuously waved the orchid offer aside, but had accepted the rest on strict condition that he took the girl away. Guess Matkins's delight! In surprise, le Strange questioned the old devil. He came back looking much relieved:

"It appears," he explained in his sober way, "old Fuka-lala is jealous. Fi-fi's influence is growing with the tribe. She's jolly shrewd, and has been using this spirit business very much to her own advantage. It's a godsend to Fuka-lala to get rid of her. He's not quite game to poison her, because she's worked her way in too well with the tribe. So he told them the Great Spirit says Fi-fi must go away with the white men. Of course, Fi-fi acted up to this. Last night the War Spirit spoke to her, and said she must go with the white men, else the pygmy tribes will hop down and slaughter the lot, not to mention a disastrous disease breaking out among the crops. The tribe are sullen, but resigned. I'm glad. I thought we were in for a brawl through that little white devil."

A few days later we broke camp. Matkins had handed over all his earthly possessions, except his rifle, to Fuka-lala, le Strange would not allow him to part with the rifle.

The tribe, after sorting out the carriers, bade us a morose good-bye. The three priceless orchids, trussed carefully up in palm-fibre from their own swamp, we would trust only our own boys to carry. Then we commenced the long climb down. It was going to take many days, but we were a highly successful expedition, and success is the breath of life. Nothing punctures a man when he is successful. In three hours we peered over the steep banks of a tearing river. At its shallow crossing-place, which was the boundary-line of the next tribe, their promised carriers were not waiting to meet us. Le Strange, always cautious, halted.

It was the searching eyes of our head boy who twigged the raft on the opposite bank.

"Bushes. close up longa fighting men," he excitedly pointed, "plenty bow an' arrer!"

Fuka-lala's carriers stealthily tried the disappearing trick. Le Strange just as quietly halted them. "Shout out and ask what this means," he ordered our head boy; A derisive yell answered. In unashamed nakedness, two hundred warriors sprang from the opposite bushes, menacingly waving spears and bows. They looked decidedly nasty, and smelt worse, having greased themselves with the fat of a dead man's body, to give them extra courage and strength. Their dress was circlets of parrot plumage, dog's-tooth necklaces, and nose-bones.

In the following haughty palaver they demanded Fi-fi unconditionally. She was to be their war-interpreting doctor. Hand Fi-fi over and they'd give us carriers to the next village. Otherwise they'd give us carriage to Paradise.

Which meant that Papua was out after our hides, and this tribe had been picked on to deliver the goods. There was no turning back, no dodging. You can't dodge on the mountain razor-backs unless you can fly down precipices. The problem was simple: win forward or perish. Cutting out le Strange's pidgin-English, this is what he said to our own trained boys:

"Sham to walk back to Fuka-lala's village. When the fools behind jump from their shelter I'll give the word. Then put down your orchids very carefully, and we'll all run back to the river-bank, and open fire. Remember each man must shoot straight. We will win easily."

The boys grinned appreciatively. When carrying a gun, the one thing in the world the Papuan desires is to shoot somebody.

We turned our backs to the enemy. They howled in exultant triumph and rushed down from the opposite bank, not intending to allow such an easily bluffed prey to sneak back to Fuka-lala and be eaten up by him. The village carriers dropped their packs and bolted, followed by the contemptuous grins of our own boys.

"Put down the orchids," said le Strange, quietly. "Carefully, now!" The thirteen of us, Fi-fi's eyes sparkling with excitement, spread out slightly and ran straight back to the bank.

We were quite an army against niggers. Even if our number, thirteen, was ominous, it was offset by Fi-fi being a spirit of war and on our side.

The would-be man-eaters were running in full view across the river. We let them have it. Their triumphant yells were instantly silenced in the echoing reports. Men spun backwards, and, like crumpled bundles, were swept away by the stream and dashed against the rocks. For a second they wavered; then, as one man, turned and ran.

And how they ran!

We whites got in some good shooting before their be-feathered bodies disappeared into the jungle. But our boys were so excited after the first volley that their guns made tremendous noise but little damage.

"Pick up the packs!" ordered le Strange. "We'll cross straightway."

Long Harry glanced soberly at all the fine orchids left strewn about by Fuka-lala's cold-footed boys. They'd have to be left behind.

"Can't be helped now," said le Strange; "but I believe we can save them."

We crossed, glancing curiously at the bronze-black forms that were now the play of the tumbling waters. Some of the boulders were sprayed with crimson drops that looked curiously warm.

We filed up the track leading to their main village. The throb of war-drums reverberated over the valleys. The peculiar, long-thrown voices of their criers wirelessed the news from mountain crag to mountain crag. Our head boy interpreted.

"They are calling all the tribes to ambush, and will pick us off one by one along the jungle. They swear we will never reach the coast."

From their biggest village, stockaded as usual, the women had already set up the hideous mourning wail. It ceased abruptly as, to our surprise, le Strange swung towards the stockade. There was not a soul among the big grass houses as we strolled cautiously through.

Again le Strange gave orders to our head boy:

"Go," he said, "and cry to these men that if they don't come straight to council we will put a fire-stick to the village and destroy the crops and gardens. Tell them that we are invincible, for the War Spirit has told Fi-fi that he is with us and will kill every enemy until we reach the coast. Tell them to cry the news to all the villages that they must also give us carriers, otherwise we'll magic their crops and the spirit-god of Fi-fi will spread many terrible diseases amongst them."

Well, that about ended it. They had taken their lesson; we had potent witchcraft with us. To the superstitious Papuan we were invulnerable. They sent back and picked up the orchids on the river-bank. From village to village we got all the carriers we wanted and finally hit the coast intact, our boys boastfully triumphant, ourselves very much relieved. And Fi-fi – she was like a lovely child that has been given the first toy of its mischievous life and to whom a wonderful new world is waiting with welcoming arms.

As I said, that was just eighteen months ago. We quietly smuggled Fi-fi across to the Australian coast. Matkins married her there, and is now a sugar-grower in the Cairns district.

The rest of us are in Sydney – and are wondering. We are sure Fi-fi is an albino – and yet We are going to know very soon.

Beche-de-mer Luggers Cooktown, N. Queensland.

GOLDEN HAIR

IT's a sporting chance," argued Leslie. "In any case we can't lose financially. You hire the diver and gear; I supply the cutter. The wreck is there. It must be an ancient craft. There are no records. I don't say there *is* treasure aboard, but it will be strange if she doesn't carry material sufficient to repay us for the very moderate outlay on the venture. Your holiday expenses to Melbourne, and back to Thursday Island, will cost you as much as the diver's fees. Make this venture your holiday instead. Even if the wreck turns out a complete dud, we can still make money by sailing to the shelling-beds and employing the diver at pearl-shelling. He'll be able to dive much deeper than my native crew; so we will work ground I've been unable to exploit before, and return loaded with pearl-shell. And that, at its present price, is as good as treasure."

"H'm," said Peters uncertainly. "Sounds all right; but I'm a business man with a reputation. How the North would laugh if I went Spanish-galleon hunting! If there we're only a successful precedent, now."

"Got you!" replied Leslie triumphantly. "There *is* a precedent. All the North knows about Jardine, of Somerset, and the old chest with £3000 odd of Spanish and Mexican dollars he recovered off the Great Barrier Reef!"

"By Jove!" exclaimed Peters. "I'd forgotten. I'll go. But for heaven's sake spread the word that we're merely cruising for new shelling-grounds with a suit diver aboard."

Far-stretching water, calm and lagoon-green, sparkling in the sun's rays. The wooded Torres Strait isles, clear-cut and beautiful; the cutter motionless, yet with an illusory air of a living thing capable of foaming life should quick need arise.

In care-free curiosity the blackboys grouped around the "Syd-nee man," Burton, donning the diving-dress. Leslie was about to adjust the helmet when the diver's half-gestures halted him. Burton gazed around as if loath to leave the beauty of the world. Almost shyly he glanced up at the immensity that receded in a superb arch of blue; then at the world into which he would disappear in the space of minutes. With an impatient smile he signalled for the helmet.

Under Leslie's supervision the boys stood by the airpump. The diver stepped overs ide and, climbing heavy-footed down the ladder, threw himself clear into the water. Slowly his cumbrous body disappeared, followed by the grotesque dome of the helmet' in a spray of air-bubbles. Diminishing ripples wavered to the cutter's side. Like a coffin of lead gently sinking, the diver faded into the darkening waters along the reef-edge. A blackboy, leaning overside, watched intently as the indistinct form merged into the depths.

As Burton slipped down into the peopled silence, he adjusted his air-valve to the differing pressures. He was going down to a great depth, so those on the cutter kept him suspended at intervals, fifteen minutes at a time, to accustom his system to the increasing pressure. His blood might "boil" otherwise.

The wreck lay at the extreme limit of diving depth.

Warily his boots came to rest on a shell-encrusted beam. Experience directed his eyes upwards. Through his face-glass he could dimly see the air-pipe and life-line stretching up through opaqueness into greenness, to merge into yellow-green towards the surface. He could distinguish the cutter's keel, and as through many fathoms of gradually lightening glass he saw the sun, a dull-red disk floating in dimmest blue. The experience was new and thrilling. At such a depth, even in the clear waters of the Coral Sea on a bright day, it was extraordinary that he could see to the lighter water above-let alone the cutter and the water-red sun. Seeking an explanation of the phenomena he gazed about him. He was in a vast crevice between two converging reefs of coral. Where the chasm had narrowed the old wreck had caught. The sun's rays shooting down directly overhead had somehow been concentrated by the magnifying properties of the water within the angle of the coral walls and helped vision amazingly.

This was Burton's first dive in the Coral Sea and he was fascinated. Already, high up around air-pipe and life-line darted a cloud of inquisitive fish, more entrancing than the shimmer of parrots through sunlight. The creamy walls, creepered with "sea ivy," rising on either side were reminiscent of moonlit medieval battlements.

A thing like a floating gossamer veil emerged from the gloom and pulsed away – a maze of cells of recurring pin-pricks of light. Burton sensed that its seeming helplessness really held power and purposeful life.

Grotesque vegetable growths flaunted from the thousand coral crannies. Some were miniature trees, with queer tapering stems that sinuously swayed where there was not the slightest movement of the water; many were plants of nightmare form and "flowers" that would surprise even in a garden of dreams. He stared as a green cabbage-like growth slowly unfolded white petals and displayed a yellow heart alive with a phosphorescent glow. An eel-shaped fish nosed towards the brilliance; instantly the petals whipped around it and closed, the disappearing tail wriggling frantically as the clenching petals dulled back to green.

Burton glanced at the wreck, now a skeleton, its ribs clothed with the life of the sea. It looked utterly forlorn in this silent, living world. And yet so rottenly dead, with all that riotous life growing in and upon and around it.

Again he glanced up. The life-line and air-pipe were sagging a little, so he signalled to take in the slack. A sagging line is a menace, for it is liable to become fouled around a block of coral or, should the diver slip into a hole in the sea then he slips straight down to the limit of the line, resulting probably in paralysis from suddenly increased water-pressure.

Cautiously Burton put foot upon what dimly suggested coral-grown timber, and gazed down at the sponges and sea-grass, trying to distinguish where might be the hold of this long-dead ship. Possibly the ship might have been Spanish; but it seemed so old that but for its size, as shown vaguely by the sea-growths, it could have been a craft of the Norsemen.

Presently he smiled. Though a riotous floral growth waved from its shell-encrusted muzzle, he recognized a drooping encrustation as an old-time cannon. The wreck was not so very old, after all. At least only a hundred years or two at most! Those vanished centuries were a bond of sympathy between man and ship. They represented a limit in time whereas this drear world of the fishes seemed to have lived on for ever and ever.

Very slowly Burton worked his way along, with a creepy feeling that if he slipped off the timbers and coral arms he would sink straight down through the vegetable life into a bottomless pit of weeds. A long shadow swept past and, lithely turning, came again. Burton was not afraid of sharks, but this fellow's movements and cold green eyes were menacing. It circled close, then almost twisted in its own length, as if reluctant to keep its jaws from claiming this new thing that was rightfully its.

Burton had met inquisitive sharks before and taken only a wary notice of them, but he disliked this one immediately. It was so plainly going to attempt a kill; it so obviously regarded the diver as prey. When the tiger of the sea came swiftly close again Burton's hand touched his air-release valve. To the spray of marvellously beautiful bubbles the shark dived convulsively and was gone. Burton laughed. After all, sharks among the coral reefs were as cowardly as those of the harbours farther south. He felt his way cautiously, reassured.

A bloated growth like a big balloon, all rainbow jelly throbbing with life, waved before him. He touched it: its colours dimmed to water-green, and it slowly disappeared within itself. Amazed, Burton watched the big thing until, small as a garden pea, it vanished within a crevice of coral.

From a cavern a hideous, moveless head watched him; glaring from unblinking eyes, crueller than the eyes of a snake. Burton recollected pearlers' tales of the giant groper; of how they had been known at a single bite to snap off the leg of a diving blackboy.

That monstrous head waited within a cavern just above the centre of the wreck. Burton touched the air-valve, the bubbles hissed up. The head never moved. Something else did. A huge fish, tiger-striped, darted past the cavern. Burton glimpsed the instant opening of rounded jaws, the gleam of many teeth that snapped – and head and tail of the striped fish floated down towards him.

Burton reflected that these brute fish must be scared of him; the diving-dress made him a hideous monster too. What he did not know was that this cruellest of things that breathe cared not at all for hideousness. He did not know that certain dangerous sea-things were not afraid of him, but that they were wary of two long slender things that stretched up to the unknown far above him; that air-pipe and life-line appeared like endless tentacles that might envelop its prey in a trap. It was the "tentacles" that dangerous fish were afraid of. Burton let those big eyes watch him, because he could not prevent them. Far away, he could hear a great heart beating, never missing its throbbing pulse. It was warmly companionable, the throb of that air-pump coming from the cutter's deck.

He peered below his feet and guessed that all hope of treasure was gone. The bottom was almost certainly out of the wreck. Treasure chests, if any, must long since have slipped down to the uttermost depths. This old ship's shell-encrusted ribs were only held together by the marine growths that had spread over and between them.

Then Burton stared amazed, for swimming – really swimming – came a fish of wonder colours, its scales flaming in phosphoric lights. It resembled a miniature ocean liner bathed in an electric glow skimming a black sea. Even at this depth he could plainly see the daintily shaped head with its great liquid eyes that stared so seriously. It disappeared and shone again; then flashed straight across a crevasse and vanished. He drew a breath of disappointment as the waters again closed solid. Burton only sensed the shape of that fish, but vividly saw that growing up from its head there bent a supple rod over the snout which flashed a little rosy lamp – a lure for inquisitive prey.

Something came floating down through the vast crack above him. Like a broad, green blanket tasselled with gold sinking slowly through the depths it covered nearly the width of the huge crack and its masses of hair-like edges drooped prettily and wavered.

"A cloud must be over the sun," thought Burton as he straightened up. Then the cloud softly enveloped him; its folds draped around him and closed him in caressingly but ardently, as if impelled by a dreadful love that would not be denied.

He stood in utter darkness, not comprehending, his heart thumping louder than the air-pump above. Then he grew aware of pressure, as if he were being squeezed by suddenly increased water-pressure. Fearfully his arms swung out, his clawing hands quite easily tore through a silken mane of hair just cosily damp. His arms swung again and went through quite freely, and again and again as he clumsily spun around. But he felt the pathways torn by his arms instantly filled up with a stronger seethe of something and sensed that soon it would demand toil to thrust his arms through this jelly-like hair wrapping ever more firmly around him. He felt his own hair bristling; his heart near bursting with horror. He struggled frantically and the hair, slipping through his clawing hands, silkily caressed his fingers and felt reluctant to slip away.

He paused, shuddering. How intensely dark! What a weight was closing around him! building him in! He was encased as if in wet cement that was fast setting.

Trembling violently, he nerved himself to stand absolutely still and think. So many years of diving experience had taught him-what? That now at two hundred feet he was at the greatest diving depths. Only slight exertion meant quick physical exhaustion. But to struggle, why that meant the brain must go almost immediately! Diver's paralysis certainly. In every such case a cool head meant the only escape from a crisis.

Gently his hand searched to his breast for the signal cord. It pushed through the outer hair, which closed caressingly around his hand. It had become appreciably harder to push through around the corslet; just like pushing through thickening cheese. His fingers spread and twisted as they tried to poke a way around the cord. Like claws they coiled around and dug an inch into the hair enwrapping the cord. It was compressing and becoming in turn harder to compress. His fingers closed, but it was as if around a stiff rubber tube. He could not close on the cord!

And the hairy mass was squeezing around his wrist and forearm; he could feel his upper arm already enveloped, his fingers now were being gripped as in thickening glue. He tried and tried to jerk. Just as his brain lost control he staggered through the plant-life down into the hold of the wreck and his weight stretched the cord.

They hauled him up, leaving him stationary at intervals, for they dare not haul him up straight away from that depth lest his blood burst. He did not answer their signals and they feared he might already be stricken by paralysis. But they did not see, as they hauled him up through the shallower water down which the sun's rays shone, a cloth of gold like finest seaweed quickly but without haste unwind from around him. It spread and grew until it was a dense blanket of gently waving hair. Then as if a thing of dreamy life, it floated, fringes prettily waving, down into the depths.

Caught Dugong, Thursday Island, 1920s.

ACCOUNT RENDERED

SNORES came from the sprawling blackboy crew on the deck for'ard, deep breathing from the two white men astern. A star-beam slanting off the polished mainmast rested steadily across Reynold's brow, its pale light appearing to divide the strong brown face. But the sleeper neither knew nor cared.

No water gurgled along the cutter's sides. The tide was at its height, stationary and silent. Nearly three miles across the channel loomed the two conical peaks of Howick Island. Above, the stars smiled down upon the sleeping waters of the Great Barrier Reef. Beyond the water but touching it, was an indistinguishable smudge like an immense patch of spilt ink-the mangrove forest sucking its life from the black mud of the ocean.

Clear and distinct came the eight sharp clangs of a ship's bell. Before the musical notes had toned away the white men were sitting up inquiringly. The black crew tossed aside their blankets, slumber-dazed. But no big ship loomed above them, no towering maze of lights, no throb of engines.

"What on earth–" began Reynolds. "Did *you* hear it?"

"Yes," answered Harris. "Eight bells! A steamer."

"Where?"

They stood up, searching the waters. But there was no steamer; only tiny Coquette Island beside them; silver water all around.

"Strange," murmured Reynolds. "I could have sworn--"

"And I too. But we *must* have been mistaken – look at the boys!"

"Turn in," advised Reynolds softly; "we don't want them catching the jim-jams. What the explanation is I'm hanged if I know, but if the boys get hearing spooks this cruise is done."

The two men were soon breathing deeply. The boys, reassured by the white men's unconcern, yawned, coiled again in their blankets and noisily went to sleep. The tide, now on the turn, sent a low, rippling laugh from bow to stern of the cutter.

Night again, and the stars, and the quiet of the Barrier Sea. A smell of opened pearl-shell from the cutter's deck mingled with the faint scent of tobacco smoke. Reynolds opened questioning eyes.

"Can't sleep," explained Harris softly. "Thinking of that bell. It was about this time last night–"

Across the waters clanged the strokes of a ship's bell. The men, white and black, sprang up, eyes wide, breath short, listening.

"Seemed to come from the heart of the mangroves on Howick Island," said Harris incredulously. "But it can't. Impossible! There's not a living soul on that speck. And there's not a ship in sight."

The crew shuffled close together for'ard. Uneasy glances were shot towards the white men. Reynolds yawned unconcernedly. "Mine been think it ship's bell wash in longa mangroves," he spoke aloud; "catch up longa tree. Wind blow him about."

Sudden relief spoke in the quick laugh for'ard. Making fun of their own fears the crew turned in.

"I can't make it out," said Reynolds thoughtfully.

"Tomorrow when I go out with the fishing-boats, you slip off in the dinghy and look over the island. There may, just possibly, be someone there. There *must* be. But why ring a ship's bell at midnight the Lord only knows!"

"There's not a sign of a living soul on the island," whispered Harris that evening. "I examined every inch of the place, walked over it all day. All except the mangroves, of course. There are a hundred acres of them, a forest of mud and crooked trees, with a few creeks from the sea running through. When the tide is out it's soft mud and water-pools. When it's in, the water rises up among the tree-branches. No human being could possibly live there."

"Of course not," said Reynolds. "I only thought some beachcomber might have squatted between the two little hills."

"The place is absolutely uninhabited," answered Harris with conviction. All hands were unusually late that evening at turning in. Seemed unwilling. But, before midnight, all hands seemed sleeping. A dead quiet hung over the little vessel.

Up for'ard a blanket was cautiously raised, a woolly head emerged. Presently the head jerked back under the blanket.

"That's bad," whispered Reynolds; "they're listening, too. They'll want to clear out of this just as we've located a payable patch of shell. I hope that–"

Clear across the waters clanged the first sharp stroke of a bell. The crew were instantly on their feet.

"You boys go to bunk," ordered Reynolds. "What damfool rot this!"

"We fright alonga bell," answered the head boy softly.

"Him only bell washed ashore longa mangroves," said Reynolds confidently. "Wind blow him."

"No wind," replied the black boy quickly.

"Tide shakem branches," answered Reynolds instantly.

"Tide no turn yet," said the boy.

The two white men made a pretence of turning in. But the crew, creeping down from for'ard drew nearer to the white men and crouched against the mainmast, blankets drawn tight around their shivering shoulders, frightened eyes peering out across the water.

"This is serious," whispered Reynolds. "All fishing is off now until we solve this mystery. There *is* someone tolling a bell among those mangroves, otherwise it could not occur always exactly at midnight. There's never a steamer visible, and the bell can't toll from the bottom of the sea!"

"Only one way to find out," answered Harris. "It is nasty – and risky too. When the tide covers both reef and mangroves, I'll take a boat and row up one of the sea-creeks between the trees."

"We'll both go," said Reynolds decidedly, "and take two of the boys. When we come back they can explain to the others what will turn out to be some simple explanation of this uncanny business."

That evening, with the incoming tide, they rowed across to the black smudge that was Howick Island. The boys at the oars, shivering quietly, cast longing glances astern at the black outline of the cutter lying by Coquette Island. Harris signalled to cease pulling while they were yet out in the channel, some little distance from the gigantic coral reef that encircles the island. A low wailing of tortured waters was rising from far in there among the trees.

"Better wait until the tide is stationary," advised Harris from the bows. "The water is still rushing over the island from every side of the sea. If we venture into that waterlogged forest we'll simply be sucked into the mangroves. And we are early yet."

When the waters had quietened, the dinghy crawled forward. Over the broad coral reef now lisped five feet of water. Behind them, the sea stretched away to merge quietly with the night. But in front, they peered at a dim outline of twisted trees behind which was blackness. Harris, peering ahead from the bows called instructions, quakingly obeyed by the boys at the oars. They crawled forward into the barely perceptible mouth of a creek in the black wall ahead. The dinghy timidly entered, and vanished, walled in by a million trees whose branches reached out overhead like a ceiling in the Pit.

A hissing stream of fire whizzed from beside the boat.

Sheeny green and yellow flame ran up the oar-blades and dropped as brilliant bubbles into the dinghy. Streaks of criss-cross fire stabbed the blackness of the creek where fish darted to escape the vicious rushes of the shark.

"A man would soon be mince-meat if he slipped overboard," growled Reynolds.

"Yes," answered Harris from the bows, "but we're not going over – unless these frightened fools capsize us on a root. But keep a look out for these branches; I can't guard against all of them."

Big fishes had followed the little fishes into this luscious feeding-ground and were fighting and feeding in a riot of harry and slaughter before the waters swirled them out to sea again.

For half an hour the dinghy crept on its twisty way, a ghostly visitant in this water-logged place of the night, its bow nosing in among the trunks, its keel grinding with eerie scrunch on roots. A blackboy whimpered. "Shut your noise!" hissed Harris.

The creek abruptly twisted and presently widened slightly, space grew broader among the trees. The darkness lightened. As gaps appeared. among the branches overhead a glimmer of sky showed a spray of stars far up. Harris rested his tired arms.

"Thank heaven!" breathed Reynolds; "at last we can see, if only in patches. This job is getting on my nerves."

"Clang! Clang!"

That bell tolled from the very sky, it throbbed among the wet tree-trunks, its tones thrown to the water and up again to echo among the trees and, whispering, die far out at sea.

"Clang, clang!" "Clang, clang!" "Clang, clang!" The night trembled to the vibrations.

The blackboys threw themselves face down into the dinghy and the white men jumped for an oar just in the nick of time as, almost imperceptibly, the dinghy swung around. Cursing in the quick relief after fright, the white men kicked the terror-stricken boys. But death itself could hardly have loosened their grip of the boat's bottom.

"No good," panted Harris. "They're done! But the bell is straight ahead. I'll pull. Quick! Keep a bright look out from the stern."

He bent to the oars, the dinghy gurgled chokingly as she lurched ahead. Reynolds's hand clenched the tiller as over Harris's shoulder there shot a gleam of light, real light, shining steadily between the branches from where the sea-creek widened out and tall, gnarled trees stood up.

Right across the creek, stretched from tree to tree, was the white bridge of a steamer; and along it walked, tall and alert, backwards and forwards, a man in the smart uniform of an ocean boat's captain. The rays of two hurricane lanterns, lashed high, gleamed on shiny buttons, peak cap, and the gold braid of his cuffs, as he turned in his parade.

Harris's hands hung limply on the oars as he stared over his shoulder, cold sweat beading his brow.

Reynolds crouched there staring as if carved in stone.

While up there among the tall trees it walked, that sea captain, backward and forward, spick and span, square-shouldered, well groomed, with greying Vandyke beard! Directly above the bridge a large ship's bell was lashed to a tree-branch. Secured to the bridge beneath a lamp was a fat, white-painted lifebelt, and the men in the dinghy below read in black letters "S.S. *Tait*."

The watchers' breath eased a little as they saw that the bridge was a framework of driftwood and wreckage built from tree to tree across the creek, and fastened to it a broad sheet of canvas formed the bridge. Close by was a whale-boat moored at stern and bows with ropes lashed to the branches above to allow her to rise and fall with the tides. They understood at last.

Invisible, insistent hands tugged at the dinghy. Harris mechanically jammed the oars in the water to steady it. The dinghy edged away as if a great hand clutched her keel and, laughing silently, dragged her back. Without looking, Reynolds stretched out an arm and clutched a twisted branch.

"Harris!" (The whisper was the voice of a man afraid of himself.) "Tell me! What do *you* see?"

Harris turned and smiled understandingly.

"It's all right, old man. I've just about got it sized up. I recognize him: Captain Tersh, of the *Tait*, He piled her up on a coral reef in the Strait just as twelve bells struck, one night in the big king tides four years ago. He raved he'd go down with his ship; but they manhandled him into the boats. Some, however, of the crew and passengers were lost. He was drunk. Lost his ticket, of course. I remember him well at the inquiry."

Reynolds drew a long, relieved breath. "But-but-what does *this* mean?"

"Looks as if he's gone clean mad and thinks he's on the bridge again – as he should have been that night. What *d'you* think?"

"Thought I'd gone crazy," Reynolds whispered. "But we'll hear *his* version. Pull up, Harris, the drag of the tide has almost got my arm pulled out."

Harris bent to the oars, Reynolds slipped his hold. Instantly the dinghy swung viciously down-stream. Straining in intense surprise, Harris forced the dinghy's head around.

"Kick up those blasted boys," he gasped. "The tide's turned with the strength of a mill-race – it's almost wrenching the oars out of my hands."

Reynolds snatched an oar and together they tugged the boat back towards the bridge.

Before they got within hail a curious change had come over the night silence. There was a whispering all round, as if everything had awakened to moving life. Now the water was humming and hissing; the millions of tree-trunks came to gurgling life. The vast sheet of water was quivering under the strain, it was spreading out, *moving*. The sea was subsiding, falling quickly many feet, and the waters on the land were straining to get back into the bosom of the mother.

Reynolds roared "Ahoy, there, ahoy!"

The figure on the bridge halted, petrified, his eyes riveted on the struggling dinghy. He dropped to his knees.

"It's all right!" bawled Reynolds. "For God's sake keep your head. We're friends! Do you want to come off in the dinghy?"

The man, ashen faced, stared down at them.

"Quick!" shouted Reynolds. "We can hardly hold her seconds longer. Quick, speak!"

"I thought–" came a quavering voice. "Are you really– I thought–"

"It's all right, Tersh," shouted Harris. "You remember me. Harris of Thursday Island. We're not ghosts! We're pearling, off Coquette Island. Come with us to the cutter for a spell, will you? But be quick."

The man rose, tall, commanding. Fury flooded his face. He clenched a fist at them.

"I thought you were *they* come up from the sea," he screamed. "Curse you! Can't you leave me alone even here? Go off into the darkness and drown, you swine! As I saw *them* drown."

"Let her go," gasped Reynolds. "Swing her nose around before we're smashed among these trees!"

Both men swung on the port oars, as she plunged halfside on into the darkness. The rushing waters spun her nose around as she sped away into the night.

"Pull in the oars," shouted Reynolds, "before they're snapped off. I'll try to steer, but I can't see far ahead. If we're dashed against the trees, cling to the branches and climb up, it will be the only chance of seeing daylight again!"

Straight down the black channel sped the dinghy, bumped aside by protruding roots, thrashed by low-lying branches. All around and far away arose one frightening, wailing sob as from the island centre the waters in a falling circle were rushing back into the sea. Dismal cries, eerie groans rose from a million tree-trunks as the sucking waters swirled and dragged among them. Drooping branches sucked under by weight of pulling water added their indecipherable cries to the din.

An irresistible force dragged the dinghy side-on against the trunks. Both men flung desperate arms around a tree as a new note stormed into the infernal orchestra. The waters had changed direction.

"It's all right," shouted Harris; "the water is flowing off wherever gravitation pulls it. As the tide lowers, it will rush back into the deep channels and must carry us out along the creek back to the sea – if we're lucky! Put life into those boys or we're done! I'll hold the dinghy."

Reynolds gripped the waist of a boy. He screamed. "Billy," said Reynolds, "I chuckem you overboard longa debil-debil fish. What say you?"

The boy sobbed, clenched his teeth in the dinghy gunwale and clawed the bottom.

"Then sit longa seat!" roared Reynolds.

"Takem oar! By-em-bye we pull out longa cutter. S'posem you no pull I chuckem you over! Which feller?"

The boy scrambled to his seat. Reynolds treated his companion likewise.

For an hour they clung there, the dinghy pressed against the trunks as by a mighty hand. Quite suddenly the pulling waters jarred the trunks as if in indecision, while a new-toned whine rose up among the trees. The dinghy eased off, gathered way and shot forward down the creek.

Harris sprang to the bows. "Make the boys backpaddle," he shouted. "If they can only steady her I'll do my best to see ahead. The thickest mass of the foam will be the channel." Reynolds clung to the tiller, peering desperately ahead as the dinghy merged into the sucking stream of wider waters.

"Port!" yelled Harris. "Port! Port!"

Reynolds threw his weight against the tiller: as with his heart in his mouth he saw a turn in the creek where the water, impatient of the restriction, screamed through the trees striving to tear a corner of them from its path.

"Keep her off the trunks," yelled Reynolds, "and we might round the turn."

Their united strength held her off from the crash and thus, pressing her back from the trees they crept around that corner foot by foot taking every advantage of the circling overflow. As they rounded the turn the dinghy was snatched away by the main course of the current.

Quivering like a terrified horse, the black shadow shot from out the trees and into the churning, milky haze that was splathering over the great reef. In moments only they were over the reef edge and out into the deep open waters of the sea.

Reynolds smiled at Harris. "By the powers that be," he said in a wondering voice. "This little old world of ours holds many surprises. And life, by God, life is good!"

Two days later, from the cutter's deck, they stared at a forlorn something drifting towards them with the current. "I don't quite sense what it is–yet," said Harris quietly. "But–you remember that night? The tide-water was right up to the bottom of the bridge. Last night saw the full height of the king tides, the anniversary, as it happens, of the night the *Tait* went down. Last night's tidewaters rose many feet higher than the night we were there. I wonder– I wonder if the old fool stood on that flimsy bridge and imagined he was going down with his boat. That water would tear his bridge away as if it was a straw."

Reynolds turned towards the dinghy. "We'll see what it is," he said.

"It" was a white-painted lifebelt carrying in bold black letters "S.S. *Tait*."

The native-built bridge at Samai, by Gunner Landtman 1908.

THE BRIDGE

A SHOT rang out – echoed and re-echoed. Wykeham stood surprised; his carriers dismayed. Sullen before, they were now only prevented from bolting by the threatening rifles of the two Tanna "boys."

Pleased interest wiped the worry from Wykeham's face, his tall figure straightened expectantly. He was in the country of the mountaineers, the "bushmen" of Santo Island and it sounded as if those irreconcilables might be all that report made them out to be.

For Santo, although the largest of the New Hebrides, is almost unknown inland. Its bushmen are naked men with beliefs so primitive that each carries a loaded Snider wheresoever he goes. The weapons were supplied by traders of other days.

Wykeham smiled reassuringly to the carriers: his tired, lean face could smile rather nicely.

"We go on now Tommy," he ordered quietly. Tommy gripped his Winchester and stepped dubiously forward. He was the pathfinder. In his blue lava-lava emphasized with a cartridge-belt and sheath-knife, he was as proud as any Tanna Island man could be, and as contemptuous of the Santo "salt-water men" in whose company he found himself.

With fiercely hissed threats Jacky, bringing up the rear, urged the carriers forward. Surlily they complied, climbing doggedly – they had been climbing these five days past-all the way from Hog Harbour. They had crossed the Jordan, climbed first the hills, then up and down from peak to mountain hemmed in by sombre forest. The cooing of many plump pigeons had at first delighted the ever hungry coastal boys, but the wealth of timbers had set Wykeham dreaming longingly.

The track was a native bushman's "pad," none but a native could quickly follow its windings. Through the forest in places it was only detected because it was impossible to walk elsewhere. Down the steep mountain slopes however and along straight spurs, it was sometimes as distinct as a man-wide cutting walled in by trees.

After climbing a precipitous spur, the party halted, panting. For Tommy was blocked by a wall of ledged rock hedged in with undergrowth in trellised masses. A gorgeous butterfly floated past his quizzically upturned face. A bird whistled far down in some hidden valley. Tommy inserted his big foot in a cleft, reached up and, grasping a root, swung himself to a jutting ledge. Wykeham followed suit, not envying the carriers, coastal men all, quite lost in this country of the mountaineers.

Laboriously they climbed the rocky ledges to the continuation of the path above. From there, as he waited, Wykeham read fear in the carriers' eyes. At the peak summit he allowed them a breather. It was good, sitting away up there on the roof of the world; the breath of the age-old forest, the quiet peep of sky, the rustling whisper from that sea of foliage – all spelt peace.

Mutinously, the carriers pushed on, hating the Tanna boys who over-seered them. Wykeham however, felt pleased – not exactly at the tough and uncertain job before him; perhaps the reaction in this hint of excitement that had eased his mind of dull care.

Wykeham's fine plantation away down on the eastern coast was, like that of other Britishers, languishing for, scarcity of native labour. Under the Condominium, the French planters could work with plentiful and cheap Tonkinese labour. But the British were bound by other laws. And now Wykeham, desperate, was seeking Wutomoli, notorious but most influential chief of the bushmen.

French and English planters alike thought Wykeham's idea hopeless. The mountains, they knew, held some thousands of bushmen, but those independent wife-stranglers spurned work; they had resisted all inducements to "sign on" these thirty years past. So Wykeham had loaded up with presents and set off into the fastnesses, alone.

They were now clambering down a mountain side which was fast developing into a precipitous gorge with a gloomy mountain opposite. Wykeham envied the carriers their sure footgrip. While he steadied himself with a hand against a tree-trunk, or snatched at a vine, they picked their way with bare feet, and carrying loads. From the invisible below arose the hum of water. They could almost peer over a precipitous lip into gloomy depths – Wykeham wondered how on earth they were going to climb down there!

Then he scrambled down to a rocky ledge and stood gazing in surprised admiration at a long suspension-bridge swung right across the gorge. Its upper cables were lengths of cane drooping down from trees on the opposite cliffs to connect with tree-branches high above his head. Those cables were thicker than a man's arm. From the looping cables was swung a trellis of cane, bottomed by a footwalk. The footwalk was only one foot wide of long cane strands interwoven with short lengths of bamboo, giving the appearance of a close-runged ladder. There was a single handrail of slender bamboo poles lashed end to end with rattan vine. Wykeham felt glad of that handrail.

This spider "web" bridge was a masterpiece of native engineering. Wykeham was astonished that such "bush rats" could and would build it. That it was built of necessity he realized as he peered over below. Without that bridge it would be impossible or else would mean hazardous hours of climbing to clear the gorge. Suddenly, the echoes of Sniders crashed down from above the very tree tops, it seemed.

"All's quiet on the Santo front!" smiled Wykeham and ducked as Tommy wheeled around and fired to a yell behind. Jacky, his face a study as he picked himself out of the bushes, blazed furiously back along the jungle path.

The carriers had bolted! Wykeham thought quickly staring at the discarded packs.

"We go straight on, Tommy. We close there now. S'pose Wutomoli sell me plenty feller boy – he send boy pickem up present belonga him quick feller time."

Tommy nodded understandingly, but his face was anxious as he stepped on to the bridge.

Wykeham admired his two Tanna men, afraid, yet game. He clung to that handrail when the bridge swayed as if it would gently slip from under. When away out in mid-air, he felt the vibration in the cable strands, heard the wind softly hissing past, reminding him of a nightmare dream at sea. Straight below yawned a sheer drop in whose gloomy depths foam flashed like tablecloths of flowers.

As they climbed the opposite peak, Wykeham's blood tingled sympathetically to the cautious body of the Tanna man creeping ahead. The peak proved to be only a spur down which they peered along a track sharply defined by walls of jungle. Wykeham sighed cheerfully. Several hours of climbing faced them again, to reach a spot that looked but a stone's throwaway.

They crept on, wary in the knowledge that they were right in a native "war." Occasional shots rang out, apparently from the tree-tops above, and were replied to from back across the gorge.

Then they saw the outpost. The peak was barely two hundred yards away by rifle-shot, but Tommy pointed excitedly before Wykeham could distinguish the black figures squatting among the rocks, each with a Snider across his knee. That those black forms crouching there were poor shots he knew and was glad. Then a shot echoed from above and a little beyond the outpost. Tommy pointed quickly and Wykeham realized the simple plan of campaign. He stared, intensely interested.

A peak top loomed above the outpost and towered beside a blue space in the sea of trees that must be the gorge edge. In a clearing was a bamboo palisade enclosing boat-like roofs of houses thatched with palm. Close by a monstrous *gamal* house, a *levine* post, forty feet in height, carved and painted in grotesque designs, could be distinguished. Long-snouted pigs rooted unconcernedly within the clearing. A puff of smoke shot from the stockade and a Snider answered it from immediately across the gorge. Two villages sniping at one another!

"More better we go back," warned Tommy. "Bushman, he fight alla time big feller fight! He proper angry feller. He no talk sign on boy now!"

Reluctantly Wykeham realized that he was beaten; for to talk of work to these bushmen savages in the throes of a bloodlust, would be worse than foolhardy.

He appreciated the strategy of that outpost commanding the only available path, placed to guard against surprise lest an enemy party swarm down and cross the bridge to take the village in the rear.

Then Jacky jerked him behind a tree. Breathing expectantly, they faced about and looked back along the track which was visible down the spur as ribbony intervals of hill-side hedged by trees.

A savage appeared in flying leaps from rock to rock, to vanish, then reappear leaping from root to log, a picture of agility, uncannily sure-footed. Wykeham gazed in sheer admiration until the man vanished near the bottom of the spur up which they had come.

The two Tanna men poked their rifle-barrels between the leaves. Wykeham checked them.

"No feller shoot!" he ordered sternly. "Let him go pass. S'posem we kill him, by-em-bye plenty feller bushmen shoot us altogether finish!"

Unheralded as an apparition the bushman appeared directly on the path before them and stood poised, looking back over his shoulder, his sinewy chest panting.

"A scout!" thought Wykeham, "and he's located something, too. As delighted as a boy – but what a cruel looking devil!"

Naked, the bushman yet was dressed. Across his buttocks shone a stick of wood shaped like a bullock's horn, and double pointed; it was held in place by a vine corded around the waist. Mottled leaves dangled from the vine and were caught up behind in a striking fashion between his legs. Wykeham had heard of that ornament from pioneers as being worn only in the old primitive days. Tufted feathers adorned the man's wild hair; curved tuskers encircled his neck, and boars' tusks his upper arms. A bamboo knife was thrust through his belt of vines, and he carried the inevitable Snider. He stared back at the spur up which he had come, his brutal face intensely animated. Then with a twisted grin he disappeared into the jungle. Wykeham thought he had quite gone, but Tommy motioned silence, pointing warningly at the foliage near by. They hardly breathed; the very forest seemed listening.

Another savage came loping along the path to crouch down, peering across at the outpost, his dark face crinkled with desire. Those black sentinels up there on the outpost never moved. Step by step the foeman in trembling eagerness crouched forward, his Snider held before him. Slowly he raised the weapon.

Between the trees, a rifle-muzzle came poking out within two feet of his back, a deafening report and the would-be sniper pitched headlong.

With a yell the hidden bushman jumped upon the body and hacked with his bamboo knife; a throaty gurgle from Tommy betrayed suppressed blood-letting awakened. The killer sprang back and peered from among the bushes, his face working with thwarted fury. He vanished – and the forest rang to his signals.

The Tannamen jumped to the path, eyes bulging, lips wide, their colour livid.

"Quick feller, we altogether finish now!" gasped Tommy.

"Run quick feller," ordered Wykeham. "You two feller run back longa bridge – sit down wait longa me – no let him any feller man cross!"

He glanced back towards the outpost; they had vanished but were coming. He laughed as a Snider-ball thumped into a tree; their shooting was comical, but he feared their quickness. He was hastened by the forest ringing to the high-pitched signal howls of men roused to the chase; they would be on him in minutes almost.

Wykeham raced when he could; leapt when he had to, with eyes and mind alert lest he miss the track – if he did that he would never find it again: He feared the bushmen might think of the bridge and cut the Tanna boys off before they could cross it.

When half-way up the opposite spur, he glanced back towards the ribbons of track down which he had come.

In the shadowy gloom were leaping figures at which he emptied his magazine. They vanished, but he fired snappily into the trees. He smiled as he panted on – one civilized man armed with modern weapons was superior to hundreds of savages with Sniders!

But now he was being hunted by invisible men against whom a machine-gun would be useless. They would slip past amongst the timber, wait for him at the bridge, and shoot from yards away. He slid down a ravine, plunged through the water and clawed up the roots at the opposite bank. He fired to right and left amongst the trees ahead as he ran. An explosion near by almost deafened him. He sprang aside. At every cleared space he wheeled around and blazed back along the track. With lungs wheezing, he still ran. Pace saved him, for the blood-crazed men who slipped past and hid down the path ahead were too excited to aim as he panted past.

From the last peak summit he looked down into the green depths from which came the sough of running waters; then scrambled down, sliding, falling, clutching vine and root. A rapid fire of Winchesters rattled up from the gorge edge, drawing an immediate howling from surprised men.

Wykeham had not sufficient breath left to shout to the Tanna men to hold on, he was coming. He staggered to the edge of the gorge and reaching the bridge-head wheeled around and fired at a score of figures, laughing at their startled disappearance and the renewed crack of Winchesters from the gorge bank behind him. He leapt for the bridge but jumped as a Snider exploded from a leafy bough overhead. With his heart pounding he gripped the bridge handrail and gazed straight ahead as he stepped urgently along that precarious foothold. He shouted hoarsely: "Fire 'em quick feller Tommy, Jacky, plenty feller shootem alla time!" and the whistle of their bullets cheered him on. He held his breath when midway across, for the bridge cables swayed back and along across the chasm. He clung to the handrail, making slow haste, not so much because of the atrociously aimed bullets from behind, but because he feared a slip. He was too preoccupied to see Tommy jump out from behind a tree and aim steadily; but he gasped to the hiss of the bullet and convulsively gripped the rail as the bridge plunged behind him. He just glimpsed a bushman spinning down into the depths. Thereafter he gripped the rail with both hands and his nerves with iron control.

Safely across, Wykeham shouted, "Quick, Tommy, Jacky, cut him bridge! Quick feller cut him altogether finish !"

From behind a tree he knelt down and blazed away to cover the Tanna boys who climbed to the tree branches and frenziedly hacked at the wood-hard cane. It would take time even with the fury of their blows to hack through that stuff, but Wykeham's position was strong as a battalion now.

The upper cable parted with a snap; the bridge drooped. For a moment there was a queer silence on the farther bank; then cries of dumbfounded rage. Snider balls whizzed among the trees as the bushmen went berserk at the sacrilege.

As the lower cables were hacked through the bridge parted with a crackling snap to hiss down into the gorge and smack against the opposite cliff. The Tanna boys flung their rifles in the air and yelled in triumph.

"Quick feller now," laughed Wykeham. "Find him track; we go quick feller before him dark-by-em-bye bushman he cross long way down – maybe other feller come down alonga nother feller hill, then we finish altogether. Quick feller, find him track now!"

And they "quick fellered."

THE RIVALS AND A DEVIL-FISH

BILLY BANNER plodded along on the floor of the sea. He was happy, this lone human, working in the relentless water world. To the animate life of that world he appeared a monstrous, unfamiliar thing, therefore not to be treated with contempt. As with heavy solemnity he appeared through the luminous gloom, his dome-like helmet looked like the head of some beast of prey. That the sea things sensed he was; a dangerous beast like themselves, and left him alone, though an odd shadow watched him with dreadful eyes that flashed green. Billy plodded on, methodically yet warily, content that he was armoured within rubber and brass, yet not treating the denizens of this underworld with any undue familiarity, for he knew that among them were some liable to call his bluff at any moment.

The sea bottom here was gravelly sand, with occasional coral patches peeping amongst the sea-gardens, "areas of grasses, delicately coloured, with strands sometimes fathoms long, fine as a girl's hair. And plant growths of shapes that must have been conceived in a devil's garden, but of colours that surely were mixed in heaven.

Billy paused, his mind momentarily "up above" where many leagues away the wind warmly swayed the grasses in a homestead paddock. Down here the grasses were also swaying, but coldly if gently. No sweet lullaby of insects, no scent of flowers, no sheen of sun. Just a ghostly tremor amidst greenish gloom.

Billy grunted disapprovingly. Every second is precious to the diver searching the ocean-bed for shell. If he day-dreams down there he is liable to be put to sleep forever. So Billy plodded on.

A "nigger-head" tall as himself loomed up, shaped and coloured like an immense mushroom. As Billy drew closer its unusual shape lured him right up to it. He stared, then suddenly smiled, for on the smooth coral "head" was roughly but plainly scratched a list, some in English characters, some in Japanese, some in Malay:

Tanaka loves Echu.
Rimadie loves Doolas.
Guichi loves Keo.
Tangona loves Percesima.

Again Billy visioned things. An old man fig-tree in a sunny Australian town; its bark scarred deeply with the names and initials of lovers. He hesitated; then, clumsily stooping, picked up a trochus-shell:

"Why not? She mightn't like her name in company with those of

Malays. But, bless it all! No matter what the colour, love the world over is all the same-even at the bottom of the sea." With the pointed shell-end he scratched deeply:

Billy loves Celia.

You may not think so, but it's a fact. Some corals are rounded and smooth as a petrified cheese might be. And it is easily possible to scratch your name on them at the bottom of the sea; and that scratch remains visible and readable for many days.

A few days later, just before they screwed down his helmet, Billy glanced casually around. He always insisted on this last glance, for – who knows? Little Cairncross Island lay hazily distant; the sky was hot and the sea-like glass. Overhead, a frigate-bird volplaned and a gull, a silver fish in its beak, somersaulted frantically to avoid the pirate. Drifting down with the tide came the *Winsome Lass,* and by the lines Billy saw that their diver was overboard, no doubt drifting too, suspended just above the bottom, searching the depths until he should signal shell.

"Pity these Japanese can't mind their own business," grumbled Billy as the big helmet cased him in. "Sure as they spy a boat working they must nose alongside to see what's doing. Japanese diver, too, I suppose." Billy had been working this "ground" for a fortnight now, and doing well, for though small in area, it was dotted with shell.

"No chance now of working out the patch ourselves," scowled the tender at the oncoming craft. Billy scowled back through his face-glass, then disappeared in a foam of silver bubbles.

Down in the silent world he picked up an odd shell, weed-covered, and fervently hoped one would hold a Christmas-box. It was ages since he'd handled a decent pearl. Just like kids and their lucky dips, this pearl-shelling was. Every dip might hold a treasure; any shell a pearl. Life itself was a lucky dip.

It seemed that his laden boots, more than his will; drew him towards the nigger-head. When it bulged eerily close, he decided to gaze on her name again.

"Cold comfort," he chuckled, "love at the bottom of the sea. Lor' love a duck, even the waters of the ocean can't cool it out of a man's system. Who'd have thought it of me!"

Gingerly he skirted a hole, its lip camouflaged by weeping ferns of the sea. The slight delay annoyed him. "Pity the sea didn't fall through its own holes," he groused. "A man would be able to pick up pearl-shell in a Ford then. My word, that Japanese has got me real nettled, right enough."

He lumbered through the luminous gloom like an elephantine shadow. A rainbow-fish pursued by a larger fish crashed against his face-glass and registered the shock of its life. So did Billy. Often things come suddenly, and all are magnified down below. But dismay awaited him by the nigger-head, for boldly scratched below his heart's confession ran the legend: *Celia loves Harry.*

Quaint perplexity followed Billy's dismay; then anger.

But he knew that air-and water-pressure play scurvy tricks with a heated man's head down below, not caring what damage is done to his heart.

What did it, mean, anyhow? He gazed upward in shocked surprise as a monstrous form sagged right atop of him. Billy shouldered back against the nigger-head as the descending diver noiselessly grounded.

Both men glared behind their thick face-glass; there was something ominous in the eyes of the newcomer as he whipped out a knife. In startled alarm Billy jerked back his air-pipe and also freed his steel, the ludicrous idea of two such monsters fighting on the sea-floor did not strike him then. What were they going to fight about anyway? Relievedly he watched the stranger scratch:

"Are you Billy Banner?"

Billy nodded within his big domed helmet.

"She's my girl!" scratched the stranger, and pointed his knife at "Celia!"

Billy scratched "Liar!"

They breathed heavily and glared behind their face-glasses; then jerked back and up in grotesque alarm as a black pall clouded the sea. They would have sped straight up to the surface if they could, for real fear gripped them.

Cruising in mid-water, casually nosing the air-pipes, was a diamond-fish; the dreaded devil-fish of the native divers, its mouth set in a malicious grin. With its ton weight of fighting strength it clove through the water as if the sea were fashioned for its exclusive pleasure. Its playfulness is its terror. It may gambol around a diver as a cat a mouse, and leave him with nothing but a heart attack. But in the whim of the moment it may hook the air-pipe between its "horns" and bolt with it and the pendant diver, as a child whips a play-string through its fingers. From near the eyes of the big fellow stubby "horns" projected.

Both men gazed up in sickly fascination, while the fish played gently and with a beautiful rhythm in its dreamy movements, nosing first one set of lines, gliding off to nuzzle the other, then leisurely circling both sets as if uncertain which to play with. It slipped between the men and the clear world above, this bat-like monster, its terrible eyes glancing at the motionless things below. They felt as the benumbed mouse must feel before the spring of a cat; waiting, not for the pounce, but for a sickening jerk and the tearing away of the air-pipes.

The fish glided above and delicately nosed the life-lines, its blanket-like flippers undulating with a slow motion which flashed a whiteness underneath, instantly swallowed in the blackness of the beating flippers.

Billy's rival, with the hope of one man moving his lines from the impending tangle so that he might be able to help the other in a crisis, started crab-edging away. His signal cord brushed the manoeuvring fish. Startled at the contact, its flat bulk flashed around straight between both sets of lines. These tickled the spreading wings and it back-kicked in a rolling somersault. Fearful now of what it did not understand, its horns engaged both sets of lines and it bolted in a furious swirl. The alarmed tenders in the luggers above jumped to make fast their respective lines, while the flapping fish, jerked suddenly aback, pivoted in terror. Two sets of lines caught within its horns had completely upset its calculations. The divers were carried off their feet to swing in water like children clinging to the ropes in a maypole dance, the circle of their swing drawing rapidly narrower as the lines twisted into one strand.

Billy hoped for a quick death while he prayed frantically for life. Disturbed sand blotted vision from the face-glass. He thudded into something solid, and gripped, and was gripped in turn. He sensed that he was staring into the face-glass of his one-time rival. The twisted diving-lines had the men locked together in mid-water.

Would the fish bolt again and, snapping the lines, deposit them in some bottomless pit of the sea? Billy's sick mind wirelessed a halcyon vision of how heavenly it would be to lie dead in the clear sunlight above. If the luggers could only haul them up!

The startled tenders were battling with every ounce of man-power at their command. But the weight of both entangled divers, added to a ton or more of fish, *plus* the enormously increased weight of its frantic wallowings, was a strain which no diving-gear has been built to stand.

The very struggles of the fish gave the men life. The jamming of the pipes between its horns cut off the air-supply, and pain roared into the ears of the divers. Then an inevitable dislocation of the gear occurred, and excess air poured down into the diving-dresses. Their roomy proportions becoming inflated, the men commenced to rise. The fish, feeling the slackening at the bottom end of this dread thing that had trapped him, instantly bolted upward, then down on a long slope. He was brought dead up with a jerk that threw him a clean head-on somersault. His horns slipped from the twisted strands and he shot out for the depths.

Released air hissed into the diving-dresses, though the dizzy men did not know it.

To the luggers, their divers emerged from the depths like bloated toads but feet first, grotesquely interlocked in one another's arms. The crews sprang overboard to help in upending the tangle, and get the helpless mass aboard.

"She's my girl!" gasped Billy as his face-glass was unscrewed.

"Liar!" denied the other in a subdued voice.

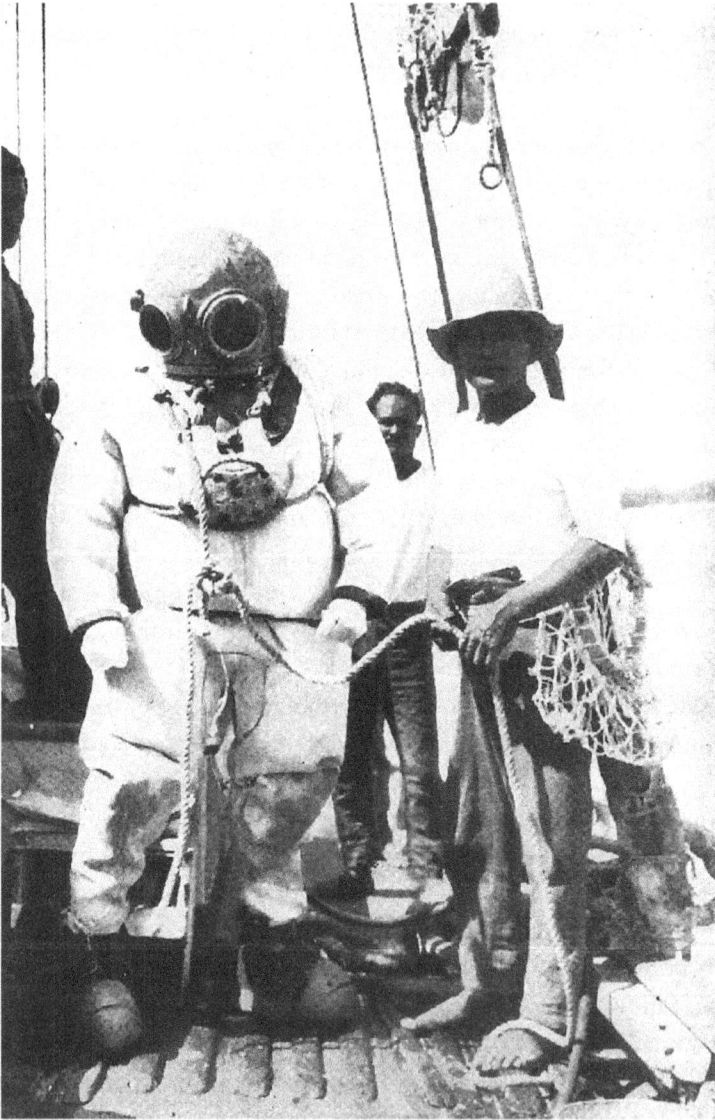

THE WOES OF
"SCANDALOUS" GRAHAM

IT was hopeless attempting sleep, so I relit the slush lamp, stoked the pipe, and wearily prepared to listen.

"Scandalous" Graham, in a Jacky Howe flannel, was sitting hunched in bunk with bony legs drawn up under the chin of his ugly face. He had just done a month as His Majesty's guest, and his head was still sore as the result of beer he had imbibed on his return to society at large.

"What I want to know is," he demanded truculently, "why do the public stand for publicans? Why don't they wipe 'em off the face of the earth! Stingers of the pockets of the poor. Money-snatchers. Cows! A man blows inter town for a hard-earned spell; passes the pub; meets the publican. Oh, a bonzer feller! Downs a few drinks; gets gay; an' that's all he remembers. Leastways until he wakes on a dusty road with a broilin' day, the leaves whisperin' the drought, the crows floppin' from tree to tree doggin' a man, carkin' for him to die. And *what* a thirst. Oh hell!"

"By-en-bye, when the body furnace cools down, he wonders if the scowlin' bloke who slung his swag an' him on to the footpath could really be that breezy publican-

"But what he properly wakes up to is his blued cheque, an' his clobber that'd break a scarecrow's heart with 'shame. He's got nothing. No money, no tucker, no brains, only a roarin' thirst that all the money in the world wouldn't drown."

Scandalous eased off for a moment. Reaching across the table he grabbed a plug of Havelock, bit off a piece, and chewed reminiscently. He spat confidently.

It may have been the lingering effects of the hops.

Anyway the beastly stuff landed on the chewer's legs. He wiped it off with hairy paws, using his flannel-tail as a towel. He was furious. He is modestly proud of that neat knack of his of squirting the juice just outside the tent door.

"You see," he resumed savagely, "that is another curse of liquor. A man loses his punch, no matter how scientific he may be. Fill a crack rifle-shot with beer, and watch him miss the target! Same with every art where judgment an' science is essentials. But as I was sayin', just look at the way those crawling beer-sellers pumped me dry this last trip to town!

"I was shrewd this time. Shied straight to the store; squared up those old bills; bought a sheikh suit and a silk handkerchief with sunflowers round it. I was some blood, believe me! The storekeeper was so surprised he murmured 'a drink.' Of course I says 'No!' We breasted the bar where the publican greets me as an old an' valued friend. But my weather eye sees he don't fancy the new clobber. Whether the suit didn't fit to his liking, or whether he reckoned the storekeeper had done him out of something, I dunno.

"However, I was soon in a breezy humour, specially when the pub girls flocked round me like the female cockatoos swarm the flash young cocky with the big yeller crest.

"There was a barmaid sluggin' the pump this time an' by evening she an' me was real tender; she murmurin' all about her troubles, due to the high cost of livin'. Well, some heavenly days blew by, then I wakes up with only half a quid in me pocket.

"Gorstruth! That cheque was to have took me to see the Melbourne Cup. Well, I soon finds the girls have sort of flown, as if my yeller comb had sort of lost its feathers.

"The barmaid was particular haughty. Seems as if I was a prize poodle today an' a worn-out worm tomorrer. She took the huff too, just becos I leaned acrost the bar and whispered somethin' in her pink ear. The publican blows along an' reckons he'd serve me with what I want, seeing as I had no respect for ladies! Not feeling too perlite meself, I tells him to hobble to hell, an' orders one of his own girls to get behind the bar an' serve me, seein' as the barmaid's got a flea in her ear.

"But he up an' snorts the likes of me makes a public bar no place for his daughter to serve behind." Scandalous glared from his bunk. "Now what do you think of that!"

"What happened next?" I inquired yawningly. "Nothin' happened," snarled Scandalous. "I pulled off me coat an' into him. He knocked me with a bottle an' bawled for the police.

"You *orter* heard the charge next mornin'! Gee-roosalem! Drunk an' disorderly; illegal language; refusin' to fight; obstructin' arrest; bashin' the King's helmet; tearin' his buttons; chewin' the publican's ear – it kept on readin' like that, on an' on, just like the candidates promises at election time!"

Scandalous's grim face wrinkled into a self-satisfied smile. "Made me sort of feel I'd done somethin' out of the ordinary. A bit of a holy terror like."

I grinned – and regretted the mistake. Scandalous leaped from the bunk and shook a knotted fist at my face.

"I'll kill a policeman!" he howled. "By hell, I'll kill a policeman. That's wot I feel like."

"Go on!" I grunted. "Get back to bunk before the cockroaches nibble your toes. You know the nearest policeman is fifty miles away, and that the first thing you'd say to him would be: 'Come an' have a drink.' You can't bluff me, Scandalous. You know very well you wouldn't willingly kill a grasshopper."

Scandalous reclined on his bunk. "Well no," he agreed amiably. "But sometimes I do believe I'd love to kill a policeman. Not exactly kill him – but yes – oh damn it all, you know what I mean!"

"Yes," I said. "You'd like to kill him, but you'd want him to wake up immediately afterwards quite all right."

"That's just it," he cried enthusiastically. "Of course I wouldn't like to hurt the poor cow."

He drew up the rough blanket and settled back in the bunk. "You're a good mate, Jack," he confided cheerfully.

"That bit of a talk you started has fixed me up great. My old dream-box is feelin' just the thing. Strike me lucky, it must be late. Hear that squawkin' mopoke, the noisy cow! Gorstruth, an' work in the mornin'."

He doubled up like a kangaroo pup, turned his back, and blanketed his head.

Thankfully I doused the glim.

189

I ON IDRIESS

'Jack' Idriess was born in 1891 and served in the 5th Light Horse in the First World War. He returned to Australia to write The Desert Column, which was published following his huge success with Prospecting for Gold. He went on to write 56 books and was largely responsible for popularising Australian writing at a time when local publishing was still not considered viable. A small wiry mild-mannered man, Idriess was a wanderer and adventurer, with a vast pride in Australia, past, present and future.

ETT IMPRINT has been publishing Idriess for over 25 years, including:

Flynn of the Inland
The Desert Column
The Red Chief
Nemarluk
Horrie the Wog Dog
Prospecting for Gold
Drums of Mer
Madman's Island
The Yellow Joss
Forty Fathoms Deep
Lasseter's Last Ride
The Cattle King (audio)
Sniping
Shoot to Kill
Guerrilla Tactics
The Wild White Man of Badu
Gold Dust and Ashes
Headhunters of the Coral Sea

THE RED CHIEF

Told by the Last of his Tribe

ION IDRIESS

In times past there was an Aboriginal man
called Cumbo Gunnerah
His people called him The Red Kangaroo.
He was a clever chief and a mighty fighter
(this man from Gunnedah)
Later, the white people of this place called him
The Red Chief.

It would be hard to find a more satisfying hero than the young warrior Red Kangaroo, who by his mental and physical prowess became a chief of his tribe - the revered and powerful Red Chief of the Gunnedah district in northern New South Wales. His story is a first-rate tale of adventure but it is something more – a true story handed down from generation to generation by its hero's tribe and given by the last survivor, King Bungaree, to the white settlers of the district.

Now in its 18th edition, 214 pages, available from ETT Imprint.

PROSPECTING FOR GOLD

ION IDRIESS

From the Dish to the Hydraulic Plant, and from the Dolly to the Stamper Battery. With chapters on Prospecting for Opal, Tin, and other Minerals; and a chapter on Prospecting for Oil, by Dr W. G. Woolnough, F.G.S., Geologist to the Commonwealth of Australia. Illustrated.

This book, written by a prospector with a lifetime's experience, will save the new chum gold-seeker much labour and time and disappointment, and will teach the old hand many a payable wrinkle.

Dr W. G. Woolnough (Geologist to the Commonwealth of Australia) :-"Your hints should be invaluable to all, beginners and experienced men alike."

Canadian Mining and Metallurgical Bulletin:-"The volume will arouse the reader's interest at the outset and hold it to the end."

Queensland Government Mining Journal :-"It tersely sums up a lifetime's knowledge gained at first hand acquired by a man well equipped to pass his experience on to others."

Engineering and Mining Journal (New York) :-"This book is replete with good methods, described simply. Lack of space forbids quoting the terse directions."

Rabaul Times (New Guinea) :-"Invaluable. Each bit of advice and information is practical, as it comes from an old-time miner himself."

Now in its 20th edition, 190 pages, available from ETT Imprint.

DRUMS OF MER

ION IDRIESS

With Foreword by Wm H. MacFarlane, Mission Priest, Torres Strait Administrator of the Diocese of Carpentaria.

Professor T. G. Tucker, Litt.D. (Camb.), Hon. Litt.D. (Dublin), writes :- "Apart from his evident knowledge of the natives and their customs, Idriess has a graphic power greater than that of any writer whom I have read for years. His accounts of a battle of canoes, the wreck of a flotilla, and other events, are the finest things of the kind that anyone out here has produced."

Christchurch Times (N.Z.) :-"Idriess's Masterpiece. To enter into the life of a savage race of a bygone age, and to make that life spring into renewed reality, so that the blood runs hot and cold in response to its splendour and its degradation-this is the feat, almost an unparalleled feat, that has been achieved by Ion Idriess in *Drums of Mer* .... Idriess must now rank as the most brilliant star in the literary galaxy of Australia, and world fame for him can only be a question of time."

Sydney Mail :-"In dramatic appeal it is superior to *Gold-Dust and Ashes* and *The Desert Column* ... that should be sufficient."

Pacific Islands Monthly:-"Mr Idriess, in the telling of his story, displays sheer genius. There is something here for the scientist, the historian, the geographer, the beauty lover, and the student of the occult. *Drums of Mer* is not only a story, it is an invaluable addition to the historical records of the Pacific Islands."

The Argus (Melbourne) :-"He has seized upon the most colourful aspects of this decayed civilization before it has been completely lost to living memory, and has dramatized them with his uncanny gift for realistic narrative writing."

Now in its 23th edition, 284 pages, available from ETT Imprint.

GOLD-DUST AND ASHES

The Romantic Story of the New Guinea Goldfields

ION IDRIESS

The 26th illustrated edition now out from ETT Imprint, Exile Bay.

Brisbane Courier :-"His latest book is really the romance of the Edie Creek and Bulolo diggings, situated inland from Salamau; and with the discovery of the field are associated the names of diggers as "Shark Eye Bill" (William Park), Matt Crowe, Jim Preston, Arthur Dowling, Frank and Jim Pryke... men who in pre-war years, crept across the frontier, defying the Germans and dodging the head-hunters... These men endured terrible hardships, and frequently faced grim tragedy. Mr Idriess writes of it all, and writes of it as if he had been with them.. What a romance! What a story! It is packed with adventure, studded with splendid pen-pictures of pioneer prospectors, airmen, and patrol officers, and told with a fascinating simplicity that is borne from something very close to genius."

LASSETER'S LAST RIDE

An epic in Central Australian Gold Discovery

ION IDRIESS

The 49th edition now out from ETT Imprint, Exile Bay, illustrated with photographs, extracts from Lasseter's Diary and letters.

Morning Post (London):-"Perhaps the greatest of Australia's real life epics."

Daily News (Perth) :-"No grimmer tragedy than Lasseter's Last Ride has been recorded in the annals of our exploratory history .... Yet Idriess manages to keep his reader wavering between laughter and tears."

Otago Daily Times (N.Z.) :-"One almost finds it difficult to believe that the story is modern and true."

Sydney Mail:-"One of the most graphic, most poignant, and most absorbingly interesting tales that the chronicles of Australian exploration - those treasure stores of dramatic adventure - have ever revealed."

The Herald (Melbourne) :-"A true story that for sheer excitement, thrills, and sustained suspense, cannot be surpassed by even the most imaginative novelist."

The Telegraph (Brisbane) :-"This thrilling book reveals in convincing colour, the details of a story that is history and that has all the elements of stark tragedy."

www.ingramcontent.com/pod-product-compliance
Lightning Source LLC
Chambersburg PA
CBHW020905100426
42737CB00043B/380